# From Nationalism to Universalism

## Vladimir (Ze'ev) Jabotinsky and the Ukrainian Question

# From Nationalism to Universalism

## Vladimir (Ze'ev) Jabotinsky and the Ukrainian Question

Israel Kleiner

With a Foreword by
Wolf Moskovich

KIУC
CIUS

Canadian Institute of Ukrainian Studies Press

Edmonton 2000 Toronto

Canadian Institute of Ukrainian Studies Press
University of Alberta
Edmonton, Alberta
CANADA T6G 2E8
University of Toronto
Toronto, Ontario
CANADA M5S 1A1


ISBN 1–895571–25–1 (c); 1–895571–33–2 (p)

**Canadian Cataloguing in Publication**

Kleiner, Izrail', 1935–
From Nationalism to Universalism: Vladimir (Ze'ev) Jabotinsky and the Ukrainian question

Translation of: Vladimir (Zeev) Zhabotins'kyi i ukrains'ke pytannia.
Includes bibliographical references and index.
ISBN 1–895571–25–1

1. Jabotinsky, Vladimir, 1880–1940. 2. Antisemitism — Ukraine — History — 20th century. 3. Ukraine — History — Autonomy and independence movements. I. Title.

DK508.835.J33K5413 1999 947.7'00492'4 C98-931682-3



Printed in Canada

To my mother,

who in her spirit so

resembled Jabotinsky

# Contents

The subject matter that follows is that of a drama in three acts, the last of which is the unfinished one now being enacted in which we, now living, are the participants.

John Dewey, *Freedom and Culture*

> But there also exists another kind of nationalism—a creative nationalism. For this kind of national awareness, national existence is a creative responsibility. This kind of national awareness not only presupposes but demands self-criticism; it calls for self-criticism and reeducation in the name of national existence. This type of national awareness is of a higher order.

Nikolai Berdiaev, *Filosofiia neravenstva*
(The Philosophy of Inequality)

# Preface

Anyone who studies the history of Ukraine or of the Jews in Ukraine through primary sources must be struck by the blatant discrepancy between historical fact and the notions that prevail today concerning the Ukrainian national-liberation movement and the history of Ukrainian-Jewish relations. This state of affairs shows that historians have failed in their appointed task of adequately informing the public about the origins and development of historical events. Objective works by such authors as Arnold Margolin, Solomon Goldelman, Joseph Schechtman, and Elias Tcherikower have been overwhelmed by a torrent of writings designed to imprint on people's minds the notion that Ukraine is a country whose history is notable only for one huge incessant pogrom.

This book has been inspired by a desire to dispel the fog of propagandistic myth and to base my interpretation on well-established historical fact. After years of effort, I have become convinced that Vladimir Jabotinsky, one of the most illustrious figures in Jewish history, grasped and sought to pass on to others a clear and unbiased view of Ukraine, its national-liberation movement, and the meaning of the Ukrainian problem for the Jewish people, for the whole of Eastern Europe, and indeed for the entire world.

I wish to express my sincere thanks to all who have helped me in this work, especially to the following individuals: Professor Manoly R. Lupul and Dr. Bohdan Krawchenko, former directors of the Canadian Institute of Ukrainian Studies in Edmonton; Dr. Yehuda Benari, Mr. Gan, Mr. Evarovich, and Mrs. Tatiana Gruz of the Jabotinsky Institute in Tel Aviv; Mr. Lev Bykovsky of Denver; Mrs. Khaliavka of the Bavarian Library in Munich; Mrs. Kaplan of the Paris University Library in Nanterre; Mrs. Maia Ulanovska of the National and University Library in Jerusalem; Mr. Petro Iosypyshyn of the Symon Petliura Library in Paris; Dr. Rubin-Jabotinsky, the niece of Jabotinsky, and her husband, Dr. Rubin; the late Professor Mikhail Frenkin of the University of Jerusalem; Mrs. Miriam Goldelman and Dr. Asher Wilcher of Jerusalem; and Mr. Moriel (Meierovich), Jabotinsky's former colleague, of Tel Aviv.

The original Ukrainian text of this book was written in Jerusalem in 1982. An English translation prepared in the 1980s by Halya Kowalsky was extensively revised by Linda Distad. In 1995, the Ukrainian text was published by the Canadian Institute of Ukrainian Studies (in Kyiv, Toronto, and Edmonton) under the title *Vladimir (Ze'ev) Zhabotyns'kyi i ukraïns'ke pytannia: vseliuds'kist' u shatakh natsionalizmu*. The introduction to that edition was written by Ivan Dziuba, author of the well-known critique *Internationalism or Russification?* (1965). Dziuba, who made a speech at Babyn Iar in 1966 condemning anti-Semitism and calling for genuine brotherhood between Ukrainians and Jews, subsequently served as Ukraine's minister of culture (1992–94). In light of editorial changes to the Ukrainian edition, the English translation was further revised by Myroslav Yurkevich for the present publication.

Washington, D.C., 1998

# Note on Transliteration

Place names in Ukraine, Belarus, and Moldova are transliterated from the languages of the countries in which they are located, hence Kyiv, not Kiev; Odesa, not Odessa; Hrodna, not Grodno; Chişinău, not Kishinev. Traditional English forms are given in parentheses on first mention in the text.

The transliteration of Ukrainian and Russian in the text follows the modified Library of Congress system (at the end of surnames, "ий" is transliterated as "y"). In bibliographic references, however, the strict Library of Congress system (omitting ligatures) is used, hence "Zhabotinskii," not "Jabotinsky."

For the transliteration of Hebrew names, the following sources have been consulted: Cecil Roth and Geoffrey Wigoder, ed., *Encyclopedia Judaica* (Jerusalem: Keter, 1972), 16 vols.; Glenda Abramson, ed., *Blackwell Companion to Jewish Culture* (Oxford: Blackwell, 1989); and Joan Comay, *Who's Who in Jewish History*, 2d ed. (New York: Oxford University Press, 1995).

# Foreword

This book appears at the end of a century that brought state independence to both Israel and Ukraine as a result of the struggle for national liberation of Jews and Ukrainians respectively.

It is time to look at the difficult relations of these peoples throughout their history, and particularly during the twentieth century. Prejudice and established negative stereotypes still divide the two nations, so that mutual understanding is not easy to achieve. This book by Israel Kleiner is a Jewish author's attempt to provide an objective appraisal of some of the problems on the road to such an understanding.

Kleiner, who has specialized since his emigration from Ukraine to Israel in 1971 in the area of ethnic relations in the former Russian Empire and Soviet Union, is definitely one of the best-informed scholars on problems of Ukrainian-Jewish relations. The appearance of his book under the imprint of a Ukrainian publisher demonstrates the will of certain Ukrainian liberal intellectual circles to give a description and explanation of historical issues that still divide Ukrainian and Jewish readers, and it must be hoped that the book will contribute to the dispelling of biases on both sides.

This book is not the first by a Jewish author to interpret the bloody historical events of the last century in a way that tries to take account of the Ukrainian position and show the actual conditions under which pogroms in Ukraine were perpetrated. Could Symon Petliura really have prevented the pogroms or not? Answers to this and similar questions are to be found in this book.

Kleiner may leave his reader convinced or unconvinced of his interpretation of events, but the reader can at least be certain that the author has left no stone unturned along the road, thoroughly researching all the relevant evidence and documentation.

The outstanding leader of the Zionist revisionist movement, Vladimir (Ze'ev) Jabotinsky, stands at the center of Kleiner's book. Jabotinsky, who was born in Odesa, had friends among Ukrainians from childhood, and supported the national aspirations of the Ukrainian people, remains a symbol of Ukrainian-Jewish dialogue and, as such, has become a cult figure in present-day Ukraine. A Ze'ev Jabotinsky foundation was established by the Ukraine-Israel Association in Kyiv in 1997. The first winner of the annual Jabotinsky prize and medal "For

International Understanding" was the prime minister of Israel, Benjamin Netanyahu, for his book *A Place among the Nations: Israel and the World.* Israel Kleiner won the prize for the Ukrainian version of the present volume in 1998.

Jabotinsky, a most original thinker, was ahead of his time. He expressed revolutionary views and was often misunderstood or undervalued. His public appearances and publications aroused discussion and disagreement. His uncompromising stand and his marginality can be explained by his rare qualities as a great national leader and prophet. Jabotinsky once defined a genius as one who sees and feels what will happen in ten years' time.

He was the first Jewish political leader to acknowledge that the solution of the Ukrainian problem would decide the fate of the Russian Empire. As the Jewish population of Ukraine sided culturally with the Russians, Jabotinsky called on the Jews to support Ukrainian national aspirations and cooperate politically with the Ukrainians, which was, in his view, in the best interests of the Jews themselves. He believed that sooner or later Ukraine would become independent, and Jews as a minority had to be prepared accordingly.

Jabotinsky correctly predicted in 1938 that a sovereign Jewish state would be proclaimed in ten years' time. In vain did he admonish the Jews of Poland in 1938–39 to emigrate immediately to Palestine, warning them of the impending holocaust. His appeal fell on deaf ears.

Jabotinsky first put forward the concept of an "iron wall" in the Jewish-Arab conflict. He claimed that the Arabs would compromise only when they discovered that they could not prevail against a strong Jewish military force. History has proved the correctness of his view: after many years, the Arabs lost hope of defeating Israel in a war and are now prepared to talk peace.

Jabotinsky was destined to become a leader of the newborn Israeli state, but adverse circumstances—his expulsion from Palestine in the 1920s and his untimely death in 1940—prevented that from happening.

Much has been written about the so-called Jabotinsky-Slavinsky agreement of 1921 on the creation of a Jewish militia to defend the Jewish population on Ukrainian territory. Jabotinsky's opponents denigrated him for concluding that agreement with Petliura's representative, Maksym Slavinsky. The blame was undeserved. In making the agreement, Jabotinsky held fast to his tenet of Jewish self-defense, maintaining that Jews had to stop relying on others and protect themselves. This principled position, which he implemented in 1920 as commander of a Jewish self-defense force repulsing an Arab pogrom mob in Jerusalem, resulted in his imprisonment and banishment from Palestine by the British authorities.

As for Jabotinsky's attitude to Petliura, who was blamed for pogroms during his rule, the Zionist leader explained that in defending the interests of the Jewish people he was prepared to speak with the devil himself. Subsequent historical events, such as Rabin's handshake with Arafat in the White House in 1993, seem to justify this pragmatic view.

If on questions of security Jabotinsky remained a staunch advocate of Jewish self-reliance and strength, and on questions of national survival he was a consistent Zionist, a proponent of Jewish national revival in the Promised Land, his positive attitude toward the national aspirations of other peoples was based on his belief in universal human rights and values.

First and foremost Jabotinsky was a liberal, a democrat, and a fighter for justice. As such, he understood and supported the national aspirations of the Ukrainian people. Jabotinsky defended the status of the Ukrainian language as separate and distinct from Russian. That question, in his view, was ultimately to be decided not by linguists but by a people that regards a language as its own. The same principle applies to the distinctiveness of a nationality. Jabotinsky included the great Ukrainian national poet Taras Shevchenko in a list of anti-Semites alongside Gogol, Pushkin, and Dostoevsky. That did not prevent him, however, from praising Shevchenko highly as a "brilliant expression of Ukrainian national and cultural vitality." "The Ukrainian people," wrote Jabotinsky, "have preserved intact the main invincible bulwark of the national soul: the village." According to Jabotinsky, Shevchenko was not a popular poet but "a national poet, and therein lies his strength...in the subjective sense, that is, a poet-nationalist, even including all the outbursts of uncontrollable hostility to the Pole, the Jew, and other neighbors."

Jabotinsky was a man of his time: his opinions were determined by his general world-view and his understanding of the interests of his people in the prevailing historical circumstances. Applied to present-day conditions, his views may sometimes appear obsolete. However, Jabotinsky's basic principles of international relations have not lost their validity. Among them is his stand on the recognition of the national rights of the Ukrainian people and his insistence on Ukrainian-Jewish dialogue and understanding.

It is within this modern context that the present volume takes on particular importance, for it contributes to a better understanding of the past.

Since the proclamation of Ukrainian independence on 24 August 1991, both peoples, Ukrainians and Jews, have developed their relations on an inter-state level. Ukraine and Israel regard each other as strategic partners. Friendly political, economic and cultural ties have been established between the two countries. State anti-Semitism does not exist in Ukraine, and Jewish cultural life has been rebuilt. Jewish emigration from Ukraine is free and unhindered. Of more than 300,000 immigrants from Ukraine to Israel who have arrived since 1989, 30,000 are ethnic Ukrainians who belong to mixed families. There is now not only a Jewish minority in Ukraine, but also a Ukrainian minority in Israel.

Negating the stereotype of Ukrainians as anti-Semites, more than a thousand Ukrainian righteous Gentiles who saved Jews during World War II, risking their lives to do so, have been recognized by the Israeli memorial institution Yad Vashem. Ukraine now holds third place in Europe with respect to the number of saviors of Jews.

Many tragedies of the passing century were common to Ukrainians and Jews, among them the Chernobyl catastrophe. Today Israel is second in the world after the CIS countries as to the number of persons whose health was affected by the Chernobyl disaster. This is a result of the mass influx of immigrants from affected areas. Israel is also providing humanitarian assistance to the victims of Chernobyl in Ukraine.

Excellent relations between Ukraine and Israel are a good omen for the future. However, among Ukrainians and Jews generally, and particularly in the diaspora, old prejudices die hard. As a new generation comes onto the scene, it must be educated in the spirit of inter-ethnic tolerance and cooperation. This is easier said than done. The revival of interest in the figure of Jabotinsky as a proponent of Ukrainian-Jewish understanding may help in achieving that arduous task.

Professor Wolf Moskovich
The Hebrew University of Jerusalem, Israel

INTRODUCTION

# The Time and the Place

Vladimir (Ze'ev) Jabotinsky,[1] one of the greatest leaders of Zionism, was born in Odesa (Odessa) on 18 October 1880. Odesa was then the great cultural, industrial, and commercial city of southern Ukraine. Established at the end of the eighteenth century as the largest Russian port on the Black Sea, with the flags of dozens of countries fluttering from ships moored there, Odesa always had a character of its own, multinational and even somewhat cosmopolitan. It was a crossroads where Russian, Western European, Jewish, and Ukrainian cultural trends influenced one another. Indeed, although it was situated on Ukrainian territory, its population and cultural atmosphere produced a city that was not genuinely Ukrainian. According to the 1897 census, 45 percent of the population was Russian and 35 percent Jewish, while Ukrainians accounted for little more than 10 percent.[2]

This situation was typical in most towns on Ukrainian territory. The villages remained almost completely Ukrainian, while the towns were culturally more or less Russified, with considerable Russian, Jewish, and sometimes Polish populations. As a rule, Ukrainians made up between 10 and 40 percent of the town population—a characteristic situation among stateless agrarian nations incorporated into great land-based empires.[3] Of all Ukraine's large cities, Odesa probably displayed the least perceptible Ukrainian influence.

Odesa's Jewish community was numerically the second largest in the empire (the largest, if Polish territories are excluded).[4] Jewish activity and cultural life pulsated through the city, although as time passed the community became more Russified and adopted typically Russian linguistic and organizational forms. Many prominent Jewish cultural and community figures came from Odesa or had links with it, including Leon Pinsker, Mendele Mokher Seforim, Ahad Ha-Am, Simon Dubnow, Chaim Nachman Bialik, and Joseph Klausner, as well as a whole generation of prominent Jewish musicians. Several prominent Russian-Jewish writers also came from Odesa, such as Isaac Babel and Eduard Bagritsky.[5]

It was precisely Odesa, with its atmosphere of relative spiritual freedom and multiplicity of trends (insofar as one can speak of freedom and diversity under conditions of authoritarian, bureaucratic tsarist rule), that was the greatest formative experience for the young Jabotinsky. An article that he wrote much later, in 1930, titled "My Capital,"[6] was a hymn in praise of Odesa. It is a tribute to youthful feelings and memories, as well as an avowal of the great influence that the city's utterly original atmosphere had on him. Throughout Jabotinsky's life, Odesa kept recurring as a theme in his writings. Many pages of his autobiography[7] were devoted to the city.

Jabotinsky was affected by the non-Ukrainian character of the city in which he spent his childhood and youth, but he could not avoid the fact that Odesa was an islet in the midst of a Ukrainian peasant sea, an environment that exerted direct or indirect influence on the social and cultural life of the city. As he wrote:

> ...Ukraine gave us sailors to man oaken dugouts and stone-masons, and above all, that salt of the earth, those pillars of the homeland, those true builders of Odesa and of the entire south whose epigones the Volga-born Gorky went in search of and found to be, even in our own times, authentic, solid people...the sentence has turned out to be a very long one, but the people I had in mind were the vagabonds. Ukraine also provided us with another type of builder, known as the *chumak*. He loaded the rye near the Dnipro rapids, urged on his oxen, and trudged along behind his creaking cart across the steppe to Peresyp. Who knows how long that journey could take on foot—weeks or even months....[8]

This excerpt interweaves humor with nostalgia and literary style with a profound and basically serious affirmation of the Ukrainian subsoil hidden under the European façade of a Russified yet cosmopolitan city.

The education received by Odesa Jews was most commonly purely Russian, and their language of daily use was generally Russian as well. Jabotinsky's education followed this pattern. An enthusiasm for literature, which is considered indispensable among educated circles in Russia and is probably the clearest evidence of membership in the intelligentsia, also made a great impact on him. At a rather early age, he began writing poetry and prose in Russian and soon gained a reputation in his circle as a *wunderkind*.

In 1898, at the age of eighteen, he became the Rome correspondent first for *Odesskii listok* (Odesa Leaflet) and then for *Odesskie novosti* (Odesa News). His reports from Italy became very popular with the readers of those papers. In 1901, having acquired a flawless command of Italian (in his mature years Jabotinsky spoke eight languages fluently), he returned to Odesa. Soon he became quite a well-known Russian political writer, poet, playwright, translator of poetry, and orator.[9]

The Russian poet and man of letters Kornei Chukovsky, with whom the young Jabotinsky was on friendly terms, retained into his old age the fondest memories of Jabotinsky. In 1965, when "Zionism" was treated as a term of abuse in the USSR and the name Jabotinsky was allowed past the censors only in a slanderous context, Chukovsky wrote the following in a letter from Moscow to Jerusalem:

> Vladimir Evgenievich's whole being exuded a certain spiritual radiance. There was something of Pushkin's Mozart[10] in him, and perhaps something of Pushkin himself. I felt myself an ignorant mediocrity alongside him. Everything

> about him enthralled me: his voice, his laugh, his thick, jet-black hair hanging in a forelock over his high forehead, his wide, fluffy eyebrows and African lips, and his chin, which jutted forward and gave him the appearance of a bully, a fighter, a brigand.... He voiced youthful, free, and outrageous ideas about conventional morality, about marriage, about rebelling against established traditions, etc.[11]

Others who commented on Jabotinsky's literary talent included Aleksandr Kuprin, Maksim Gorky, and Leonid Andreev,[12] but he was not destined to become a prominent Russian writer. One of the waves of anti-Jewish pogroms that swept through many of the cities and towns of the empire at the beginning of the twentieth century drove him forever off the rails of Russian cultural life and brought him face to face with his people.

At that time, at the turn of the century, about 5,200,000 Jews lived in the Russian Empire, including 1,300,000 in that part of Polish territory incorporated into tsarist Russia after the partitions of Poland at the end of the eighteenth century. By 1917, the Jewish population of the empire (excluding the Polish territories) had risen, owing to natural increase, by about 650,000.[13] In 1903, Jews within the tsarist state made up almost 48 percent of world Jewry. In 1911 the proportion was about 44 percent—a decrease due mainly to Jewish emigration to the United States.[14]

It is important to bear in mind that about 94 percent of the Jewish population of the Russian Empire lived in ethnically non-Russian territories—mainly among Ukrainians, Poles, Belarusians, Lithuanians, and Moldavians. The law stipulated that Jews were allowed to live only in the so-called Pale of Settlement, and within that region, only in the towns. Since these areas lay mainly outside Russian ethnic territory, the number of Jews in territories populated by Russians was very small. For example, in Moscow gubernia (including the city of Moscow), there were only 8,500 Jews out of a total population of 2,500,000. In every gubernia of ethnic Russia, Jews constituted less than 0.5 percent of the population.[15]

The civil and national rights of Jews within the Russian Empire were very limited, much more than those of any other national or religious group. Moreover, those restrictions had an exclusively religious basis, for baptized Jews automatically gained all the rights recognized by imperial law.[16] Laws curtailed the right of Jews to move and settle freely, to obtain an education, to own real estate, to hold official posts, and to rise within the ranks of the military. It would be difficult to find any sector of social or economic life in which there were no restrictions on Jews. They had the right to live in only twenty-five gubernias—a Pale of Settlement including ten gubernias in Poland and fifteen in Ukraine, Belarus, the Baltic region, and Bessarabia. It is, however, true that Jews who had obtained a higher education, or were wealthy merchants, artisans of certain types or former soldiers in the tsarist army could, though with significant restrictions, live beyond the Pale of Settlement. In 1917, when the Provisional Government of Russia turned its attention to ending legal discrimination, it had to repeal 140 laws restricting Jewish rights.[17]

In the gubernias within the Pale of Settlement, Jews constituted, on average, 11 percent of the population, ranging from 18 percent in Warsaw and Hrodna (Grodno) gubernias to 4 percent in Poltava gubernia.[18] Moreover, the Jews in those gubernias were allowed to settle only in the cities and towns, not in the villages. A *numerus clausus* restricted the entry of Jews into institutions of secondary and higher education.[19] In every respect, Jews were the most disenfranchised and oppressed group within the population. Despite the presence of a quite significant stratum of wealthy Jews, the economic situation of the Jewish population as a whole was very difficult. Most Jews in the Russian Empire lived in small towns beset by overcrowding, distress, and frequent calamity. Typically, those towns had mixed populations of Jews and Gentiles, but some of them were totally or almost entirely Jewish.[20]

*Evreiskaia ėntsiklopediia* (The Jewish Encyclopedia), published in St. Petersburg shortly before the First World War, offers the following picture of Jewish life in Russia:

> All one's life as a Jew is spent in a permanent quest to be allowed those things that other subjects are granted as the natural right of every human being. From one's first conscious steps right up until death, the Jew is confronted with a dilemma: either to endure humiliation, suffering, and material deprivation, to deny himself an education, a cherished profession, an occupation, an office, an activity, and to live under the constant threat of eviction and ruin, or to renounce his faith and become a citizen with equal rights. The legal status of Jews has greatly worsened since the government identified them as the main participants in the revolutionary movement, which has gained strength especially since 1904 and has led to changes in Russia's system of government.[21] After the suppression of this movement in 1907, the reaction was directed mainly against the Jews. Their lack of rights, the roundups, the evictions, and so on lead the surrounding population to think of the Jews as people stripped of all legal protection. That image, associated with the taunts in anti-Semitic newspapers, leaflets, and pamphlets, leads to pogroms. Plunged into despair, the Jews are emigrating en masse to other countries....[22]

Jewish emigration from the empire began in the mid-nineteenth century, sharply increased after the pogroms of 1881, and acquired a mass character from the mid-nineties onward. It was a direct response to the disenfranchised status of the Jews in Russia and continued until the outbreak of the First World War. From 1897 to mid-1915, about 1,400,000 Jews left the empire, of whom 1,100,000 went to the United States. Today, they and their descendants constitute a large proportion of American Jewry.[23] Only an insignificant number of Jews chose baptism as a way out of oppression. From 1836 (when an accurate register of baptisms was begun) until the 1917 revolution, the average number of baptisms per year rarely exceeded 1,000 (although in 1854 it rose to almost 4,500, and averaged 2,300 annually between 1851 and 1855). In any case, even in the "record" year of 1854, the number of baptized Jews accounted for only a tiny fraction of the Jewish population in Russia, which was several million strong.[24]

Jewish participation in oppositional and revolutionary movements was a natural and utterly comprehensible reaction to disenfranchisement and the government's anti-Jewish policies. Jews were active in all opposition movements, contrary to the later myth that they were mainly involved in the Bolshevik party. But the assertion that Jews were the *main* driving force of revolution, advanced by the tsarist government to justify its anti-Jewish policies, was completely false.[25] In fact, a tangle of unresolved social and national problems was responsible for the revolutionary situation. Almost 500 years of territorial expansion had turned a Russian state that originated as a small principality centered in Moscow and dependent on the Mongols into an enormous continental empire inhabited by more than 100 peoples of many races, religions, and cultures—all at widely differing stages of cultural development.[26] Russia's imperial rulers never acknowledged the idea of civil equality or that of equal rights for all religions and peoples. It could thus be said that the main driving force of the revolution was the tsarist regime itself, whose deeply reactionary incompetence precluded a solution to any of the empire's difficult social and national problems. Among those problems, the Jewish question was of secondary importance (however characteristic and symptomatic it may have been). The revolutionary activity of a certain proportion of educated Jews was a component and a consequence of the general revolutionary process, not the reason for it.

Representatives of all the developed peoples of the European part of the empire and of the Caucasus participated in oppositional and revolutionary movements. Alongside political parties and movements operating throughout the empire, strong national movements existed in particular areas, especially in Poland, Ukraine, the Baltic region, and the Caucasus. The Poles, Ukrainians, and Georgians, as well as the Jews, were very active, both in their own national movements and in the all-empire parties and movements.

When Jabotinsky began his political activity, the Jewish national movement already influenced a significant section of the Jewish population of the empire and was divided into several currents and parties, both Zionist and non-Zionist. The Jewish Social-Democratic Party (the Bund), formed at the end of the nineteenth century, was quite strong. It opposed Zionism, supporting the theory of class struggle and "international proletarian solidarity." The Po'alei Zion Party, precursor of socialist parties in contemporary Israel, attempted to fuse socialist ideology with Zionist principles. At the beginning of the twentieth century it existed in Russia as a loose association of groups and organizations, but they were later consolidated into one party. The comparatively small Jewish Socialist Workers' Party (the so-called "Sejmists") had a non-Zionist program and concentrated its efforts on fighting for the national rights of the Jewish people within the Russian Empire. The party's aim was to create a single national union that would develop into an autonomous extraterritorial national body extending across the state with its own supreme organ, a national Sejm. The Jewish People's Party (Folkspartei), formed in 1906 mainly through the efforts of Simon Dubnow, was also non-Zionist but at the same time non-socialist. It focused on defending the national rights of Jews in Russia on the basis of general democratic principles and national-cultural autonomy. The political center of Jewish assimilators was the Union for the Attainment of Full Civil Rights for the Jewish People in Russia, formed in 1905 and soon renamed the Society for the Attainment of Full Civil Rights for the Jewish People in Russia. The Union's political program was very close to that of the Russian Party of Popular Freedom (Constitutional Democrats or Cadets), and it was led by one of the most prominent activists in that party, Maxim Vinawer. This stronghold of the assimilators ceased its existence in 1907. Finally, the Zionist organization in Russia, reorganized as a party in 1906, had a non-socialist orientation and fought for the greatest possible political rights for Jews in order to consolidate and preserve the Jewish people in preparation for future resettlement in Palestine. The Jewish religious parties and groups kept somewhat to themselves and included both Zionists and anti-Zionists. In addition, there were several Jewish political groups and parties that split, fused, and joined the larger parties or again split away from them.[27]

Underlying this changeable political scene were some constant principal forces—Zionist non-socialists; Zionist socialists; socialist non-Zionists; parties whose main aim was to achieve equal rights or national and cultural autonomy for Jews; and assimilators who found no place for themselves within the Jewish national movement and eventually joined the various Russian opposition parties. Thus, when extraordinarily dangerous revolutionary cataclysms began to shake the empire, Jewry found itself in a state of political division and divagation, and the effects of this were soon felt.

The first Russian Revolution of 1905 forced Tsar Nicholas II to issue the Manifesto of 17 October, in which he promised to recognize all civil rights throughout the territory of the empire. The State Duma, a parliament with limited legislative functions, was created. Jews could participate in elections to the Duma, but the tsarist government and reactionary circles were able to use various procedural machinations and administrative measures continually to restrict both Jewish electoral participation and the number of Jews elected as deputies. None of the four Dumas that existed between 1906 and 1917 (the first two of which were illegally and prematurely dissolved by the tsarist government) was able to improve the legal situation of the Jewish people.[28]

The October Manifesto did, however, bring a certain degree of liberalization. It was swiftly followed by the stormy rise of political activity within the empire as numerous political organizations were formed and the opposition press, including the Jewish press, flourished. Far from stemming the revolutionary processes, that limited and involuntary liberalization created conditions for the growth of revolutionary activity. The last decade of the tsarist regime passed amid a widespread premonition of an inevitable revolutionary explosion.

That spectre of revolution elicited an anti-Semitic reaction from the defenders of the imperial order, who had no positive ideas with which to counter the revolutionary movement. The only means the tsarist government was able to find to combat the revolutionary mood within the state was to support the Russian chauvinist and extremely anti-Semitic organizations known as the Black Hundreds (the Union of the Russian People, the Union of the Archangel Michael, and various others), which arose toward the end of 1905. The Black Hundreds were ferocious enemies not only of the Jewish people but of all oppositional and national-liberation movements, but the Jews were the main target of their attacks.[29]

In the elections to the Second Duma, the program of the Union of the Russian People stated:

> For many years, and especially during the last two years, the Jews have expressed in full their irreconcilable hatred for Russia and everything Russian. They have expressed their incredible hatred of humanity, their total alienation from other nationalities, and their peculiar Judaic views, according to which only a Jew can be considered a neighbor. As for Christian Gentiles, they [Jews] allow any kind of illegality and violence, even murder, to be perpetrated against them [Christians].
>
> It is well known, and has often been stated by the Jews themselves in their "manifestos" and proclamations, that the current antagonisms and the revolutionary movement in Russia in general—with the daily murders of dozens of honest servants of the TSAR and their fatherland, loyal to their duties and oaths—can be laid almost exclusively at the door of the Jews and have been financed by Jewish money.[30]

About half of this program was taken up with attacks on Jews and with the list of legal restrictions on Jews that the Union of the Russian People wanted introduced. Yet only seven lines in the program were devoted to the labor question, one of the most important issues in the country at that time. Five extremely clear lines were devoted to the status of the empire's non-Russian colonies:

> The Union of the Russian People resolutely proclaims and publicly affirms the indivisibility of the Russian Empire and of its present boundaries, and establishes as its sacred and ineluctable duty to use all its strength to ensure that those lands, conquered by the blood of our ancestors, will always remain *an integral part of the Russian state*, and that all attempts to dismember Russia under any guise *will be decisively and unconditionally defeated.*[31]

Emperor Nicholas II and his circle openly, even demonstratively, supported the Black Hundred movement. The emperor received delegations from the Black Hundreds on many occasions and always expressed his personal support. He even wore the badge of the Union of the Russian People on his uniform, thus manifesting his own membership in the organization, and he spent considerable sums on the publication of Black Hundred literature.[32] The Ministry of Internal Affairs, its police, and the local organs of state in many gubernias and towns worked in close cooperation with Black Hundred organizations and financed them.

Using extensive anti-Jewish propaganda, the Black Hundreds managed to strengthen anti-Semitic sentiment greatly, and in 1905–6 they organized a wave of pogroms with the direct support of the authorities. The pogroms began on 18 October, the day after the tsar's manifesto, which promised freedom to the population of the empire, was published. Policemen, soldiers, and Orthodox priests took part in preparing and directly carrying out many of the pogroms, and did so generally with the full support of higher civil, police, and military authorities. A clear example of this was the Białystok pogrom of June 1906, in which the most active role was played by the police and the army. Delegations of Jews had appealed to the Hrodna governor, Kister, before the pogrom there, yet far from preventing it, he actually expressed solidarity with those who carried out the pogroms.[33] Frequently official investigating bodies falsified evidence and depositions concerning pogroms, thereby imputing blame not to those who carried them out, but to the Jews themselves. The official *Pravitel'stvennyi vestnik* (Government Courier) expressed the view that the Jews themselves were to blame for anti-Semitic outrages.[34]

The Black Hundreds set up an armed organization with a proliferation of branches. Ostensibly secret, it was in fact well known to, and supported by, the police. It was this organization that took part in the pogroms. It also resorted to individual acts of terrorism and murdered, among others, two deputies of the State Duma—Mikhail Herzenstein (of Jewish descent) and G. B. Yollos (a Jew), both members of the Cadet party.

One of the largest centers of such Black Hundred activity was Odesa, whose administration, both civil and military, was particularly enthusiastic in its support for the Black Hundreds. Indeed, Odesa acted as a virtual training ground where the Black Hundreds could be schooled in elaborating and executing such diverse activities as pogroms (the first pogrom of 1905 in Odesa occurred three days after the tsar's manifesto), beatings of Jews and high-school and university students on the streets, attacks on workers, and fights in theaters. Besides the Union of the Russian People, other organizations operating in Odesa at various times included the Union of the Archangel Michael, the Southern Monarchist Union, and the Union of the Russian People, as well as a special Odesa Black Hundred organization, the White Two-Headed Eagle, and even a Union of Janitors. In 1913, through the use of terror and ballot fraud, the Black Hundreds won the elections to the Odesa city council.[35]

The Black Hundreds constantly sought to charge Jews with the ritual use of non-Jewish blood. The 1911–13 trial of the Kyivan Jew Mendel Beilis on a charge of such ritual practices provoked a wave of public outcries from the opposition press, particularly the Ukrainian press of the empire, and from liberal circles throughout the world.[36]

The activity of the Black Hundreds, backed by the regime, gave rise to the atmosphere that facilitated the terrible mass pogroms of the following decades. A fatal precedent was thus created by the authorities. It turned the empire into an *Unrechtsstaat* in which the authorities defied their own laws by failing to guarantee the defense of the honor, life, and property of a whole group of subjects. This practice exerted a powerfully corrosive influence on public consciousness and psychologically prepared the way for the explosion of violence during the revolution and civil war.

This was the background against which Jabotinsky's political activity began. His childhood and youth spanned the period between the comparatively small wave of pogroms of 1881 and the 1903 pogrom in the Bessarabian city of Chişinău (Kishinev), a "dress rehearsal" for the mass pogroms of 1905–6. This was a period of legal restrictions on the rights of Jews in the empire and of deepening social and national conflicts. Within the Jewish communities, important parallel social processes were taking place:

1. Assimilation—acceptance of the Russian language and culture and a simultaneous withdrawal from the Jewish language, culture, and religion; assimilation was the product of an aspiration for national emancipation;
2. Dissemination of Zionist ideas and the creation and development of Zionist organizations;
3. The spread of socialist and revolutionary ideas, which led Jews to participate in Russian, Jewish, and, in some rare instances, local (Ukrainian, Polish, etc.) political parties and movements.[37]

Although Jabotinsky's parents did not take part in political activity, they were touched by this process of imaginary emancipation—imaginary, for genuine emancipation was impossible in a situation of thoroughgoing legal restriction—and were involved in the common pattern of linguistic and cultural assimilation. They reared their children in a Russian spirit. In 1905, when Jabotinsky was already a Zionist, he described the psychological condition that led Jews into the camp of the assimilators:

> We, the Jews of the current transitional period, are growing up as if on the frontier between two worlds: on one side, Jewry; on the other, Russian culture. I mean precisely Russian culture, not the Russian people, for we hardly ever see the people, hardly ever have any contact with it—even the most "assimilated" among us almost never have close friends among the Russians. We acquaint ourselves with the Russian people through its culture—mainly through its writers, that is, through the best, highest, purest expressions of the Russian

> spirit. It is precisely because we do not know the Russian way of life, the day-to-day realities of Russian existence, that our notions about the Russian people are based on its geniuses and leaders, and the picture we have is obviously one of a wonderful fairy tale. I do not know whether we all love Russia, but I can state without any doubt that all of us children of Jewish intelligentsia circles are enamored of Russian culture to the point of intoxication and self-abasement, and through it with the whole Russian world; that we draw our conclusions about that world only through its culture. This infatuation is utterly natural, because the Jewish world on this side of the divide could not compete in our souls with the enchantment of the "other side." On the contrary, from our early childhood we perceive Jewry not in its highest manifestations, but through its everyday life and philistinism. We live within this ghetto and at every step we see its ugly impoverishment, created by centuries of oppression; and it is so unattractive, so unpleasant.... Whereas what is truly sublime and majestic in our heritage—Jewish culture—is what we do not perceive.[38]

The Jews' infatuation with Russian culture and their linguistic and cultural Russification created the conditions in which the non-Russian peoples of the empire viewed the Jews as bearers of what they considered hostile to them—Russian influence as an instrument of Russification. Russification, in turn, was the most important factor of imperialist policy in the non-Russian territories. As we shall see, Jabotinsky later declared war on the assimilation of the Jews and on their role as Russifiers in the non-Russian lands.

But why did Jews in most parts of the empire accept the Russian language and culture so readily and gladly while living amid non-Russian peoples whose cultural influence they were far less prepared to recognize? The answer lies in the fact that the Jews aspired to emancipation, and the *illusion* of emancipation required association with the ruling culture. Associating with an oppressed and half-forbidden culture was no equivalent of emancipation, and the most oppressed and semi-forbidden cultures under tsarist Russia were those of the Ukrainian and Belarusian peoples. The same, or only slightly better, conditions applied to most of the other peoples of the empire. Only the Poles, the Finns, and to some extent the Caucasian and Central Asian peoples were able to preserve, either juridically or in practice, certain elements of cultural autonomy on their territories. Besides this, the Jews needed the Russian language for purely practical purposes—to communicate with official functionaries, for appearances in court, for industrial and commercial matters, and for gaining an education. A somewhat analogous situation obtained and continues to obtain in many countries for Jews and other national minorities who have lost territorial compactness. But recognition of this fact does not constitute acceptance, and the Zionists were those who fought resolutely against assimilation.

In 1903, Jabotinsky underwent a spiritual metamorphosis involving a transformation of his world-view similar to that experienced by some of his predecessors in the Zionist movement. Leon Pinsker, the linguistically and culturally assimilated Jew who had called for the creation of a Jewish state fourteen years before Herzl, came to the idea of Zionism as a result of the wave of pogroms in 1881. Theodor Herzl, the Jew assimilated into German culture, had returned to his people under the influence of the Dreyfus trial in France.[39] For Jabotinsky, such an impulse came from the Chişinău pogrom. Chukovsky, who witnessed Jabotinsky's spiritual evolution, wrote of it as follows:

> He seemed to me as radiant as the sun, delighting in life. I gloried in his friendship and was certain that a broad literary avenue lay before him, but then in Chişinău came the thunder of the pogrom. Volodia Jabotinsky changed utterly. He started learning his native language, broke his ties with his former circles, and soon stopped writing for the general press. I had already scrutinized him from every angle. He was the most educated and most talented of all my friends, but I then drew even closer to him.... Until then I had not known that a person could change so completely.[40] Jabotinsky himself wrote about the influence of the Chişinău pogrom on Jewish awareness in tsarist Russia: "The future historian of the Jewish National Movement will certainly recognize those three days of massacre in the Bessarabian capital as marking, in many ways, the birth of a new Jewish mentality."[41] The Chişinău pogrom was the first mass pogrom following two decades during which there had been no pogroms on such a scale, which is why it had such an enormous impact on the Jewish community. This pogrom, in a city where Jews constituted almost half of the population (46.3 percent, according to the 1897 census[42]), bore for Jews all those especially disturbing hallmarks that were characteristic of the later wave of pogroms in 1905–6: the active incitement from local anti-Semitic circles and from the press (the well-known and extremely anti-Semitic Pavolaki Krushevan and his newspaper *Bessarabets* [The Bessarabian]); the authorities' indulgence toward, or even support for, the anti-Semites; and the military command's disinclination to defend the Jewish population against those who carried out the pogrom.[43] In Chişinău about fifty Jews were killed and several hundred wounded. It was the beginning of a tragic century for the Jews (and not for them alone).
>
> In 1903 Jabotinsky became a Zionist, and from that time until his death each step he took and every word he wrote were directed toward a single goal. There are very few figures in world history who devoted themselves to a single idea and a single cause as completely as Jabotinsky. In a 1904 article devoted to the memory of Theodor Herzl, who had died shortly before, Jabotinsky dedicated some profoundly felt lines to the condition of Jewry before Zionism emerged and to the metamorphosis that Zionism had produced among Jews. These lines are in great part autobiographical:

We were sitting at the time in the gutter, at the end of the great highway of life, and on this road we watched the majestic procession of nations on their way to their historic destinies. And we were sitting aside, like beggars with outstretched

> hands, begging for alms and swearing in different languages that we merited the charitable offering. Sometimes it was given to us, and then we imagined that we were pleased and contented because the master was in a good mood and had thrown us a gnawed bone. So it only appeared, for deep in our souls was growing a repulsive disgust for the beggar's spot in the gutter and for the outstretched hand, and we felt a confused attraction for the great highway, a desire to walk upon it like others, not to beg but to build our own happiness.
>
> Then he [Herzl] appeared and, responding to the vague impulsive yearning of our souls, spoke to us: "Create your own history; step out on the arena and see to it that from now on your destiny shall be created by you only." Never did an echo on earth bear such a resemblance to the voice that caused it as did his response to our expectations. And hence, never did mortal words have such a regenerating influence upon a generation.
>
> We changed; we were brought to life by touching the earth upon which he moved. It is only recently that I felt that earth, and it is only from that moment that I understood what it meant to live and breathe—and if on the morrow I should have awakened to learn that this was merely a dream, that I am what I had been, and that the ground is not and cannot be under my feet, I would have killed myself, for it is impossible for one who has breathed the mountain air to return and be reconciled to sprawl once more in the gutter.[44]

It was entirely natural that the first significant concern of Jabotinsky the Zionist should have been his involvement in the formation of a Jewish self-defense organization against pogroms in Odesa. He did not view self-defense only as a means of combating pogroms, for clearly in conditions where the authorities and police supported those who carried out the pogroms, the efficacy of self-defense would hardly be adequate to the purpose. He saw it also as the Jewish people's assertion of personal dignity and national pride—those qualities that Jabotinsky himself exhibited in the highest degree. He considered that Jewish armed detachments, no matter how small or weak, would inspire the Jewish masses with a faith in their own strength that would assist the growth of national consciousness and national consolidation.

Throughout his life, Jabotinsky fervently supported the creation of Jewish armed forces—a self-defense force; the Jewish Legion (which he later created within the framework of the British army); a Jewish gendarmerie within the Ukrainian army (which he attempted to create in 1921; see chapter 3); the Jewish armed organizations Haganah and Etzel, on whose creation in Palestine he had a decisive influence; and his call, upon the outbreak of World War II, for the creation of a Jewish army. His "militarism" was never an end in itself. He saw it always as simply a means whereby the Jewish people could secure a chance to live, preserve national awareness and identity, and fight for its future.[45] As a deeply civilized and humane individual, Jabotinsky could not in any way be a militarist in the ordinary and negative sense of the word. For him militarism meant force in the service of a practical policy that was called forth by the terrible threat to the life of the Jewish people. After breathing the atmosphere of this threat in Russia and feeling its approach in Western Europe, Jabotinsky sought to create Jewish armed forces to meet that danger not as the Jews had met it in Chişinău in 1903, but with dignity, with proudly uplifted heads, and with weapons in hand.

Having become a Zionist, Jabotinsky conceived of Zionism as Jewish nationalism. Although it may seem self-evident that every national movement is an expression of nationalism, the term was already quite compromised by the beginning of the twentieth century, and later developments in Europe even gave it sinister connotations. This has led many authors to seek to downplay the fact that Zionism is nothing other than Jewish nationalism. Yet Jabotinsky never hesitated to call himself a nationalist, and many of his works hail nationalism as a great life-giving and *liberal* idea that has nothing in common with chauvinism, racism or national arrogance. Whether one agrees with this view or not, one cannot fail to recognize the integrity, logic, and moral beauty embodied in Jabotinsky's interpretation of nationalism.

"Mrakobes" (The Obscurantist), his essay dedicated to the great Italian national leader Giuseppe Garibaldi, was an emotional hymn to liberal nationalism. Jabotinsky noted bitterly that in the eyes of contemporary left-wing political activists, who proclaimed slogans of proletarian internationalism and class struggle, Garibaldi was an obscurantist for demanding national independence instead of a solution to class antagonisms or other social problems. He put words into Garibaldi's mouth that could equally be seen as expressions of his own convictions:

> I dedicated my life to Italy, yet Herzen[46] called me a knight of humanity. I was indeed a knight of humanity and of humanitarianism, capable of loving and understanding all peoples, with my heart on the side of the oppressed in every struggle. But more than anything on earth I loved my people and its country, and when necessary I was capable of hating a foreign enslaver.... Yes, I was a knight of humanity, but I taught my fellow compatriots to believe that there is no greater good in the world than one's own nation and fatherland, and to acknowledge that there is no God for whose sake it would be worth sacrificing those two treasures. So my creation lies before me. I created this beautiful third Rome; I created this new, young life; this new center of creativity whose name is Italy. And I believe that my monument on the mountaintop is visible not only in Rome but throughout the world. In every corner of the world my call is still heard and remembered, and in time, wherever there exists an oppressed tribe with a great past and a bitter present, there also the struggle for *my* ideal will flare up....[47]

Jabotinsky's character and world-view incorporated two main features—an innate aristocratic nobility that impelled him to value personal and national dignity above everything else ("it is better not to live at all than to live without self-respect and pride," he wrote),[48] and a profoundly liberal outlook that he dubbed the "nineteenth-century world-view." Those two elements, aristocratism and liberalism, which in many instances can be opposites, were united in Jabotinsky together with his diverse talents and his intellectuality to form an individual of singular integrity. He was endowed with such attractive power that his onetime colleague Arthur Koestler spoke of "Jabotinsky's magnetism."[49]

Jabotinsky gave luminous expression to his credo in 1927, writing in memory of the eminent Italian liberal politician Luigi Luzzatti, who was of Jewish origin: "I will thus avail myself of comrade Luzzatti's death to attest my unwavering loyalty to the 'ideology of the nineteenth century.' I believe in the sacred immortality of those scraps from the pantry—freedom of speech, association, assembly and the press; democracy; universal suffrage; the equality of all before the law; and in a state above classes. I intensely, fastidiously, and derisively despise all other ideologies."[50] The somewhat ironic tone ("comrade Luzzatti," "scraps from the pantry"), highly characteristic of Jabotinsky, is merely a stylistic device concealing Jabotinsky's profound lifelong faith in the fundamental importance of liberal-democratic principles.

In the twentieth century, the epithet "nationalist" does not go unpunished. Jabotinsky's political opponents made demagogic use of the negative connotations associated with the idea of nationalism, connotations arising from the activities of fascists and racists in various countries, to bring charges against him that had no bearing on his ideology or practical activity. Jabotinsky's colleague and biographer, Joseph Schechtman, wrote bitterly: "This man, reared in the best traditions of nineteenth-century liberalism, was later decried as a Fascist and militarist."[51]

Jabotinsky became a nationalist in the Russian Empire, a state whose unique ethnic relations left their particular imprint on every expression of national consciousness and on the very concept of nationalism. Every people in the empire experienced restrictions, if not in the field of civil rights, then in such matters as free national and cultural development and the use of a native language. In every respect, tsarist Russia was a "prison-house of nations," as the representatives of various opposition movements often called it.

There is nothing odd about the fact that the status of the non-Russian peoples within the empire provoked their opposition. At the turn of the century, many national movements were already operating among the various peoples. Those movements became involved with the general all-empire opposition or revolutionary organizations (i.e., those basically Russian movements that operated not only on Russian ethnic territory but throughout the state), cooperating with them or confronting them. Together they comprised that extraordinarily complex patchwork of strained, explosive relations that finally erupted in a catastrophic revolution and civil war.

From the very beginning of his political activity, Jabotinsky understood that the resolution of Jewish nationality problems in Russia—preventing assimilation, putting a stop to persecution, and creating opportunities for untrammeled ethnic and cultural development—was only possible within the framework of the overall resolution of the empire's nationality problems. He considered it very harmful that Jewish civic forces were being dissipated in various political movements, Jewish and non-Jewish, whose main aim was not the resolution of nationality problems. Jabotinsky drew particular attention to this problem at the Third Zionist Conference (of Zionists in Russia), which was held in Helsinki in 1906. *Evreiskaia mysl'* (Jewish Thought) provided an account: "In the speaker's [Jabotinsky's] opinion, the Jews are unable to play a determining, creative role in the liberation movement as such because of their politically slight specific weight. The only realm in which they could say something distinctive would be that of the nationality question, the problem of building a multiracial state, especially and above all on the issue of national minorities."[52]

Only the Zionists adhered to the view that Jews should withdraw from active participation in the all-empire political movements and focus on the resolution of the nationality question; most of the Jewish revolutionary intelligentsia utterly rejected that view. For this very reason, Jabotinsky frequently repeated the idea in an effort to make it understood and accepted in wider Jewish circles: "We should...renounce all claims to be in the 'front ranks' of this struggle against the regime, which does not depend on the Jews. Pride of place should be given to the masters! ...Our independent, initiative and creative role in the liberation movement in Russia is entirely and exclusively concerned with the nationality question, and in that field we still need to stake out our plot."[53]

This was a prophetic idea, but at the time it did not meet with understanding and acceptance beyond the circles of non-socialist Zionists. Undoubtedly the revolution would have brought positive results for the Jews (abolition of the Pale of Settlement, enactment of legal equality for the Jewish people) even if the Jews had not taken such an active part in it, while the negative consequences of that participation have left their mark to this day. In the first place, participation by the most active sections of the Jewish intelligentsia in the revolutionary movements divided Jewish civic and intellectual forces, which left Jewry as a whole unprepared and defenseless during the bloody events of the revolution and civil war. In the second place, the presence of large numbers of Jews among the leaders of the revolutionary parties gave the tsarist regime and anti-Semitic circles a pretext for unleashing frenzied anti-Jewish activity.

Jabotinsky was one of the first to demand systematically that the Zionist organization take the most active part in the empire's political life with a single aim—the defense of the national rights of the Jewish people, as well as the preservation of its ethnic and cultural identity and national consciousness in order to create the conditions for future emigration from Russia to Palestine. In 1906, in a series of articles under the common title of "Our Tasks," Jabotinsky put forward an entire program to solve the Jewish question in Russia. Pride of place was given to equal rights for the nationalities and national autonomy for the

Jews.[54] In the same year, those programmatic demands were incorporated into the Helsinki Program adopted at the Zionist conference. Jabotinsky constantly emphasized that there was no contradiction between the two tasks of creating a national center in Palestine and fighting for Jewish rights in the Diaspora. According to him, the struggle for Jewish rights in the Diaspora would make it possible to gather forces, consolidate the nation, provide it with political education, organize it, and enable it to undertake autonomous political activity:[55]

> What is Zionism? It is the ideal and future outcome of a *Jewish national policy* (emphasis added—I.K.). A national policy worthy of the name is possible only when the nation is united, in the first place by a common awareness, and in the second place by common institutions. The first condition is called nationalization; the second, organization.... Both points together are necessary preconditions for a national policy and thus for Zionism. If we do not create them in exile, we shall never find our way out of exile. So what should our demands here, that is, our creative work in exile, lead toward? Toward the creation of those preconditions.[56]

After working out a program of Jewish tasks within the Russian Empire and gaining its adoption by the Zionist conference, Jabotinsky had solid grounds for stating: "Neither before the Helsinki conference nor since has any group in Jewry posed the question of equal rights for the Jewish people so comprehensively and demanded such an exhaustive response."[57] Jabotinsky understood that Jewish national policy was only beginning to take shape. Realizing that Zionism required a theoretical elaboration of nationality problems, he devoted a great deal of time to the study of theory and eventually became an eminent authority on the question of nationalities.

Karl Renner (Rudolf Springer), a prominent Austrian socialist, made a deep impression on Jabotinsky through his works on the nationality question.[58] Although never a socialist and later a convinced anti-socialist, Jabotinsky paid great attention to Renner's views, which, with some modifications, formed the basis of the nationality programs of socialist parties in various countries and the nationality programs of some Jewish and non-Jewish socialist parties and groups in Russia. However, Jabotinsky understood that Renner's nationality program was not readily applicable to the situation in Russia. In his introduction to the Russian translation of Renner's *State and Nation*, Jabotinsky wrote: "National distinctions in Russia are much deeper [than in Austria-Hungary]; the forms of national hostility are much sharper. To respond to Jewish pogroms or to the Armenian massacre with 'cultural' autonomy would simply be a joke. Nationalities must have effective means to secure their national inviolability."[59] Having distanced himself from Renner's formulae, Jabotinsky made a profound study of the problems of national minorities in multinational states. His article on "The Self-Government of a National Minority" (1913) was the outcome of some years' reflection and research.[60]

The situation in tsarist Russia provided a wealth of material and examples for the study of problems of inter-ethnic relations. In Ukraine especially there was a superabundance of such material. Even though he had had very little contact with the Ukrainian national element during his childhood and youth, Jabotinsky expressed great interest in Ukrainian national problems. His first references to the Ukrainian theme are to be found in articles published in 1904.[61] From the very outset of his activity concerning the nationality question, Jabotinsky expressed the conviction that in the struggle for its national goals, Jewry within the Russian Empire had to seek allies among the empire's oppressed peoples or, more precisely, among liberal-democratic circles in the national-liberation movements of those peoples. In "Our Tasks," he addressed that question as well: "By analyzing Jewish national demands, one can delineate the general principles upon which they are based. These must then take root in the consciousness of the predominant political spheres in Russia. We must find and unite with allies whose interests overlap to some extent with ours. Herein lie our tasks in the *general political* arena."[62]

The need to "find and unite with allies" quickly brought Jabotinsky to the principled political position that Jewish social life and national policy must (in the interest of Jews themselves) be coordinated with the social and political life of the non-Jewish environment. Much later, in 1930, he expressed this principle as follows: "We still have to live with [other] peoples and reckon with their ideals."[63] The principle may seem perfectly obvious, but in the conditions of the Russian Empire it was neither simple to grasp nor easy to adopt. Jewry within the empire was a national minority among peoples that themselves were national minorities within a huge multinational state. The long-standing, difficult, and complex relations between the imperial rulers and the non-Russian peoples could not but leave their mark on the fate of Jewry. With whom should the Jewish people live in peace and with whose ideals should they reckon—with those of the imperial rulers, with those of Russification and denationalization of the non-Russian peoples or, on the contrary, with the ideals of the latter and of their national movements?

Abnormal social conditions created a situation in which Jews involuntarily and almost unconsciously functioned as an instrument of the imperial policy of Russification, which was hateful to the indigenous peoples. It would be difficult to imagine a more unnatural situation than one in which a people hated and brutally repressed by a regime is at the same time this regime's faithful tool in its drive against other oppressed peoples. Indeed, the presence in large non-Russian territories of a significant national minority that was actively being Russified and that accepted and propagated Russian culture—Russian theater, the Russian press, Russian books—was bound to provoke opposition from nationally conscious elements among the indigenous peoples.

Jabotinsky was acutely conscious of the artificiality and danger inherent in such a situation. He put forward the idea that the Jewish national movement should support the indigenous national movements. Most of all, he was concerned to support the Ukrainian national movement, a concern that he expressed with particular clarity in the collection *Fel'etony* (Feuilletons).[64] He was most concerned with the Ukrainian national movement not just because he had been born in Ukraine, but because Ukraine occupied a special and very important position within the whole complex of the Russian Empire. The southwestern portion of the Russian Empire, with a territory approximately the size of France, was the richest and most fertile area in the state, the main supplier of grain, sugar, coal, and iron ore; a land where industry and trade were developing rapidly. At the end of the nineteenth century, Ukraine became the largest granary in Europe. Part of Ukraine's ethnic territory, Eastern Galicia, was ruled by Austria-Hungary, and its three million Ukrainians were under Polish influence. Smaller portions of Ukrainian ethnic territory controlled by Austria-Hungary were in zones of Slovak, Hungarian and Romanian influence. At the turn of the century, all Ukraine's ethnic territories comprised a population of about 36 million, of whom some 75 percent were Ukrainians.[65]

In every respect, Ukraine was one of the most important parts of the empire, second only to the central Russian regions. At the same time, Ukraine was of prime importance from a strategic perspective. Bordering what were then Austria-Hungary and Romania, Ukraine was the exit to Central and Southeastern Europe. Since it encompassed the northern shore of the Black Sea, Ukraine guaranteed the Russian Empire's sway over that sea and also gave it an exit through the Black Sea to the Mediterranean Sea and the Near and Middle East—regions that had long been objects of Russian imperialist encroachment. Over the centuries, Russia had fought Poland, Turkey, and Turkey's vassals, the Crimean khans, for mastery of Ukraine and the Black Sea coast. The struggle ended with Russia's total victory. By seizing this vast and rich land and thereby gaining a commanding strategic position, Russia moved into the ranks of the major European powers.

Ukraine was drawn into the Russian Empire's orbit gradually after 1654. At that time, following a long struggle with Poland, Hetman Bohdan Khmelnytsky concluded a military and political alliance with Muscovy. This was the start of a process that continued right up to the end of World War II, when the last portions of Ukrainian ethnic territory were annexed to the USSR. Russia's westward drive was a great historical victory, involving the domination of Ukraine, Belarus, and the states of the Eastern Baltic, as well as the destruction of Poland as a large, independent, and ambitious power. A significant role in this victory was played by the military struggle of the Ukrainian Cossacks and peasant insurgents against Polish domination. Having helped Russia destroy

Poland, the Ukrainians found themselves even worse off economically, socially, and politically in the Russian Empire. As the great Ukrainian poet Taras Shevchenko wrote:

> And you boast that we
> Once felled Poland!...
> The truth is yours: Poland fell,
> And crushed you with it![66]

Although Ukraine entered an association with Russia as an autonomous Cossack state, it gradually lost all elements of national and political autonomy and was transformed into a component of the Russian Empire, divided into several gubernias. Even the name "Ukraine" was not acknowledged by the tsarist authorities, who called it "Malaia Rossiia" (Little Russia) instead."

In pursuit of its policy of Russification, the tsarist government declared the Ukrainian and Belarusian peoples to be part of the Russian people, claiming that their languages were dialects of Russian, although such a classification has no basis from a philological or historical point of view. It was only in 1905 that the St. Petersburg Academy of Sciences recognized the independence of the Ukrainian language as the distinct language of a separate Slavic people.[67] Ever since the Valuev circular of 1863 (named after the minister of internal affairs, who issued it), the government had officially restricted the publication of Ukrainian books and the use of the Ukrainian language. In 1876, Tsar Alexander II's Ems Ukase introduced even tighter restrictions by forbidding the import of Ukrainian books and the staging of theatrical performances in Ukrainian.[68] Official restrictions on Ukrainian publishing and theater were not formally abolished until the 1917 Revolution, although in practice they had been significantly weakened after 1905.

The declaration that Ukrainians and Belarusians were part of the Russian people was a measure of the utmost importance for imperial interests. It meant that the Russian (Great Russian) people, a numerical minority within the empire's total population (about 43 percent, according to the 1897 census),[69] could appear as a large majority when counted together with the Ukrainians and Belarusians. Such a large Russian majority could be used to justify Russian cultural dominance within the empire, since that dominance would be due not to political coercion but to the numerical preponderance of Russians. The fusion of the three East Slavic peoples could create the indispensable basis for imperial rule that the Russians alone could not provide. The Zionist activist Joseph Schechtman, who later became Jabotinsky's associate and biographer, wrote in 1917:

> The traditional policy of Russification was applied with particular force and intensity against the Ukrainian people. In 1863, Minister of Internal Affairs Valuev said: "No Ukrainian language ever existed, exists today or will ever

> exist." This categorical repudiation, which was extended to cover the entire Ukrainian national identity, became the guiding principle of all government policy on the Ukrainian question. At a time when the national identities of other nationalities were recognized and those peoples were subject only to Russification, the position on Ukraine involved a complete denial of its national existence. The 30 million Ukrainians were registered en masse as "Russians"; every expression of national distinctiveness was viewed as an act of malicious separatism and *Mazepinstvo*[70] fostered by "Austrian intrigue." The Ukrainians' ethnic and cultural affinity with the Russians turned out to be their special *privilegium odiosum.*
>
> This view of Ukraine as an offshoot of the Great Russian nation was shared not only by the old regime but by reactionary intellectual forces [Iuzefovich, Shulgin] and progressive ones [Struve] as well. The regime fought ruthlessly against the Ukrainian movement as an active national force.[71]

The Ukrainian people's manifest national consciousness and its stubborn refusal to merge with the Poles or with the Russians led to numerous conflicts. The national-liberation struggle in Ukraine lasted for centuries, often assuming violent and bloody forms. That struggle also inscribed several tragic pages in the history of the Jewish people. Having no land of their own, the Jews were forced into commercial occupations, as well as intermediary and handicraft activities. In the eyes of the local population, the Jewish middlemen and traders appeared as servants of foreign exploiters, and every popular uprising against foreign domination was accompanied by destruction directed not only against foreign lords, but also against the local Jews. Since the Jews were more defenseless than the Polish lords, they often suffered more. In this way, anti-Semitism and anti-Jewish outrages were always linked to, and by-products of, social conflicts in Ukraine (as opposed to Russia). Unless that fundamental fact is understood, it is impossible to explore the status and history of the Jews in Ukraine.

Anti-Jewish outrages could indubitably provide an outlet for popular feeling, but they could in no way help to resolve social and national problems. Even if all the Jews in Ukraine had been exterminated in the course of national uprisings, that would not have altered the sociopolitical and national status of the Ukrainian people in the slightest. In fact, the Jewish pogroms in Ukraine, which took place during popular uprisings, were evidence of the political immaturity of the popular masses—an inability to recognize the true enemy, a sign of readiness to take revenge on the first available scapegoat. It is no secret that the Jews fit the bill as scapegoats better than anyone else.

In the historical memory of the Jewish people lie two unhealed wounds, remembered as Jewish tragedies that occurred during two mass popular uprisings in Ukraine: the Cossack-peasant uprising led by Bohdan Khmelnytsky in the mid-seventeenth century, and the peasant uprising led by the haidamakas (the so-called Koliivshchyna rebellion) in 1768, at whose head were Maksym Zalizniak and Ivan Gonta.[72] Nathan Hanover, a witness to the Ukrainian uprising in the mid-seventeenth century, gives a very vivid impression of the magnitude and horror of the tragedy, and there is no shortage of other testimonies.[73]

It should be noted that the eighteenth-century haidamaka uprisings in Right-Bank Ukraine, which was under Poland at that time, were in some instances inspired and incited by the Russian government, which sought to exploit them in order to weaken Poland.[74] Before the partitions of Poland at the end of the eighteenth century, there were hardly any Jews in Russia, and the tsarist government tried various means to restrict the number of Jews on its territory. As a result of Poland's partition, Russia gained large territories populated by Ukrainians, Belarusians, Poles, and Lithuanians, as well as by the Jews who lived there. This obliged the government to pay more attention to the Jewish problem, although legal restrictions against Jews remained the cornerstone of government policy. In particular, the Russian government always attempted to keep Jews within the bounds of those lands where they had lived under Polish rule, and it did not envisage the resettlement of a large number of Jews on ethnic Russian territories. Although in the period from the partitions of Poland until 1917 there were various partial twists and turns of policy, the general trend involved more extensive and oppressive restrictions on Jewish rights within the territories where they were allowed to live.

To understand anti-Semitism in Russia, it is important to be aware of the difference in principle between the anti-Semitism of the Russians and that of the non-Russian peoples such as the Ukrainians, Poles, and Lithuanians. Anti-Semitism among the non-Russian peoples arose out of the process of living with Jews on the same territory, associating with them, and engaging in economic competition and social conflict. The non-Russian peoples saw in the Jews and Jewry nothing mystical, mysterious or supernatural. The Jew could evoke dissatisfaction as an economic rival, hatred as a servant (real or imaginary) of foreign or local oppressors, and exasperation as the bearer of a different religion or mentality, but that was all. In more peaceful historical periods Ukrainians, Belarusians, Poles, and Lithuanians could live peaceably together with the Jews. They felt no mutual repulsion strong enough to disrupt the daily need for practical interaction that served mutual convenience.

Russian anti-Semitism has a completely different character. The mystical and messianic psychology peculiar to the Russians and so beautifully analyzed by the Russian philosopher Nikolai Berdiaev[75] provides the subsoil for the growth of a typically Russian mystical anti-Semitism. Russians rarely encountered Jews in everyday life, hence they drew their ideas about Jews most frequently from assertions about their role in crucifying Christ, as well as from home-grown or foreign anti-Semitic legends. All of this led to the rise of fantastic notions about Jewry as the incarnation of universal evil. These notions drew inspiration from mystical Russian messianic consciousness and took on such horrifying dimensions that the extremely anti-Jewish Black Hundred elements among the Russians completely lost contact with reality. Their writings on the Jewish question displayed this unreality, as witness their "theories" about the "worldwide Jewish-Masonic conspiracy" aimed at undermining or destroying all non-Jews; their notion that Jews systematically used human blood for ritual purposes and murdered Christian children massively and bestially; their idea that Jews had infiltrated all governments, parliaments, parties, and social organizations in the world; and their contention that Jews had already seized control of the world economy. All these and many other concoctions, advanced in Black Hundred writings with all seriousness and in language designed to beggar the imagination, reached heights far beyond the bounds of malicious political demagogy and gave the impression that they were created by a diseased psyche.[76]

It is interesting to note that philo-Semitism, which sometimes appears among the best-educated and mainly pro-Western Russian intelligentsia, often also has a mystical character. It is based on the notion of a chosen people that has some sort of special link with God and a particular destiny in the spiritual and religious development of humanity. Berdiaev exemplified this:

> The Jews have played an all-important role in history. They are preeminently a historical people and their destiny reflects the indestructibility of the divine decrees. Their destiny is too imbued with the "metaphysical" to be explained either in material or positive-historical terms. Moreover, it presents no sign of that antithesis between the metaphysical and the historical which I regard as an obstacle to the apprehension of the inner significance of history. I remember how the materialist interpretation of history, when I attempted in my youth to verify it by applying it to the destinies of peoples, broke down in the case of the Jews....[77]

However, such a positive-mystical approach to Jewry has been and still remains peculiar to only a small number of representatives of the Russian intelligentsia. Among the broad masses in Russia, as well as among semi-educated and educated circles, a negative-mystical attitude toward the Jewish people predominates.

Without doubt, the Russian Black Hundreds' anti-Jewish activity had consequences far beyond Russia's borders. Their efforts spawned a whole anti-Semitic school whose main "achievements" were later assimilated by Hitler and his circle. A prominent role in this was played by the Nazi ideologue Alfred Rosenberg (originally a Baltic German born and educated in the Russian Empire), who was very familiar with Black Hundred literature. Other Germans from Russia's Baltic region also played a part in ensuring that the "science" of the Russian Black Hundreds took root in German soil during the Nazi period.[78] Nevertheless, Nazi anti-Jewish writings are rather pale imitations of Black Hundred writings. The Nazis, with the practical German bent of their character, could vastly outdo Russian anti-Semites in the technical and organizational aspects of the mass extermination of Jews, but the "theoretical" writings of the Russian Black Hundreds are in many cases matchless models of anti-Jewish propaganda that could hardly be surpassed.[79] It is no accident that they were so readily exploited not only by Nazi but also by Soviet "anti-Zionist" propaganda.[80] It is important to note that the Ukrainian and other non-Russian national movements within the Russian Empire were never the source of such propaganda. It is particularly characteristic and suggestive that anti-Semitic propaganda in the USSR was consistently linked to propaganda against Ukrainian nationalism. The phrase "the criminal alliance between Zionism and Ukrainian bourgeois nationalism" became a stock in trade of Soviet propaganda.[81]

The tsarist regime's support for the Black Hundreds opened the way for mystical anti-Semitism to become a significant part of the ruling imperial ideology, whereas in the earlier period tsarist policy toward the Jews and the ideology associated with it had been considered of secondary importance. Inasmuch as mystical anti-Semitism was an irrational phenomenon, so also the domestic policy of the tsarist regime in the twentieth century was, to a significant degree, irrational and thus doomed to defeat. Since the great majority of Jews lived in the western and southwestern regions of the European part of the empire, it was there that the Black Hundreds developed their activity to the greatest extent. While they concentrated on disseminating and inciting anti-Semitism, they simultaneously opposed all the national-liberation movements and the national consciousness of all the non-Russian peoples in the empire, especially those of the Ukrainians and Belarusians, who were legally denied their identity, distinct from that of the Russians.

One result of this was the emergence of an important factor with major consequences: a common agenda of struggle against Black Hundred activity opened up before both the Jewish national movement and the national movements of other peoples in the empire. Certainly, as soon as the Black Hundred movement emerged, the Ukrainian national movement came out strongly against it. Especially consistent and uncompromising in its opposition to the Black Hundreds was the Russian-language *Ukrainskii vestnik* (Ukrainian Herald), established in St. Petersburg in 1906 by the eminent Ukrainian historian Mykhailo Hrushevsky. At that time, Hrushevsky was acclaimed as the leader of the Ukrainian movement. In 1908 he joined the governing council of the Society of Ukrainian Progressives, which comprised several Ukrainian political groups that stood for constitutional parliamentarism and Ukrainian autonomy.[82]

At the turn of the century a Revolutionary Ukrainian Party (RUP) also existed, which later developed along Marxist lines and transformed itself in 1905 into the Ukrainian Social Democratic Party. A Ukrainian People's Party was formed in 1902; it was later renamed the Ukrainian Party of Socialists-Independentists. This comparatively small party came out, from the start, for a completely independent

Ukraine—this at a time when the Ukrainian movement as a whole was advocating greater or lesser autonomy within the framework of a future democratic Russian state. There were also other Ukrainian parties and movements, most of which shared one form or another of socialist ideology.[83]

Individual Jews played an active part in the Ukrainian movement from its organizational beginnings in the 1860s. Thus Vsevolod Rubinshtein and Viliam Berenshtam were active in the Kyiv (Kiev) Hromada, a cultural and political organization of the Ukrainian intelligentsia. Quite a few Jews were involved in the RUP, and in the town of Makariv, in Kyiv gubernia, Jews even formed a RUP circle, while the journalistic efforts of Jewish political writer Maksym Hekhter were based on that party's program.[84] Although the majority of Jews in Ukraine maintained a certain distance from the Ukrainian movement, contacts always existed.

Substantially different conditions prevailed in the western part of Ukraine's ethnic territory, which was part of the Austro-Hungarian Empire until 1918. In Eastern Galicia, most of the population was Ukrainian (about 3 million Ukrainians or roughly 10 percent of the entire Ukrainian people). Galicia's capital, Lviv, is located in the eastern, that is, Ukrainian part of Galicia, but the city was almost completely Polonized. The process of Polonization in Galicia's Ukrainian towns was similar to that of Russification in Ukrainian towns within the Russian Empire.

Within Austria-Hungary Ukrainians experienced significantly fewer cultural restrictions than in the tsarist state. There were Ukrainian schools, publishers, and theaters, as well as cultural, educational and social organizations. The confrontation was less between Ukrainians and the Austrian authorities than between Ukrainians and Poles, who were trying to make their sway over Eastern Galicia permanent and to Polonize the Ukrainian population. Ukrainian-Jewish relations in Galicia were the subject of lively debate in both the Jewish and the Ukrainian press. (For Jabotinsky's participation in this discussion, see chapter 1.)

At the end of the nineteenth century, 1.8 million Jews inhabited the Ukrainian territories of the tsarist empire, while more than 600,000 Jews lived in Eastern Galicia. In 1897, almost 3 million Jews lived on Ukrainian ethnic territories as a whole.[85] Thus, at the turn of the century, about 28 percent of world Jewry was living on Ukrainian ethnic territories, was experiencing Ukrainian cultural influences, was being pulled willy-nilly into the social conflicts in those lands, and was being forced to reckon with conditions in its Ukrainian environment.

This, in general terms, was the political arena where Vladimir Jabotinsky began his activity. Even in his youth he had a sufficiently developed political sense to grasp that the Ukrainian question was the key problem that would largely determine the Russian Empire's future and consequently the fate of the Jews on that territory. He therefore understood that one could not develop a Jewish national policy in Ukraine, or more generally for the whole empire, without linking it to the problems of Ukraine and without deeply probing the essence of those problems. He saw also that the aims of the Ukrainian national movement—democratization of public life, recognition of national equality, and broad cultural and national autonomy—were analogous to the goals of the Zionist movement within the Russian Empire. So Jabotinsky set out resolutely on the path of support for Ukrainian national demands. The path was long and difficult, but Jabotinsky never deviated from it.

The history of Jabotinsky's dealings with Ukrainian problems can be divided, sometimes rather tentatively, into a few distinct periods. Each one is rich in courage, determination, and inner drama. The "Ukrainian pages" of Jabotinsky's biography as a politician and political writer highlight not only his attitude to the Ukrainian question, but also numerous facets of his political teachings and personal profile. I shall now proceed to examine, in chronological order, these "Ukrainian pages" in the life of a great Zionist leader.

# Notes

1. Jabotinsky generally used the Russian form of his first name, Vladimir; on occasion, especially when he wrote in Hebrew, he used the Hebrew equivalent, Ze'ev. Ukrainian political writers often Ukrainize his first name to Volodymyr. In the present work, I use the form of the name that Jabotinsky himself used.

   In bibliographic references to Jabotinsky's Russian-language writings, the Russian form of his surname, Zhabotinskii, is used in the present work.

2. *Entsyklopediia ukraïnoznavstva*, part 2, ed. Volodymyr Kubijovyč, 10 vols. (Paris and New York, 1955–84), 5: 1817; *Evreiskoe naselenie Rossii po dannym perepisi 1917 g. i po noveishim istochnikam* (Petrograd, 1917), p. 72 (henceforth *Evreiskoe naselenie*). Cf. *Encyclopedia of Ukraine*, ed. Volodymyr Kubijovyč and Danylo Husar Struk, 5 vols. (Toronto, 1984–93), 3: 654.

3. *Entsyklopediia ukraïnoznavstva*, part 1, ed. Volodymyr Kubijovyč and Zenon Kuzelia, 3 vols. (Munich and New York, 1949), 1: 158. A similar situation existed, particularly in some areas of the former Austro-Hungarian Empire, wherever a high percentage of Germans lived in towns on Slavic and Hungarian territories. Prague, the capital of the Czech lands, was almost completely Germanized until the mid-nineteenth century.

4. According to the census of 1897, in Odesa there were about 140,000 Jews out of a total population of approximately 404,000; that number increased to 152,000 on the eve of World War I (*Evreiskoe naselenie*, p. 72). The largest Jewish community in the empire, numbering 219,000, lived in Warsaw—the figure is given in *Evreiskaia ėntsiklopediia*, ed. L. I. Katsenel'son et al., 16 vols. (St. Petersburg, [1906–1913]), 5: 327. However, in proportion to the general population, the percentage of Jews was higher in Odesa than in Warsaw—35 percent in Odesa, about 32 percent in Warsaw.

5. Leon (Lev, Leib) Pinsker (1821–91), one of the first Zionists. In his book *Self-Emancipation* (1881), he argued for the idea of creating a Jewish state in Palestine fourteen years before Herzl did.

   Mendele Mokher Seforim (Shalom Abramovich, 1836–1927), prominent Jewish writer in Yiddish and Hebrew.

   Ahad Ha-Am (Asher Ginsberg, 1856–1927), Jewish philosopher and essayist. Known as the "father of spiritual Zionism," he wrote only in Hebrew. He considered that the spiritual rebirth of Jewry must be the basis and precondition for the creation of a Jewish state, which would be the spiritual center of world Jewry.

   Simon Dubnow (1860–1941), Jewish historian and sociopolitical leader. He wrote the multi-volume *Istoriia evreiskogo naroda* (History of the Jewish People) and many other works.

   Chaim Nachman Bialik (1873–1934), great Jewish poet who wrote mainly in Hebrew.

Joseph Klausner (1874–1958), prominent Jewish historian and literary scholar.

Isaac Babel (1894–1941), prominent Soviet Russian writer of Jewish origin. Many of his works depict the Jewish lower strata of Odesa in a humorous vein.

Eduard Bagritsky (Eduard Dziubin, 1895–1934), Soviet Russian poet of Jewish origin.

On Jewish intellectual life in Odesa, see A. Orbach, "Jewish Intellectuals in Odesa in the Late Nineteenth Century: The Nationalist Theories of Ahad Ha'am and Simon Dubnov," *Nationalities Papers* 6, no. 2 (Fall 1978).

6. V. Zhabotinskii, "Moia stolitsa," in *Causeries* (Paris, 1930), pp. 75–85.

7. V. Jabotinsky, *Avtobiografia* (Jerusalem, 1947).

8. V. Zhabotinskii, "Moia stolitsa," 78. *Chumaky* were wagoners and traders who dealt mainly in salt and fish. Peresyp is a district of Odesa.

9. At the beginning of the century, two of Jabotinsky's plays were performed in Odesa—*Krov'* (Blood) and *Ladno* (All Right). His poetic talent was well demonstrated in the poem "Bednaia Sharlotta" (Poor Charlotte, 1902, about Marat's murderer, Charlotte Corday). His translations into Russian of Edgar Allan Poe and Chaim Nachman Bialik remain unsurpassed to this day. He also translated many other poets. Later, Jabotinsky also wrote novels (*Samson-Nazorei* [Samson the Nazarene], 1927; *Piatero* [Five], 1936). His own poems also deserve attention.

10. A reference to the image of Mozart in Pushkin's "little tragedy" "Motsart i Sal'eri."

11. *Rakhel' Pavlovna Margolina i ee perepiska s Korneem Ivanovichem Chukovskim* (Jerusalem, 1978), p. 20.

12. Joseph B. Schechtman, *Rebel and Statesman: The Vladimir Jabotinsky Story*, vol. 1, *The Early Years* (New York, 1956), pp. 67, 108–9; Yehuda Benari, *Zeev Vladimir Jabotinsky: A Biographical Sketch* (Tel Aviv, 1977), p. 6.

13. *Evreiskoe naselenie*, pp. ix, x; *Evreiskaia ėntsiklopediia*, 11: 527–30.

14. *Evreiskoe naselenie*, pp. ix, x; *Evreiskaia ėntsiklopediia*, 11: 527–30. Since many countries did not conduct censuses, the quoted percentages should be considered approximations.

15. *Evreiskoe naselenie*, p. 55; *Evreiskaia ėntsiklopediia*, 11: 537.

16. Herein lies the main difference between the situation of Jews in tsarist Russia and in the USSR: in tsarist Russia discrimination against Jews existed officially according to the religious criterion, but in the USSR it existed unofficially and exclusively according to the criterion of ethnic origin. See Shmuel Ettinger, ed., *Anti-Semitism in the Soviet Union: Its Roots and Consequences*, 3 vols. (Jerusalem, 1979–83); Aleksander Voronel and Viktor Yakhot, ed., *I Am a Jew: Essays on Jewish Identity in the Soviet Union* (New York, 1973); and Israel Kleiner, *Natsional'ni problemy ostann'oï imperiï: natsional'ne pytannia v SRSR ochyma radians'kykh dysydentiv* (Paris, 1978), pp. 219–55.

17. *Novyi zhurnal*, no. 109 (1972): 209; Mikhail Frenkin, *Zakhvat vlasti bol'shevikami v Rossii i rol' tylovykh garnizonov armii: podgotovka i provedenie oktiabr'skogo miatezha, 1917–1918 gg.* (Jerusalem, 1982), p. 148.

18. *Evreiskaia ėntsiklopediia*, 11: 536–37.

19. The quota for Jews in higher educational institutions was 3 percent in St. Petersburg and Moscow, 5 percent in other cities outside the Pale of Settlement, and 10 percent in the Pale of Settlement. The corresponding quotas for secondary educational institutions were 5, 10, and 15 percent respectively (*Evreiskaia ėntsiklopediia*, 13: 55).

20. *Evreiskoe naselenie*, pp. 1–76, tables. For the economic situation of Jews in Russia, see D. S. Pasmanik, "Ėkonomicheskoe polozhenie russkogo evreistva," *Evreiskaia zhizn'*, nos. 11 and 12 (November and December 1904); and *Sbornik materialov ob ėkonomicheskom polozhenii evreev v Rossii*, 2 vols. (St. Petersburg, 1904).

21. A reference to the parliamentary system introduced by the tsar in 1905 as a result of the first Russian Revolution.

22. *Evreiskaia ėntsiklopediia*, 13: 626.

23. *Evreiskoe naselenie*, pp. v-x.

24. *Evreiskaia ėntsiklopediia*, 9: 894–95.

25. There has always been a great deal of controversy and speculation about the degree and significance of Jewish participation in revolutionary events in the Russian Empire, which has given rise to a considerable literature on the subject. See especially: D. S. Pasmanik, *Russkaia revoliutsiia i evreistvo: bol'shevizm i iudaizm* (Paris, 1923); I. M. Bikerman, "Rossiia i russkoe evreistvo," in *Rossiia i evrei* (Berlin, 1923), pp. 9–96; I. O. Levin, "Evrei v revoliutsii," in *Rossiia i evrei*, pp. 121–38; David Shub, "Evrei v russkoi revoliutsii" in *Politicheskie deiateli Rossii (1850-kh—1920-kh g.g.)* (New York, 1969), pp. 353–76; Leonard Schapiro, "The Role of the Jews in the Russian Revolutionary Movement," *Slavic and East European Journal* 11, no. 94 (December 1961); Mikhail Frenkin, "Some Observations on Russian Jewry and Russia's Political Parties (1917–1921)," *Crossroads*, no. 3 (Spring 1979): 103–38.

26. See especially Kleiner, *Natsional'ni problemy*, pp. 9–27, 256–74.

27. G. A. Landau, "Revoliutsionnye idei v evreiskoi obshchestvennosti," in *Rossiia i evrei*, pp. 97–120; Yitzhak Maor, *Gatnua gatsionit berusiia* (The Zionist Movement in Russia) (Jerusalem, 1973); *Revoliutsionnoe dvizhenie sredi evreev: sbornik pervyi* (Moscow, 1930); A. Margolin, *Natsional'noe dvizhenie v evreistve, 1881–1913* (Petrograd, 1917).

28. *Evreiskaia ėntsiklopediia*, 7: 369–75; *The Jewish Question in the Duma: Speeches by Deputies* (London, 1915).

29. The most important source for the study of the Russian Black Hundred movement is A. Chernovskii, *Soiuz russkogo naroda: po materialam Chrezvychainoi sledstvennoi komissii Vremennogo pravitel'stva 1917 g.*, ed. and intro. by V. P. Viktorov (Moscow, 1929).

30. "Russkomu narodu" (St. Petersburg, 2 September 1906). This was the program of the Union of the Russian People, issued as a four-page broadsheet.

31. Ibid. Emphasis in original.

32. *Dnevnik imperatora Nikolaia II* (Berlin, 1923), pp. 229, 232; *Soiuz russkogo naroda*; Salo W. Baron, *The Russian Jew under Tsars and Soviets* (New York and London, 1964), pp. 74–76.

33. *Khronika evreskoi zhizni* (St. Petersburg), no. 23 (15 June 1906): 4–18, and no. 24 (22 June 1906): 10–18; *Pogromy v Rossii (po ofitsial'nym dokumentam)* (Berlin, n.d.), pp. 445–51 (a speech by State Duma member Makushin at a meeting on 29 June 1906); "Belostokskii pogrom," *Evreiskaia ėntsiklopediia*, 5: 170–74; and "Pogromy v Rossii," *Evreiskaia ėntsiklopediia*, 13: 611–22.

34. *Osvobozhdenie*, no. 12 (36) (24 November 1903): 206–9.

35. *Soiuz russkogo naroda*, pp. 257–65.

36. A characteristic example of Black Hundred anti-Jewish propaganda about the myth of ritual murders is the pamphlet *Istoricheskaia spravka (o ritual'nykh ubiistvakh)* (St. Petersburg, 1911), with an appendix of "A List of Ritual Murders."
On the Beilis trial, see V. Zhabotinskii, "O ritual'nom ubiistve," *Odesskie novosti*, 14, 15, 17, and 19–22 September 1913; idem, "Delo bez Beilisa," *Odesskie novosti*, 27 September 1913; idem, "Vmesto apologii," in *Fel'etony* (St. Petersburg, 1913), pp. 195–205; L. I. Petrazhitskii, *O ritual'nykh ubiistvakh i dele Beilisa* (St. Petersburg, 1913); Mendel Beilis, *The Story of My Sufferings* (New York, 1926); and Maurice Samuel, *Blood Accusation: The Strange History of the Beiliss Case* (New York, 1966).

37. Landau, "Revoliutsionnye idei"; Maor, *Gatnua gatsionit berusiia*; *Revoliutsionnoe dvizhenie sredi evreev*; and Margolin, *Natsional'noe dvizhenie v evreistve*.

38. V. Zhabotinskii, *Evreiskoe vospitanie* (Odesa, 1905), pp. 10–11.

39. Highly interesting in this connection is an article by Martin Buber, "Die drängende Stunde (über Leo Pinsker und Theodor Herzl)," in M. Buber, *Israel und Palästina* (Zurich, 1950). For an English translation, see M. Buber, *On Zion: The History of an Idea*, trans. Stanley Godman (New York, 1973), pp. 123–42.

40. *Rakhel' Pavlovna Margolina i ee perepiska*, pp. 11–12.

41. Chaim Nachman Bialik, *Poems from the Hebrew* (London, 1924), intro. by Vladimir Jabotinsky, p. xiv.

42. *Evreiskoe naselenie*, p. 2.

43. *Evreiskaia ėntsiklopediia*, 9: 506–7.

44. "Shiva," in *From the Pen of Jabotinsky* (Capetown, 1941), pp. 30–31.

45. V. Zhabotinskii, *Slovo o polku: istoriia evreiskogo legiona po vospominaniiam ego initsiatora* (Paris, 1928); Schechtman, *Rebel and Statesman*, 1: 201–86; V. Jabotinsky, *Die Idee des Betar* (Lyck, 1935), especially the chapter "Legionismus."

46. Aleksandr Ivanovich Herzen (1812–70), Russian political writer and liberal oppositionist. He played an enormous role in the development of Russian oppositional thought, but spent a large part of his adult life abroad as editor of the journal *Kolokol* (The Bell, 1857–67).

47. V. Zhabotinskii, "Mrakobes" in *Fel'etony*, p. 274.

48. V. Zhabotinskii, *Nedrugam Siona* (Odesa, 1905), p. 4.

49. Arthur Koestler, "The Magnetism of Jabotinsky," *The Jewish Herald* (Johannesburg, 1954), p. 25.

50. V. Zhabotinskii, "My burzhui," *Rassvet* (Paris), nos. 15–16 (17 April 1927).

51. Schechtman, *Rebel and Statesman*, 1: 16.

52. *Evreiskaia mysl'* (Odesa), 7 December 1906, p. 18.

53. V. Zhabotinskii, "Nashi zadachi," *Khronika evreskoi zhizni* (St. Petersburg), no. 27 (13 July 1906): 7–8.

54. V. Zhabotinskii, "Nashi zadachi," *Khronika evreiskoii zhizni*, no. 23 (15 June 1906), no. 25 (29 June 1906), no. 26 (6 July 1906), no. 27 (13 July 1906), and no. 28 (20 July 1906).

55. V. Zhabotinskii, "Gel'singforskaia programma," *Odesskie novosti*, 12 August 1912, p. 4. See also V. Zhabotinskii, "Nashi zadachi."

56. V. Zhabotinskii, "Nashi zadachi," *Khronika evreiskoii zhizni*, no. 23 (15 June 1906): 20.

57. V. Zhabotinskii, "Gel'singforskaia programma," p. 4.

58. Karl Renner (Rudolf Springer, Sinoptikus, 1870–1950), Austrian social-democratic politician. He held high government positions and during the last five years of his life was the federal president of Austria. He is also well known for his work on the nationality question.

59. V. Zhabotinskii, intro. to R. Springer, *Gosudarstvo i natsiia* (Odesa, 1906), p. 4.

60. V. Zhabotinskii, "Samoupravlenie natsional'nogo men'shinstva," *Vestnik Evropy* (St. Petersburg, September 1913): 117–38; (October 1913): 131–58.

61. An interesting treatment of the Ukrainian theme, with an expression of sympathy for the fate of the Ukrainian language and culture, which were being subjected to Russification, appears in V. Zhabotinskii, "K voprosu o natsionalizme (Otvet g. Izgoevu)," *Obrazovanie* (St. Petersburg), no. 10 (October 1904): 87–98.

62. V. Zhabotinskii, "Nashi zadachi," *Khronika evreiskoii zhizni*, no. 27 (13 July 1906): 8.

63. V. Zhabotinskii, "D. S. Pasmanik," *Rassvet*, no. 28 (13 July 1930): 7.

64. V. Zhabotinskii, *Fel'etony* (St. Petersburg, 1913). A second edition was published in Berlin in 1922, but it did not include all of of the articles in the first edition, some of which touched on the Ukrainian question. "Urok iubileia Shevchenko" is a passionate defense of Ukrainian political and cultural particularity. Other articles in the collection largely devoted to the Ukrainian question are: "Fal'sifikatsiia shkoly," "Na lozhnom puti," and "O iazykakh i prochem." For further details, see chapter 2 of the present work.

65. *Entsyklopediia ukraïnoznavstva*, part 1, 1: 134, 157–70; 3: 1035–36. Cf. *Encyclopedia of Ukraine*, 4: 148–49.

66. From Shevchenko's poem "I mertvym, i zhyvym, i nenarozhdennym zemliakam moïm v Ukraini i ne v Ukraini moie druzhnieie poslaniie" (To My Dead, Living, and Unborn Countrymen Both in Ukraine and outside It—My Friendly Epistle) (1845).

67. *Peterburz'ka Akademiia Nauk v spravi znesennia zaborony ukraïns'koho slova* (Lviv, 1905).

68. *Entsyklopediia ukraïnoznavstva*, part 2, 1: 205, 2: 637–38; *Encyclopedia of Ukraine*, 1: 824–25; 5: 552–53.

69. *Obshchii svod po imperii rezul'tatov razrabotki dannykh pervoi vse-obshchei perepisi naseleniia, proizvedennoi 28 ianvaria 1897 g.*, ed. N. A. Troinitskii (St. Petersburg, 1905), 1: 82–86, tables 41–43.

70. *Mazepinstvo* (Mazepism) was a derogatory name for Ukrainian national aspirations applied by Russian imperialists. It is derived from the name of the Ukrainian hetman Ivan Mazepa (1639–1709), who attempted to separate Ukraine from Russia at the beginning of the eighteenth century.

71. I. Shekhtman, *Evrei i ukraintsy* (Odesa, 1917), pp. 2–3. Iosef (Iosif, Joseph) Schechtman (1891–1970), Zionist leader and political writer born in Odesa. He was Jabotinsky's colleague in the Zionist Revisionist movement and on the journal *Rassvet*. He wrote a two-volume biography of Jabotinsky, as well as books on the nationality question, the history of Ukrainian-Jewish relations, and many other topics.

72. V. Antonovich (Volodymyr Antonovych), "Poslednie vremena kazachestva na pravoi storone Dnepra," *Arkhiv Iugo-Zapadnoi Rossii* (Kyiv), part 3, vol. 2 (1868): 1–787; Dmytro Doroshenko, *Narys istorii Ukraïny*, 2: 247–67; Simon Dubnow, *Die Weltgeschichte des jüdischen Volkes* (Berlin, 1925–30), 7: 157–69.

73. *Bogdan Khmel'nitskii: Letopis' evreia-sovremennika Natana Gannovera* (Leipzig, 1883); and Dubnow, *Weltgeschichte*, 7: 16–30.

Bernard Weinryb has established that the contemporary accounts by Hanover and other authors of Jewish chronicles are not completely objective and exaggerate evidence on the scale of the pogroms and the number of Jewish victims. Bernard D. Weinryb, "The Hebrew Chronicles on Bohdan Khmel'nyts'kyi and the Cossack-Polish War," *Harvard Ukrainian Studies* 1, no. 2 (June 1977): 153–77. However, the fact remains that the Khmelnytsky uprising was and remains one of the greatest national tragedies in Jewish historical memory.

74. V. Antonovich (Volodymyr Antonovych), "Akty o gaidamakakh (1700–1768)," *Arkhiv Iugo-Zapadnoi Rossii* (Kyiv), part 3, vol. 2 (1876): 128–897; Doroshenko, *Narys istorii Ukraïny*, 2: 247–66.

75. Nikolai Berdiaev, *Istoki i smysl russkogo kommunizma* (Paris, 1955); *Filosofiia neravenstva* (Paris, 1970); and *Smysl istorii* (Paris, 1969), pp. 65–106.

76. See, for example, G. Butmi, *Oblichitel'nye rechi: Vragi roda chelovecheskogo. Posviashchaetsia Soiuzu Russkogo Naroda* (St. Petersburg, 1906). Some typical excerpts from this work:

The tribe of Judas and his Elders is called "The Serpent," and its secret government, which is engaging in activities according to a preordained goal, is the "head of the Serpent."...

The task is expressed clearly: the enslavement of all humanity by the tribe of Judas, simultaneously crushing the Cross and the Christian religion and replacing them with the Kingdom of the Serpent. The Serpent is identified with the tribe of Judas, with finance capital, and with idolatry of the Golden Lamb. (p. 95)

That is how great nations decline at the touch of the Judeans. That is the harm caused by Judeans, despite themselves, which is due solely to the corrupting influence of their characteristic spiritual turpitude. Like the plague, it is passed on to every society that has dealings with the Judeans.

The harm caused by this spiritual plague, spread quite unconsciously by the Judeans, is aggravated by the conscious actions carried out by every Judean in accordance with a thoroughly predetermined hellish plan intended to subjugate all of humanity.

Everyone who wishes to save himself, his Nation, and his Homeland from total enslavement by the enemies of the human race must familiarize himself with this hellish plan, the exposition of which constitutes the second and most important section of our book. (p. 10)

77. Nikolai Berdiaev, *The Meaning of History*, trans. George Reavey (Cleveland and New York, 1962), p. 82.

78. *Encyclopaedia Judaica*, ed. Cecil Roth and Geoffrey Wigoder, 16 vols. (Jerusalem, 1972), 14: 275–76, 15: 1538, 16: 581–83; and Norman Cohn, *Warrant for Genocide: The Myth of the Jewish World-Conspiracy and the Protocols of the Elders of Zion* (Chico, CA, 1981), pp. 43, 98, 138–41, and passim.

79. An example of such a fabrication is the *Protokoly sionskikh mudretsov* (The Protocols of the Elders of Zion), widely used by the Russian Black Hundreds, the Nazis, and by anti-Semites in many countries today. See, especially, *Protocols of the Meetings of the Learned Elders of Zion* (London, 1925).

    Written by Sergei Nilus and first published in Russia in 1902, this fabrication became the prototype of all the Black Hundred and Nazi anti-Semitic theories.

80. Trokhym Kychko's book, *Iudaïzm bez prykras* (Kyiv: V-vo Akademiï nauk URSR, 1963), provoked indignation throughout the world because of its extreme anti-Jewish content and obvious similarity (both in text and illustrations) to the Black Hundred and Nazi anti-Jewish publications. The Soviet authorities deliberately tried to enlist authors of Jewish origin to write such anti-Jewish works. Tsezar' Solodar' became particularly infamous for his reckless anti-Jewish slanders. The quantity of "anti-Zionist" books, pamphlets, and articles published in the USSR comprised several hundred titles, and it is impossible to list them here. Relevant titles include Iu. S. Ivanov, *Ostorozhno: sionizm!* (Moscow: Izd-vo politicheskoi literatury, 1971); V. Skurlatov, *Sionizm i aparteid* (Kyiv: Izd-vo politicheskoi literatury Ukrainy, 1975); V. V. Bol'shakov, *Sionizm na sluzhbe antikommunizma* (Moscow: Izd-vo politicheskoi literatury, 1972); Ts. S. Solodar', *Dikaia polyn'* (Moscow: Sovetskaia Rossiia, 1977), *Tovar* (Moscow: Izd-vo Pravda, 1979), and *Temnaia zavesa* (Moscow: Molodaia gvardiia, 1979); T. K. Kychko, *Sionizm—voroh molodi* (Kyiv: Molod', 1972); G. Plotkin, *Poezdka v Izrail'* (Moscow: Izd-vo Literaturnoi gazety, 1959); and V. Bolchakov, *L'anti-communisme, profession des sionistes* (Moscow: Editions de l'Agence de Presse Novosti, 1972).

    See also "A Short List of Anti-Semitic and Anti-Israeli Publications in the USSR in the 1960s and 1970s," *Anti-Semitism in the Soviet Union: Its Roots and Consequences*, 1: 345–52.

81. Israel Kleiner, "The Soviet Ukrainian Press on Zionism and Israel," *Soviet Jewish Affairs* 4, no. 2 (1974): 46–52.

82. *Encyclopedia of Ukraine*, 5: 478; *Entsyklopediia ukraïnoznavstva*, part 1, 2: 476.

83. *Encyclopedia of Ukraine*, 4: 361–62, 5: 420–21; *Entsyklopediia ukraïnoznavstva*, part 1, 2: 472–76.

84. *Encyclopedia of Ukraine*, 2: 244–45; *Entsyklopediia ukraïnoznavstva*, part 1, 2: 473.

85. *Evreiskaia ėntsiklopediia*, 6: 98, 11: 527–30; *Entsyklopediia ukraïnoznavstva*, part 2, 2: 675; *Evreiskoe naselenie*, pp. ix-x.

CHAPTER 1

# Early Years: Concurrence and Divergence of National Destinies

The study of Jabotinsky's creative legacy leads one to the conclusion that he was not only a talented writer and an outstanding political leader, but also a prominent expert in a quite specific field—the theory of inter-ethnic relations. At the start of his political career, in 1906, he wrote that "the struggle of nations should be free from elements of violence, arbitrariness, and oppression."[1] In 1940, the last year of his life, he wrote: "Grecian or Bantu, Nordic or Eskimo. They were all formed in God's image: that is what we have learned from the Bible's first chapter. The Bible goes even beyond mere royal majesty: it hints that men are almost gods, or demigods."[2] Jabotinsky had to apply these noble and elevated ideas about nations and their mutual relations (to which he adhered throughout his life) to the complex relations among peoples in tsarist Russia, where his own people experienced not only legal restrictions and economic distress, but threats to its physical existence that were supported by the authorities.

After the 1903 pogrom in the Moldavian city of Chişinău, Jabotinsky surveyed the situation from his new standpoint of a patriot of his own nation, but a patriot without a *patria*. He saw his own people's dispersal among the numerous others of the empire. What conclusion followed from this? To a Zionist who was worried about his people's assimilation and indignant about anti-Semitism and its horrific consequences, the pogroms, it might have appeared self-evident that it was necessary to oppose the non-Jewish environment, to isolate oneself from it in order to preserve national identity for future resettlement in Palestine. Indeed, such self-isolation was to be found in the centuries-old Jewish ghetto, from which the Jewish people within the Russian Empire were only beginning to emerge. Would self-isolation save them from anti-Semitism? Did it guarantee the normal spiritual development of the nation? Historical experience showed that the ghetto neither gave refuge from anti-Semitism nor guaranteed, from the eighteenth century onwards, the normal national, cultural and religious development of the Jewish people.[3]

The Zionist movement originated at a time when Jewry in Europe and America was in a state of profound religious, national, and cultural crisis. Assimilation was both a consequence and, at the same time, one of the components of that crisis. Those Jews who rejected assimilation and searched for a way out found hope along the path of Zionism. The father of political Zionism,

Theodor Herzl, considered the final goal to be a Jewish state, while the father of "spiritual Zionism," Ahad Ha-Am, believed that the creation of a state would acquire meaning only in the context of a spiritual renewal of Jewry.[4]

Jabotinsky's ideology combined the main premises of political Zionism with some of the ideas embodied in spiritual Zionism. He considered that the political solution, the creation of a state, would be both the basis and the guarantee for the further spiritual and cultural development of the Jewish people.

Later, when the onslaught of Nazism threatened the physical survival as well as the national and cultural existence of European Jewry, Jabotinsky advanced the evacuation of the Jews from Europe to Palestine as the main aim. At the beginning of the twentieth century, however, the main threat came from assimilation. One of the predominant factors facilitating assimilation was the lack of an independent Jewish national policy. This stemmed from the inadequate political principles of Jewish political circles, whose thinking often revolved within the orbit of social utopias and did not attain a level on which their own national political principles could be elaborated consciously. Jabotinsky was, in fact, the first to emphasize the importance of working out such principles, and ultimately he formulated them as an ordered programmatic system and world-view.

An aristocrat in spirit, Jabotinsky made the principle of national dignity the cornerstone of his political program, the precondition for Jewry's national preservation before its return to the historical homeland, Eretz Israel (the Land of Israel). Is it possible for a people dispersed among other peoples to preserve and foster its own national dignity while simultaneously failing to recognize their national dignity and failing to respect them and to take into account their national interests? To this question Jabotinsky would have replied with a decisive "No!" He would also have added one especially important rider: respect other peoples, take their interests into account, but only insofar as they adopt the same attitude toward the Jews, respecting Jewish dignity and taking Jewish national interests into account.

Thus did Jabotinsky bring to the relations between his people in the Diaspora and neighboring peoples those principles that usually apply to normal relations between sovereign nation-states, that is, mutual recognition of national rights and interests, mutual respect and assistance, and the diplomatic principle of "reciprocity of treatment." He considered that the only way in which the Jewish nation could gain the right to fully equal status as a national body in its own eyes and in those of the world, thereby preparing the ground for its future recognition as a nation-state with equal rights.

Jabotinsky expressed his demand for obligatory reciprocity in relations between nations in many of his works and in various contexts, but his most important formulation of that principle was in the area of Polish-Jewish and Ukrainian-Jewish relations. At that very time, the Polish national struggle was gaining strength. Both in the Russian Empire and in Austria-Hungary, the Polish people were making the broadest possible demands for greater national, cultural and administrative autonomy. In fighting for their own national rights, all the Polish national parties categorically refused to recognize the national rights of the Jewish minority in Poland. Jabotinsky wrote about this frequently. In one of the most characteristic expressions of his views, he said:

> I absolutely refuse to understand how one can take account of the national demands of a people that refuses in principle to reckon with the Jewish people's national rights. None of the leading Polish parties recognizes the Jews as a people with equal rights, and none recognizes their right to a national culture. The Poles protest against the Russification of Jews only because they demand their Polonization. This forces us into an utterly unique relationship in which it would be foolish and absurd for us to take Polish national demands into account. In politics, considerate behavior is inadmissible unless it is mutual. For there can be only two options: either all nationalities have an equal right to their cultures and the national sentiments of each are sacred and inviolable, or there are no such rights at all, in which case the national sentiments of the Poles are as little sacred as those of the Jews. Equality is for all or for none.[5]

This was Jabotinsky's fundamental principle, which should be termed the principle of national dignity and national sovereignty.

In contrast with Polish-Jewish relations, Jabotinsky gave his readers the example of the position taken by the Ukrainian national parties, which fully recognized Jewish national rights: "The leading parties of the Ukrainian national movement recognize the Jews' right to their national culture...and welcome every sign of the national awakening of Jewry."[6] Because of the Ukrainian movement's position, Jabotinsky called on Jewish national circles to pay close attention to nationally conscious Ukrainianism as an ally in the struggle for national rights.

It would be useful to digress a little by posing a question of great importance to the understanding of Jabotinsky's personality and his political activity. He was, above all, a striking personality, so colorful that countless other talented, creative people around him, who worked with him in the Zionist-Revisionist movement that he built, fade almost completely from view. Was the multi-ethnic environment that shaped his personality so strongly reflected in his emotional and spiritual makeup that it prevented him from dealing with other peoples within the framework of polite "reciprocity of treatment?" In what was probably Jabotinsky's first pronouncement on the Ukrainian theme, in 1904, he evinced profound regret that the Ukrainian vernacular was being corrupted by Russian influence. Even in this early article, his particular universalist humanism found expression:

> While traveling in the third-class carriage of a train, I listened attentively to this degradation of the Ukrainian language [the great number of Russian words and expressions that Jabotinsky heard in the language of Ukrainian peasants on the

> train], and although I myself am neither a Little Russian nor a Slav, I wanted to shout to the entire Slavic world, "Why are you allowing this to happen? What is occurring before your very eyes is the destruction and loss of Slavic wealth!"
>
> Only mutual respect and full recognition of the individual rights of every member of the family will make for peace and harmony within this family. All of us dream of the days when all the people on earth will become brothers to one another, but such a call for brotherhood would sound hollow if one were to say to another: "I have nothing against you rejecting your individuality and becoming a duplicate of myself, and then we shall be brothers." I would feel a complete repudiation of brotherhood in such a formula....[7]

Here Jabotinsky had in mind the official policy of Russification in Russia and the attempted Polonization in Polish and western Ukrainian territories, a policy from which both Ukrainians and Jews suffered. Jabotinsky's unequivocal condemnation of such a policy was one of the first political axioms on which he based his theory of the nation: "Every nation, large or small, wherever it may be, requires the right and opportunity to exist, remain itself, and proclaim its national identity openly: only under such conditions can there be true brotherhood between it and people of different blood."[8]

A problem that was always of the greatest interest to Jabotinsky was the attitude of Jews in the Diaspora to the country in which they lived and to the people who surrounded them:

> Is it possible to devote one's efforts to benefiting the country in which one lives and to be satisfied by this? Many of us act in this way, because all of us, consciously or unconsciously, love this country sincerely and tenderly. Despite everything, we love the people that lives there and the language in which it converses. But that love is not reciprocated, and that is why it is bitterly wounding to one's self-esteem. Thus, attempting to impose one's friendship upon those who do not wish it is like an impassioned declaration to a woman who is beautiful but indifferent. The country itself is rich in spiritual resources. It does not request our services, and when we nonetheless wish to serve it, we are involuntarily viewed with cold amazement and with a shrug of the shoulders, as if to say, "Why do those people care about us?"
>
> What a strange desire—to be the unfailing defenders of foreign causes.[9]

This was written in a pamphlet that was an apologia for Zionism, a movement whose aim is to leave the Diaspora. What has that aim to do with loving countries that the Jews are supposed to leave? Yet Jabotinsky writes precisely about love. Obviously, in order to write this he must have experienced both love itself and the bitter disillusionment that came from discovering that the love was not for his own, but for something foreign, and that it was not requited.

Even in Jabotinsky's most ardent appeals for the rebirth of Jewish national awareness and for a Jewish state, there remained the clear imprint of his love for the countries and national cultures in the Diaspora. He was obviously not completely sincere when he wrote, much later, that his emotional attitude to all other nations was one of polite indifference.[10] Such an attitude may have accorded with some political aim or other, but it was not intrinsic to his personality. It was, rather, an artificial shield to protect a vulnerable spirit. For Jabotinsky was a gifted writer in Russian; he wrote with great sympathy about the Ukrainian genius Taras Shevchenko; he welcomed the achievements of Norwegian literature; he was thrilled by the Italian language and even called Italy his "spiritual homeland"; he was indignant over the discrimination against African-Americans; he was highly fluent in many languages; and he possessed an encyclopedic knowledge of world culture. It was as if his timid apprehension that other nations would sneer at his love for them and brutally reject it made him turn his love toward his own nation in the hope of finding responsiveness, understanding, and resonance. His was a sad fate shared by many sincere and unself-seeking people. Many representatives of the Jewish people have bowed, and some still do, before the anti-Semitic Karl Marx, who was of Jewish origin, rather than before Jabotinsky, who was both a Jewish patriot and an altruist.

Jabotinsky's nationalism was in no way a betrayal of altruism. He became a nationalist through the conviction that national cultures are of fundamental value and that there is only one way to serve universal culture—by serving the culture of one's own nation. Not self-isolation, but sovereign, active, and worthy participation in the universal community of nations—that was his principle. In "A Reply to M. M. Vinawer" (1907), Jabotinsky wrote about the attitudes of Jews toward the countries in which they lived. He thought that Jews should not feel like foreigners in the countries of the Diaspora:

> Our grandfathers lived in many parts of Russia [the whole territory of the empire, not ethnic Russia] for hundreds of years before today's masters came here. We contributed to its economic growth, created its enormous trade in the southwest [Ukraine], and animated and enriched the towns in those borderlands. Our people made many—perhaps too many—sacrifices of our young sons. We are neither strays nor foreigners; we are primordial citizens of this country. We wish to carry out all the responsibilities and work obligations that are assigned to all its citizens and we demand for ourselves the whole plenitude of rights that other citizens are given.[11]

Thus Jews should be full-fledged citizens with all the attendant consequences, but Jews should be aware, continued Jabotinsky, that they are not the masters of the countries of the Diaspora and thus have not created the national and social atmosphere prevailing there. Accordingly, those Jews who wish to remain Jews will always experience a certain amount of social rejection in every country of the Diaspora. Those who cannot tolerate such a situation must fight for a Jewish state in Palestine. A few years later, in 1912, Jabotinsky expressed a similar thought:

> I, a nationalist, refuse, no matter what, to consider myself a second-class citizen in Russia. I consider myself, in principle, as much the master in this state as the Russian is. I want to speak, study, write, appear in court, and participate in government in my native language. I do not intend to truckle or adapt myself to anyone, and I demand that the state adapt itself to my national demands every bit as much as it has to adapt itself to the demands of Russians, Ukrainians, Poles, Tatars, and others.[12]

The Jew must be a first-class citizen, but Jabotinsky went on to emphasize that this in no way meant he should be a first-class *Russian*, with the implication that he was equal to the Russians (or to the representatives of other peoples in any other country of the Diaspora) in his right to take part in creating the national cultural values of a foreign people:

> A foreign national character, a foreign psyche, and a culture saturated with it cannot really be assimilated even in a whole generation or in several generations. The accent in speech remains, as does the particular "accent" of the spirit. The question of whether those nuances may completely disappear many, many years later is a different matter that I do not wish to touch on here, but as long as those nuances are present, I am doomed to be considered an inauthentic and less than full-fledged Russian, a probationary Russian, an apprentice in the Russian cultural workshop. Whether people like me or not is irrelevant. What remains crystal-clear is that the source and core of Russian culture lies not among the neophytes but within the masses, with whom the neophyte can only attempt to merge. When people feel the need for authentic Russian creativity, they will push aside the neophyte's product and say: this may be very nice; it may even be better than the genuine article, but—excuse us—we require the authentic Russian work. That is what it means to be a second-class Russian.[13]

Such were the fundamental principles of Jabotinsky's outlook on the "personal" relations between the Jews and the countries and peoples of the Diaspora. In general outline, his views had already taken shape by 1904 and did not subsequently undergo any major change.

As noted earlier, the Polish national movement in Russia and Austria-Hungary was gaining strength at the start of the twentieth century. The Polish national struggle was conducted mainly by legal means: creating Polish national parties and social organizations, broadening their activity, publishing articles in the Polish press, and exploiting the influence of Polish deputies in the elective organs of both empires. Polish nationalists of all persuasions and parties adopted a maximalist position—Poland for the Poles—and refused to recognize the national rights of national minorities on all the territories that were regarded as Polish. The largest national minorities in those lands were Ukrainians and Jews. In Eastern Galicia, which the Poles also considered their own territory, Ukrainians constituted a huge majority.

In the Polish-Ukrainian dispute over Galicia, Jabotinsky was unreservedly on the Ukrainian side. It is interesting that in the manner of giving the Polish people equal national rights and the broadest possible national autonomy, whether in Russia or Austria-Hungary, Jabotinsky was on the side of the Poles, but on the issue of the national rights of minorities on Polish territories, he was on the side of the minorities in their struggle against the Poles. There is no contradiction within this position, for Jabotinsky was always on the side of the weaker and oppressed nation in its struggle against imperialist encroachment on the part of the larger and stronger nation. Poles were weaker and oppressed in the Russian Empire (in Austria-Hungary they had many more rights), but the Jews and Ukrainians were a minority and faced national oppression at the hands of the Poles on Polish territory.

Let us cite a typical expression of Jabotinsky's views on the situation in Galicia:

> The Ukrainians in Galicia are oppressed—that is beyond dispute. According to the 1900 census there were 3,998,702 Poles and 3,074,449 Ruthenians [i.e., Ukrainians] in the country. Moreover, in evaluating this Polish majority we must take into account the fact that there are 820,000 Jews in Galicia, who were not counted as a separate nationality in the census, since almost all of them are judged to be Poles in line with the authorities' wishes. The actual number of Poles and Ruthenians in the country is equal. Here is a thumbnail sketch of how the blessings of this world are distributed between these two peoples, according to the 1904 statistics. The number of elementary schools was almost equal, but the *number of classes* was as follows: 5,440 for Poles, 3,200 for Ruthenians. The number of teachers: 6,197 Poles and 1,803 Ruthenians; school inspectors: 70 Poles, 4 Ruthenians.
>
> The government spends 67,000 crowns annually on Polish textbooks and 25,000 on Ruthenian ones. The Sejm's subsidy for educational institutions is divided thus: 92 percent to Polish institutions and 8 percent to Ruthenian ones; there were 44 Polish *gymnasia* and 4 Ruthenian ones (now I believe there are 5). There were eleven Polish *Realschulen* and no Ukrainian ones. One Polish deputy in the Reichsrat represented 46,000 Poles; one Ruthenian represented 124,000 Ruthenians. Only a few days ago, when electoral reforms were being drawn up for the Galician Sejm, the leaders of the Polish parties proposed to the Ruthenians that they be satisfied in future with 46 deputies out of a total of 192—of course, the Ruthenians did not accept that proposal. And so on and so on. Thus the Ukrainian people lives badly in Galicia.[14]

This article of Jabotinsky's was mainly devoted to a question of importance to Ukrainians and to all other non-Russian peoples in the empire, namely the attempts by Russian imperialist circles to exploit Polish-Ukrainian tensions in Galicia in order to incline the sympathies of Ukrainians in Austria-Hungary to Russia's side. Although Ukrainians in the Russian Empire at that time did not have even a small proportion of the national and cultural rights exercised by

Ukrainians in Galicia, the Russian chauvinists raised an uproar in the press about the oppression of Ukrainians in Austria-Hungary. Jabotinsky had a sure grasp of the meaning of this political game. Having declared the national struggle of Galician Ukrainians a just cause, he urged them "to rap the knuckles of those offering unsolicited laments" and "to show the door" to those who were even more ruthlessly oppressing Ukrainians in Eastern Ukraine as they dreamt of expanding their rule into Galicia. The events in Galicia, that region of discord among peoples and of imperialist encroachments, were the example on the basis of which the young Jabotinsky developed his principled anti-imperialism:

> Misfortunes and insults make all of us abandon our scruples and welcome any hand extended in sympathy, regardless of whose hand it may be. Yet it may, in some cases, be the hand of one's fiercest enemy, aiming to turn our misfortune to his own political advantage.... For the Great Russian chauvinists, this is merely a fresh pretext for a new effort to pull the Galician Ruthenians, whom they call, for reasons of brevity, "Russians," into their own "sphere of influence."[15]

Jabotinsky expressed his attitude toward the Polish-Ukrainian conflict in greatest detail on the pages of the Ukrainian press. In July 1906 he published two articles, "Dotting the 'i'" and "Non multum, sed multa," in *Ukrainskii vestnik*, the journal edited by Mykhailo Hrushevsky, who would head the Ukrainian Central Rada in 1917 and become president of the Ukrainian People's Republic (Ukrains'ka Narodnia Respublika, UNR) in 1918.[16]

Today, some Jews are pained by such *open* cooperation between a prominent Jewish political figure and Ukrainian nationalists. Jabotinsky himself is obviously not to blame for the fact that the issue became painful. Historically it has turned out that the very mention of Ukrainian nationalism distresses many Jews, who treat "Ukrainian nationalism" and "pogrom" as virtual synonyms. Such an utterly mistaken view of the organized Ukrainian political movement in the twentieth century has been based on misunderstanding, inadequate information, and anti-Ukrainian propaganda. It is equally mistaken to see Zionism as a variant of racism, and it is no accident that the slanders against Ukrainian nationalism and Zionism most frequently originate from the same sources. To equate Ukrainians who carried out pogroms with the entire Ukrainian political movement is as senseless as to equate Theodor Herzl with the prominent Odesa bandit Mishka Iaponchik on the grounds that both were Jews.[17]

Despite this, Jabotinsky's cooperation with the Ukrainian nationalist press and his later contacts with the Ukrainian government of Symon Petliura remain compromising and even scandalous facts for many Jews. Jabotinsky's later biographers and commentators on his creative work have felt constrained to remain silent about his cooperation with Ukrainian nationalists or to make awkward justifications for it (that is how his followers and sympathizers have proceeded) or to attack it almost as if it were a crime (as his opponents have claimed). Matters have been further aggravated by the fact that Jabotinsky cooperated not only with *Ukrainskii vestnik* (Ukrainian Herald), whose director was the eminent and universally respected historian Hrushevsky, but also with *Ukrainskaia zhizn'* (Ukrainian Life), whose editor was Symon Petliura. The subsequent leader of the "Petliurists" (another synonym for "those who carried out pogroms") is one of the most hateful historical figures for many Jews. In some Jewish circles, a Jewish political leader's cooperation with Petliura is sufficiently scandalous to destroy that leader's reputation, even if he is someone of Jabotinsky's stature. However, any examination of Jabotinsky's activities cannot overlook his cooperation with the Ukrainian nationalist press. Indeed, this very cooperation illuminates aspects of his political views that are not apparent from other facets of his activity.

Jabotinsky began to cooperate with *Ukrainskii vestnik* in 1906 and with *Ukrainskaia zhizn'* in 1912, that is, in the years when those journals were founded. Both had similar goals, which were formulated in *Ukrainskaia zhizn'* as follows: "The task of *Ukrainskaia zhizn'* is to serve the interests and needs of the 30–million-strong Ukrainian people and to acquaint society with the Ukrainian national movement."[18] Each issue of *Ukrainskaia zhizn'* contained a list of its most prominent contributors, and that list always included the name V. E. Jabotinsky. Obviously, the editorial board could not have included his name without his permission. Could there be circumstances that might mitigate Jabotinsky's "crime"?

In 1912 Jabotinsky could not have known that Petliura was not simply the editor of a Ukrainian national-democratic journal, but the future leader of the "Petliurists." Neither could he have known that Soviet propaganda and numerous Jewish authors in the West would flood the market with works blaming the pogroms in Ukraine on Petliura. One such work by a Western author, the American academic Saul Friedman—an English-language book with the Russian title *Pogromchik*[19]—depicts Petliura as a satanic figure who could be compared only with the likes of Hitler. Fortunately, no one has thought of blaming Herzl for Mishka Iaponchik's "exploits," but propaganda from Soviet and other analogous sources has used very similar phrases to blame Zionism and "Ukrainian bourgeois nationalism" for the most terrible crimes of racism and genocide. Furthermore, Soviet sources developed the theory of a "criminal alliance between Zionism and Ukrainian bourgeois nationalism." In this scheme, Jabotinsky is none other than the founder of the "criminal alliance." Such propositions should prompt Western authors to wonder how much truth there is in propaganda against Ukrainian nationalism and whether it would not be worth examining the meaning of historical events more closely instead of vilifying a people numbering many millions and its national movement, which may seem convenient from some angles. It might also be worth taking into account the actual views of Jabotinsky, who would not, of course, have maintained good relations with the Ukrainian movement if everything that is now written about it were true.

A close look at the essence of Jabotinsky's cooperation with the Ukrainian press makes that cooperation seem both natural and self-explanatory. For at that time the political views and immediate political goals of liberal and social-democratic Ukrainian and Jewish nationalist Zionist political circles were in many respects very similar. It is true that Jabotinsky went further than many other Zionists of that time in his sympathy for the Ukrainian national movement, but far from departing from the basic positions of Zionism, he sought instead to make use of the national-liberation struggle of the peoples of the Russian Empire in order to promote Jewish national and Zionist interests. A favorable attitude toward other peoples' struggles for freedom and national liberation was always a part of the Jewish intellectual tradition, but Jabotinsky tried to make that attitude an inseparable part of the Zionist world-view—to the extent, of course, that the aspirations of other peoples did not deny national rights to the Jewish people, as was the case with the Polish national movement. Since Ukrainians constituted the largest non-Russian people within the Russian Empire, and since the majority of Jews in the empire (as well as in Austria-Hungary) lived on Ukrainian territory, cooperation between the national-liberation forces of both peoples seemed not only desirable but necessary. Moreover, this view was later recognized and fully accepted by the absolute majority of Jewish political forces in Ukraine, which supported the Ukrainian national government during the revolution and civil war between 1917 and 1920.[20]

Jabotinsky was, of course, aware of Petliura's personal opinions and of the fact that as a youth he had been reputed to be an unreserved Semitophile. Also, *Ukrainskaia zhizn'*, along with most of the Ukrainian press at that time, expressed such pro-Jewish attitudes that it could scarcely be distinguished from Jewish periodicals. When the Black Hundreds provoked the "Beilis affair" (the court case against the Kyiv Jew Menahem Mendel Beilis, accused of the ritual murder of a Christian boy, began in 1911; Beilis was acquitted in 1913 by a jury of Ukrainian peasants),[21] *Ukrainskaia zhizn'* wrote as follows:

> The first Christians were subjected to great persecution on the basis of charges that they were using human blood. In our time, two-legged animals who have insidiously appropriated the name of Christians are bringing the same kinds of charges against Jews and using them to carry out a persecution just as ruthless as that undergone by the followers of the Galilean Teacher. There is, however, an essential difference here: the persecution of the Jews, with all the horror and savagery of pogroms and ritual trials, is taking place not at the dawn of the Christian era, but almost 2,000 years after the creation of the religion of love. Shameful preeminence in this belongs to Russia, where another trial will soon take place, a trial produced by a ruthless, anti-Christian slander against Jews who supposedly carried out a ritual murder of a Christian boy, Iushchynsky, in Kyiv.[22]

And here is what Petliura himself wrote in an introduction to a play, *The Jews,* by the Russian author Evgenii Chirikov, published in Ukrainian translation in Kyiv in 1907:

> We would very much like this work, which is suffused with the author's deep sympathy for the ancient martyr people, to become more than an item for the Ukrainian public to read. One must thrice hope that the Ukrainian theatre will stage the translation of Chirikov's play.
>
> ...The suffering of Nachman in Chirikov's *The Jews* will evoke profound sympathy in all who do not belong to that nation, which by the will of historical destiny has been fated to bear a heavy cross of oppression and violence. For all the martyrs of the contemporary capitalist order are united by a golden thread of solidarity, by a single fate, by the same hopes and strivings. If perhaps not everyone will agree with Nachman's view that the particular medicines with which he hopes to heal his people's wounds will have the desired results, all will nonetheless feel the need to pour healing balsam on those wounds.[23]

It is important to note that Ukrainian patriotic circles in 1907 were greatly concerned with the rebirth of the Ukrainian theatre, which had been banned for many years. They entrusted it with the task of promoting the development of the Ukrainian people's national consciousness. If, in such circumstances, they were concerned to enrich the Ukrainian theatre with a play portraying the Jewish people most favorably, then that testified to their desire to oppose the Black Hundreds' anti-Semitic propaganda and to prevent the spread of anti-Semitic sentiments among the Ukrainian masses. By contributing to the publication of that play in Ukrainian translation and writing an introduction to it, Petliura was working precisely along those lines.

If the socialist thesis regarding the "martyrs of the capitalist order" were removed from that quotation (for Jabotinsky never favored a socialist outlook), then what did it contain that could have driven him away from those who spoke out so fervently to the Jewish people's advantage? It should also be borne in mind that the Black Hundreds' savage anti-Jewish and anti-Ukrainian activity impelled Jewish and Ukrainian national circles toward understanding and cooperation. To be sure, some researchers have paid much more attention to the Black Hundreds' anti-Semitism than to their anti-Ukrainianism, yet one of the Black Hundreds' main tasks was to nip in the bud the possibility of Ukraine's separation from the empire. With that aim in mind, they fought ferociously against the Ukrainian national movement.[24] Thus, the presence of a dangerous common enemy gave Jewish and Ukrainian national forces a strong incentive to cooperate. Since the Black Hundreds' basic instrument of activity was unrestrained anti-Semitic propaganda, Ukrainian national circles felt it necessary to fight anti-Semitism and did so consistently through their publications.

Yet it was not only practical necessity that impelled Ukrainian national-democratic activists to protest against anti-Semitism. From their liberal or liberal-socialist standpoint, they viewed anti-Semitism as an expression of extreme reaction, considering the Jewish people a natural ally of the oppressed and disenfranchised in the struggle for human and national rights. The Ukrainian activists thus had ideological as well as practical motives for their struggle against anti-Semitism. Of the many examples that could be adduced, let us limit ourselves to the Ukrainian democrats' resolution on the pogroms in Białystok, published in *Ukrainskii vestnik* in 1906:

> We now know very well that pogroms of Jews have been organized by government agents, who have been staging them, with the help of the "Black Hundreds," "against ten or against a thousand people."
>
> We cannot escape the conclusion that the "Black Hundreds" appeared because some government functionaries called upon certain people to engage in "black deeds" and rewarded them for their bestial actions against defenseless people.
>
> That is why we consider that the pogroms of Jews were terrible: not only because innocent people were killed and exterminated, but also because they corrupted Christians themselves, arousing bestial emotions within them. We were horrified to hear about the Białystok pogrom and we protest with a sense of tremendous outrage against such murder, expressing our fervent sympathy and sorrow to the Jewish people.[25]

This resolution was published in the journal's sixth issue, and Jabotinsky's article, "Dotting the 'i,'" appeared in the seventh. The editor of *Ukrainskii vestnik* at that time was Jabotinsky's friend from Odesa, Maksym Slavinsky, with whom Jabotinsky was to make an agreement fifteen years later to organize a Jewish gendarmerie, attached to the Ukrainian army, to combat pogroms.[26]

There is thus nothing unusual about the fact that Jabotinsky cooperated with such liberal and pro-Jewish periodicals. For him it was also important that the basic theme of the Ukrainian journals was the nationality question in the Russian Empire. It was precisely to that question, both in its narrow, Jewish aspect and in its wider theoretical and practical dimensions, that Jabotinsky dedicated his work. Of even greater importance was Jabotinsky's position on the nationality question, which was very close to that of the Ukrainian national-democratic press. By studying that press and comparing it with Jabotinsky's writings, one can identify some of the fundamental ideas that they held in common:

(1) The culture of every nation is a unique and irreplaceable part of human culture; every national culture should enjoy the best possible circumstances for its free, all-round development in the interests of both the nation and humanity.
(2) Every national group should have the right to self-determination as a separate nation, and no one but the nation itself has the right to declare it

part of another nation. (That point had an urgent significance in the context of the Russian nationalists' stubborn attempts to proclaim the Ukrainian and Belarusian peoples part of the Russian people.)

(3) Every nation must have the broadest possible cultural and administrative autonomy. (At that time, complete separation from the empire was not yet on the agenda of most non-Russian national movements.)

(4) In its own interests Russia should elaborate and implement, in cooperation with all the national movements, a new liberal and democratic nationality policy, without which its normal existence as a multi-ethnic state would be impossible.

Jabotinsky was the first on the Jewish side to emphasize the importance in principle of a positive resolution to the Ukrainian problem as a precondition for resolving the problems of all the other peoples in the empire. Much later, in 1936, he again confirmed that at the start of his political activity, cooperation with other national minorities in the empire was at the center of his attention: "In the field of local politics I demanded unity with the national minorities; I demanded negotiations with the Ukrainians and Lithuanians; I even took steps in that direction. I had many friends among the Ukrainians, because I supported their movement in the pages of *Odesskie novosti* [Odessa News], but the other Zionist activists reacted to the steps I took with obvious indifference or even derision."[27]

It was precisely in that way—with obvious indifference or even with derision—that the leaders of the Zionist movement (as well as the leaders of other Jewish political parties) treated Jabotinsky's calls for cooperation with the national political forces of other peoples suffering discrimination. However, within a comparatively short time—about ten years—this idea gained general recognition. At the moment when mutual sympathy between Jewish and Ukrainian national forces reached its climax, in 1917, a prominent Zionist activist and future colleague of Jabotinsky's, Joseph Schechtman, wrote:

> From the Jewish side, Ukrainian national aspirations met with the natural sympathy that Jewry traditionally expresses toward all oppressed elements fighting for their liberation. The leading Ukrainian circles in their turn had a thoughtful and sympathetic attitude toward the Jewish national movement.... The Jewish people's national demands...undoubtedly correspond to the national political attitudes toward national minorities that are now being expressed by a renascent Ukrainianism. A broad path of national cooperation lies before the Jews and the Ukrainians. There was so much sincerity and authenticity in the welcoming speech given by the Hechover [Jewish student organization] representative, a student called Nus, at the Ukrainian student conference in Kyiv. He began his speech in Ukrainian and ended it in Hebrew:
>
> "Who if not we, children of an oppressed people, can grasp the feelings and sufferings of a neighbor who has, along with us, borne the abuse and insults of the old regime? We have been united by common dreams and common aims. The moment has arrived when our dreams are close to coming true. There is still a long path ahead of us, but we believe that a free Ukrainian people will support us along that path."[28]

Such unreserved optimism, contrasting with the earlier indifference, was extraordinarily widespread in Jewish circles during the first months of the revolution that began on the territory of the Russian Empire in the spring of 1917. That brief period of rosy idealism and luminous hope for altruistic brotherhood among peoples was filled with expressions of fellow-feeling and sympathy on the part of Jewish and Ukrainian national political forces, who worked shoulder to shoulder in the government institutions created by the Ukrainian People's Republic. At the start of Jabotinsky's political career, however, there was no question of cooperation between Jewish and Ukrainian national forces (apart from some elements of such cooperation in Galicia), and Jabotinsky had to overcome rather stiff opposition within his own circles to demonstrate the community of interests among the oppressed peoples of the empire.

The situation in Galicia gave him an excellent opportunity to express his new ideas, unusual at that time within Jewish circles. All the elements of his position, and indeed the elements of the theory that he developed concerning relations between the Jewish people and the surrounding non-Jewish peoples, were expressed in "Non multum, sed multa," which appeared in Hrushevsky's journal in 1906.

Jabotinsky began by stating that Jewry in the Diaspora often found itself in a situation where stronger national, political or economic groups exploited the Jews to the detriment of weaker national, political or economic groups. He thus examined the question at the level of the role that Jewry in fact played, whether it wanted to or not, in social relations, in order to lead the reader toward conclusions about the role it should actually play in light of its national interests:

> When the struggle began among different nationalities that possessed either territorial bases or some kind of territorial support, even here Jewry was allotted the hated role of a tool, an instrument for someone else's gain. In every single instance, the side whose influence or wealth gave it stronger means of exerting pressure forced local Jews to join it in the subjugation of another nationality. In Galicia this stronger side was that of the Poles, who took extensive "advantage" of the downtrodden, uneducated Galician Jews and "utilized" them for the national oppression of the Ukrainian people.[29]

Jabotinsky never sought to deny or somehow gloss over what was, for the Jews, the unpleasant fact that in many countries, especially Galicia, they played the role of auxiliaries to economic and national oppressors. He believed that Jewry did not need to justify itself to anyone, or deny any obvious social facts, or foster illusions within itself or in others about its status and role. This does not mean that Jabotinsky joined forces with those who stressed and exaggerated the role of the Jews as lackeys of the exploiters in order to justify anti-Semitism and pogroms. Actually, only a fairly insignificant number of Jews acted as middlemen between foreign exploiters and the local population. The majority of Jews always consisted of artisans and tradespeople who facilitated the economic development of the countries of the Diaspora.[30] However, throughout the centuries of life in the Diaspora, there were few occasions when Jewry was not dependent on the will, interests or whims of those exercising power and authority. Because Jews felt this enforced condition to be an evil for themselves, they were deeply wounded by the reluctance of surrounding peoples to understand that evil and express at least a shade of sympathy. Jews thought elementary common sense should have led the Gentiles to grasp that a people cannot be blamed for the misfortunes that befall it. In this way a vicious circle of mutual misunderstanding took shape between Jewry and the surrounding peoples.

Jabotinsky's understanding of this led him to try to cut the Gordian knot by concluding that Jewry needed its own national policy. The adoption of such a policy in turn required a realistic perception of Jewry's social role and of the reaction of surrounding peoples. Only by adopting its own national standpoint could Jewry cease to be a pawn in a game between mutually antagonistic forces and begin to act as a subject equal to others.

Jabotinsky used events in Galicia to demonstrate how Jewry should behave in a concrete political situation. There, in many electoral districts, the Poles constituted a minority and could gain majorities in elections only with the aid of Jewish votes. Once these were gained, the Poles had no wish to take account of Jewish national rights or to give Jewish deputies proportional representation on elected bodies. When the Galician Ukrainians grasped the importance of Jewish votes, they sought to win the Jews over to their side, promising to support their national demands and the principle of proportional Jewish representation. At the beginning of the twentieth century the first signs appeared that Galician Jewry was beginning to move away from its traditional pro-Polish position and was becoming disposed toward joining the Ukrainians in their struggle for national rights.

For Jabotinsky, that experience was a model of the correct principles of Jewish policy. In his article "Jews and Ruthenians," published in 1906, he wrote:

> One of the most heartening aspects of the contemporary Jewish movement in Galicia is precisely its refusal to allow Jewish votes to be "used" to strengthen Polish dominance over the Ruthenian population. The roles of slave and of assistant in the enslavement of others have evidently become equally loathsome to our brothers in the Pidvolochysk area. Ruthenians have understood that as well. The reader may perhaps remember how their deputies, Vasylko and Romanchuk, supported the demand for separate representation for Jews.[31]

Having analyzed the political situation in Galicia, Jabotinsky went on to write, in the same article, about "the concurrence of interests that is undoubtedly impelling Ruthenians and Jews toward a political alliance."

In "Non multum, sed multa" he analyzed, in greater detail, the significance of Jewish-Ukrainian cooperation in Galicia and the changes in Jewish attitudes toward the Ukrainians:

> The significance of this change has been appreciated—though with differing feelings—by both Ukrainians and Poles. The former have understood very well that in dozens of mixed constituencies, where the Polish minority achieved a majority thanks only to Jewish votes, the ascendancy of the nobility was coming to an end, and that through agreement with the Jews, they could divide up those deputies' seats proportionally. It is for this reason that the Ukrainian deputy Dr. Romanchuk spoke up in the Reichsrat as a committed supporter of Jewish demands. In various parts of Galicia, Ukrainian meetings approved resolutions along similar lines.[32]

It should be noted that other Jewish community activists and political writers besides Jabotinsky were sympathetic to a Ukrainian-Jewish rapprochement in Galicia, although by no means all of them shared Jabotinsky's views on the fundamental need to support the Ukrainian movement throughout Ukraine, not just in the Austro-Hungarian lands. For instance, Daniil Pasmanik, whom Jabotinsky quoted in "Non multum, sed multa," wrote:

> Who has taken a sympathetic attitude toward the Jews?
>
> The first and strongest support came from the representatives of those nations in Austria that are, after the Jews, the most oppressed—representatives of the Ruthenians long enslaved by the Polish nobility. At the same time, the Ruthenians make no attempt to conceal their motives. They do not speak of their love for the Jews; some do not even conceal their anti-Semitism, but they advance ordinary political interests. The Ruthenians, accustomed to viewing the Jews as servants of the ruling Polish nobility, were happy to discover that the Jews no longer want to play that shameful role, but want to demand national independence together with them.[33]

Thus Jabotinsky was not alone in recognizing the advantage, in principle, of cooperation between the Jews and other oppressed peoples in the struggle for national interests. Moreover, Zionists considered it self-evident that Zionism, as a national-liberation movement of the Jewish people, was in essence analogous to the national movements of other peoples, welcoming international solidarity, equality, and mutual respect among all peoples. The Zionist leader Grigorii Abramovich (Abramowitz) expressed it thus:

> The complete victory of nationalism is the complete defeat of chauvinism, *because there can be no oppressors when there are no oppressed.*
>
> The liberation of all oppressed nationalities will create the only real basis for their rapprochement: as long as there are oppressed nationalities, chauvinism will grow and develop, and in such conditions, the realization of internationalism would be the purest utopia. Only the triumph of nationalism prepares and facilitates the triumph of internationalism![34]

Such indubitably sincere calls for cooperation among peoples should have resulted in a rapprochement between Zionists and the Ukrainian national movement. There were, however, strong and widespread anti-Ukrainian sentiments among the Jewish masses, which were the product of a sad history. Such sentiments prevented the majority of Zionist leaders from cooperating with the Ukrainian movement for quite a long time. Only Jabotinsky was consistent to the end and fought actively for cooperation, but he also understood that the historical background was by no means favorable for persuading the Jewish side to express feelings of brotherhood or love toward Ukrainians. He emphasized above all the community of interests between the Ukrainian and Jewish peoples in Ukraine as a whole and in Galicia in particular. He thus maintained the same attitude as those representatives of the Ukrainian community in Galicia who supported cooperation with Jewry:

> I am not an optimist and I do not believe in "love" between nations. In particular I do not in any way conceal from myself the fact that a certain antagonism exists between the Jews and Ukrainians in Galicia, one that sometimes takes on uncivilized forms. I am certain that those uncultured forms will disappear with the growth of education, but tribal conflicts will persist until there are fundamental changes in the political and ethnographic map of the world and in the socio-economic system.
>
> But I am not appealing here for "love." I am stating that at this moment there is a concurrence of interests between Galician Ukrainians and Galician Jews. While each pursues an individual course, they can today assist each other. That is what needs to be done.[35]

"Each pursues an individual course" expresses the essence of Jabotinsky's concept. He goes on to develop it as follows:

> What should Jewish assistance to the Galician Ukrainians consist of? It means in the first place a complete break with the Poles—*obviously not in order to hand over votes to the Ukrainians, but to live and develop independently and in our own way*, preventing anyone from "taking advantage" of us so as to enslave another group. In the second place, it means doing joint work with Ukrainian populists for the complete democratization of the corrupt political order in Austria generally, and in Galicia in particular. In the third place, it means supporting the Eastern Galician autonomists, who are demanding home rule for the Ukrainian half of today's "Crown" Galicia.[36]

These "first," "second," and "third" places constitute a whole political program that could be expanded in many directions without altering those fundamentals. An independent and endogenous national position, support for the democratization of society, and a joint struggle with other national groups for national autonomy—these were the three buttresses of Jabotinsky's entire concept of Jewish national policy in the countries of the Diaspora. That program did not, in fact, differ from the program of the Ukrainian national parties, and thus Jabotinsky's article once more demonstrated the community of interests and tasks shared by the Ukrainian and Jewish national movements.

Adhering to his principle of reciprocity in relations between nations, Jabotinsky proceeded to define precisely what kind of assistance the Jews expected from the Galician Ukrainians:

> What should Ukrainian assistance to the Austrian Jews consist of? One thing alone: that Jewry in Austria be granted the rights of a national entity. A landless nationality cannot lay claim to "autonomy," but it does have the right to demand self-government as regards its national way of life and just representation both in the Reichsrat and in the Sejms. The Jewish population's language should have equal status with the eight languages already recognized in Austrian institutions, courts, and schools. When Eastern Galicia finally disengages to become a separate, autonomous province, those rights of national minorities should be preserved intact there, and—let the Ruthenians beware!—in the western half as well, where groups of Ukrainians will remain scattered among the Polish majority.[37]

What Jabotinsky meant when he stated that "a landless nationality cannot lay claim to 'autonomy'" was *territorial* autonomy. What he did demand was, in fact, national-personal autonomy—self-government as regards national ways of life and fair representation in elected bodies. Such national-personal autonomy was proclaimed for all national minorities in the Ukrainian People's Republic in 1918.[38] Jabotinsky took the principle of reciprocity to its logical conclusion—recognition of the right to self-government for Jews and the same recognition of the right to self-government for the Ukrainian minority that was scattered among the Poles in Western Galicia.

Jabotinsky's numerous attacks on Polish hegemonism may give the impression that he was generally hostile to the Poles, but other remarks prove that such an impression would be completely false:

> In the summer of 1905 I visited Warsaw, probably for the first time. Since childhood I had loved Poland, and there was nothing strange about that, for such an attitude toward Poland was a general tradition in progressive society both in Russia and throughout the world.
>
> ...We went to Hrodna [Grodno]...[where] we decided to visit the famous Polish writer Eliza Orzeszkowa, a friend of the Jews and in general a noble representative of the naive generation of nineteenth-century humanists. A Polish flag with a white eagle in the center hung on the wall of her reception room.... She said to me in Polish: "I saw your article in the last issue of *Głos Żydowski* [Jewish Voice]. Are you opposed to an independent Poland?"
>
> I replied, "That depends on one condition: I am prepared to welcome Poland's rebirth with all my heart...provided that Polish society supports equality for the Jews in two fields: civil and national rights. In Warsaw society, the opposing

> aspiration predominates: Mr. Dmowski[39] frankly declares that his faction will make use of autonomy first and foremost to crush the Jews. Would you say, Madame, that in such circumstances we should support his claim to power?"[40]

In fact, in many of his works Jabotinsky combined categorical rejection of the views of Polish political parties on the Jewish question with his sympathy for the Polish people's struggle for national rights and for Polish culture. Here is one example of many that could be adduced:

> It would be unfair to consider any of my sympathizers to be vulgar Polonophobes, and in particular the author of these lines would protest against such an allegation. I would dare claim to be a fervent supporter of Polish national character, Polish civilization, and Polish literature. I recognize and respect the high tragic drama of Polish history, as well as Poland's role, in the era of the great French Revolution, of "Winkelried among the nations."[41]

There is thus no basis for claims that Jabotinsky was hostile to Poland or to the Poles. His attacks on Polish hegemonism were nothing more than an appropriate response to the Polish national political forces' hostility toward the national rights of the Jewish and other minorities on Polish territory.

In "Non multum, sed multa," Jabotinsky expressed both hostility to Polish hegemonism and fundamental support for Polish national rights, as well as the rights of all other peoples. He also broadened the scope of the discussion, moving from the nationality problems of Austria-Hungary to the question of how to resolve nationality problems in tsarist Russia:

> When the time comes for the *Russian* parliament to discuss Poland's autonomy, both the Ukrainians and the Jews will remember Galicia and remind others of it. Neither of them will let slip a word of opposition to the broadest possible authority for the Sejm in Warsaw. The Kingdom of Poland must be just as autonomous as Lithuania, Ukraine, and Belarus, but the question of the inviolable rights of national minorities should be decided *in advance, in an all-empire* parliament, and should cover the entire territory of the state.[42]

Jabotinsky was quite right to consider Galicia an example of relations among peoples of which both Jews and non-Jews should be reminded time and again. Over the years he kept returning to the situation in Galicia, using it to illustrate the problem of inter-ethnic relations and to substantiate his view of an appropriate Jewish policy toward other peoples. Nonetheless, Jabotinsky's ideas went far beyond conditions in the Austro-Hungarian and Russian empires. He sought to explain to the Jewish community the principle that should guide its behavior toward other peoples—the positive principle of cooperation with healthy and progressive national forces even when those peoples were temporarily oppressed and deprived of independent statehood. That principle was designed to replace the policy of self-isolation or the practice of enforced service on behalf of the stronger group against the weaker.

Most of world Jewry then lived among the many stateless peoples of Eastern Europe, and there the question of "whose side to be on" was fundamental. The destiny of the Jews depended on the answer to it. At a time when the stateless peoples of the Russian and Austro-Hungarian empires were awakening to independent national life, it was not merely improvident but even mortally dangerous not to grapple with that problem. It was necessary to seek out one's own worthy and promising place amid the ferment of those young and powerful national forces that were making ready to shake the foundations of empires.

For many years, Jabotinsky promoted the idea that after enduring centuries of oppression, the Jews should have a better understanding of the position of stateless peoples in Eastern Europe. That was what so angered him about the stance of the Polish national forces, which represented an oppressed nation but simultaneously crushed the national minorities that had ended up within their sphere of influence. In 1910 he wrote:

> Only in the Old Testament is it written, "Do not oppress the stranger, for you too were a stranger in the land of Egypt" [Exodus 22: 21]. In today's morality, there is no place for such slobbering humanism.
>
> People go even further. Not only is the memory of past suffering no obstacle to their beating others in the very place where they themselves were mercilessly beaten. Even worse things happen. It happens that a people that to this day suffers and cries to heaven for justice *simultaneously* contrives to crush a weaker group. Take those same Poles in Galicia, where they feel at least a little like masters! In Vienna the Ruthenians publish a special journal in German called *Ukrainische Rundschau*, 75 percent of which consists of lists of infamies perpetrated by the Polish administration in that crown land.[43]

While he sharply criticized the attitude of the Poles toward national minorities, Jabotinsky was even more unsparing in upbraiding what he viewed as the shortsighted behaviour of Jews who did not make the effort to take an appropriate stand in inter-ethnic conflicts. To discredit such Jewish behavior, he resorted to the literary device of using a tragicomic character named Moshko, the servant of a nobleman. He referred to "Moshko" in many articles, adapting a rhyme by the Ukrainian poet Taras Shevchenko for that purpose.[44]

For Jabotinsky, the pitiful figure of Moshko symbolized both the oppressed condition of the Diaspora Jews and their utterly mistaken line of behaviour. He returned to the image in 1912 in relation to Galicia:

> The groveling depths to which the Galician assimilator, the infamous Moshko, has now descended are well known. He runs hither and thither, ready to offer his soul for Poland. He will crush both Ruthenian and Jew for the sake of Polish culture. As for the Germans, who are oppressing "his brothers" in Poznań, he hates them beyond all measure. Do you not wish to know the history of this enthusiasm for being Polish? The late deputy Emil Byk offers a trans-

parent example of it. He died a determined Polonizer and a member of the Polish circle in 1906. Yet back in 1873 he was German to the depths of his soul and traveled through Galicia agitating for Jews to join the German party. But when he took a closer look and saw which way the wind was blowing, he "left off" being German and "transformed himself" into a Pole.... From then on, the Poles had no more faithful lackey in Galicia and the Germans had no fiercer enemy. The entire older generation of assimilators ran the course of this evolution.[45]

With his characteristic perseverance, Jabotinsky returned time and again to the theme of support for the Ukrainian position in Galicia, but always from an essentially Jewish standpoint. The way of a Moshko or an Emil Byk was to switch allegiance completely to the foreigner, while for Jabotinsky a truly Jewish policy involved honest cooperation between peoples on equal terms:

The Poles in Galicia no longer fear the Germans, but a new enemy. A new claimant is taking the stage ever more decisively—the Ruthenians. They number 3 million in Galicia, and in its eastern portion they are the vast majority. Lviv lies in Eastern Galicia, and that is why they lay the most resolute claim to it. It is neither Lemberg nor Lwów but Lviv, they say, the capital of Austrian Ukraine. That should be our place; the Ukrainian language should rule in the courts, the police force, and in the university. There's enough room in Cracow for Polish.... The spiritual brothers of Emil Byk shout the slogań, "Haidamakas out!" with the lack of foresight typical of all renegades—forgetting that in thirty years those "haidamakas" will inevitably become full masters of Eastern Galicia.... Still, what is the problem? Moshko will then become a turncoat to a third nationality.[46]

This characterization of the behavior of Diaspora Jews may seem too harsh, and if something of the kind were to be said by a Gentile, he would probably be considered an anti-Semite, but Jabotinsky's sharp criticism of such Jewish behavior could only spring from feelings that are, from any point of view, the antithesis of anti-Semitism.

Study of Jabotinsky's political and literary works shows that his critiques of the policies of this or that political circle among the various peoples were always framed in such a way as to refute any notion that the given policy was the product of some sort of negative feature inherent within the people as a whole. For Jabotinsky there was no such category as a "good" or "bad" people. Such a conviction was undoubtedly a tribute to his civility, but it was also the expression of a doctrine that constituted one of the foundations of his world-view. He believed that every people could find within its history facts it should be ashamed of, but also that every people contributed, or at least could contribute, its own unique and irreplaceable augmentation to world culture. The world community should therefore preserve and cherish, as a cell within its own organism, the individuality of every nation. From this standpoint, the life of humanity can be seen as coexistence and cooperation among nations, which work together to create human culture. Such a world should be characterized by mutual respect among nations and by the self-improvement of every nation, but there should be no room for ferreting out other nations' shortcomings in order to proclaim one's own superiority. In short, this doctrine was the complete antithesis of chauvinism.

It may be that Jabotinsky's repeated insistence on agreement and cooperation with the Ukrainian people—whose history of relations with the Jews seemed rather grim—was in some measure deliberately provocative. It was as if he were emphasizing that relations among peoples could not be based upon historical memory, and that the new, dignified, and independent Jewish national policy he advocated would facilitate successful relations with any people, regardless of the state of those relations in the past. From the beginning to the end of his career he stuck to the principle that "Jews still have to live with other peoples and reckon with their ideals."

It would be very easy to say that such views on cooperation among peoples show Jabotinsky himself to have been a member of the "naive generation of nineteenth-century humanists" in which he enlisted Eliza Orzeszkowa. For the ideal vision of peaceful coexistence among a world family of national co-creators of culture is infinitely distant from what history has offered up to now. Equally, however, neither culture nor history itself would exist if history did not also contain elements of coexistence, cooperation, and joint creativity alongside its manifestations of military rivalry and violence. Jabotinsky dreamed of conditions in which the creative elements within the historical process would become determinant and dominant. (His calls for the arming of Jews in the face of mortal danger do not contradict this. He would obviously have made the same appeal on behalf of any gravely threatened people. A nation, as a unique entity, has the right to self-defense.) Although he was an idealist, he was not a utopian but a sober pragmatist. Yet whatever the difficulties, he sought to realize lofty, idealistic goals. Jabotinsky believed that only elevated ideological goals could inspire the progress of any nation or political movement, and even if in practice one could only partially and imperfectly approach that goal, one could still move some way toward it.

Jabotinsky did not feel isolated in his lofty idealism. Numerous national movements that loudly proclaimed their demands after the 1905 revolution also cherished noble, idealistic sentiments and hopes. This was also characteristic of the Ukrainian movement. Expressing his own and the Ukrainian movement's credo, Maksym Slavinsky wrote in the first issue of *Ukrainskii vestnik*: "[The State Duma] will turn slavery into freedom, poverty and wealth into an egalitarian distribution of proprietary goods, centralism into oblast and national autonomy, Russification into the free development of peoples, and the autocratic Russian Empire into a constitutional empire of nations."[47]

When one surveys Jabotinsky's early period of political activity and writing, it becomes apparent that the very similarity of ideas and goals impelled him to adopt a favourable attitude toward the Ukrainian national movement. The various reasons and stimuli for his pro-Ukrainian declarations may be summarized as follows:

(1) The elements of similarity in the national destinies of the Jewish and Ukrainian peoples, both stateless for centuries and both attempting to preserve their national and cultural identities;
(2) The similar features of their positions in the Russian and Austro-Hungarian empires, where both, though for different reasons and to differing degrees, were discriminated against;
(3) The similarities in the ideological foundations and immediate goals of the Jewish and Ukrainian national movements, which at that time aspired to a fundamental democratization of the tsarist empire in order to bring about national liberation;
(4) The presence of a common enemy—the Russian chauvinist Black Hundreds in Russia and the Polish hegemonists in both the Russian and Austrian parts of Poland;
(5) The presence of a large Jewish population on Ukrainian ethnic territories and the value of Jewish-Ukrainian cooperation as an example of the elaboration of an independent Jewish national policy;
(6) The fact that Ukrainian patriotic circles at that time took a positive attitude toward Jewish national demands stimulated Jabotinsky to adopt a pro-Ukrainian position.

From 1910 onward, the Ukrainian theme in Jabotinsky's works, which until then had mainly revolved around Jewish-Ukrainian cooperation in Galicia, expanded both in geography and in content. The spur to this was the celebration of the anniversary of the Ukrainian national poet, Taras Shevchenko, and the discussion provoked by the anniversary in the Ukrainian and Russian press. In order to understand that discussion, it is necessary to pay closer attention to certain features of social and political life in Russia that we shall proceed to explore in the following chapter.

# Notes

1. V. Zhabotinskii, intro. to R. Springer, *Gosudarstvo i natsiia* (Odesa, 1906), p. 7.

2. *From the Pen of Jabotinsky* (Cape Town, 1941), p. 60.

3. For more on the national and religious crisis of Jewry, see Max Nordau, *Evreistvo v XIX i XX stoletiiakh* (Odesa, 1912) and "Speech to the First Zionist Congress (1897)" in *The Zionist Idea: A Historical Analysis and Reader*, ed. and intro. by Arthur Hertzberg (New York, 1971), pp. 235–41; A. Idel'son, "Samosokhranenie natsii," *Natsional'nyi vopros* (Petrograd, 1917), pp. 32–50; Simon Dubnow, *Noveishaia istoriia evreiskogo naroda*, 3 vols. (Berlin, 1923), 3: 163–76; and Artur Ruppin, *Evrei nashego vremeni* (Moscow, 1918), pp. 6–10, 14–20, 25–32.

4. Ahad Ha-Am (Asher Ginsberg, 1856–1927), Jewish philosopher and essayist. See Introduction, n. 5.

5. V. Zhabotinskii, "Otpor," in *Poliaki i evrei* (St. Petersburg, 1913), pp. 65–66.

6. Ibid., p. 65.

7. V. Zhabotinskii, "K voprosu o natsionalizme (Otvet g. Izgoievu)," *Obrazovanie* (St. Petersburg), no. 10 (October 1904): 98.

8. Ibid.

9. V. Zhabotinskii, *Nedrugam Siona* (Odesa, 1905), p. 2.

10. V. Zhabotinskii, "O zheleznoi stene," *Rassvet* (Berlin), nos. 42–43 (4 October 1923): 2.

11. V. Zhabotinskii, "Otvet M. M. Vinaveru," *Evreiskaia mysl'* (Odesa), no. 3 (25 January 1907): 7.

    M. M. Vinawer (1862–1926), leading figure in the Russian Party of Popular Freedom (Constitutional Democratic Party). He was a member of the first State Duma and a founder of the Union for the Attainment of Full Civil Rights for the Jewish People in Russia. A supporter of assimilation, he believed that once the Russian intelligentsia had achieved the democratization of the state, it would simultaneously demand equal rights for the Jewish people. From 1920 he lived abroad and continued his political activity among Russian emigrants.

12. V. Zhabotinskii, "Na lozhnom puti," in *Fel'etony*, pp. 253–54.

13. Ibid., p. 254.

14. V. Zhabotinskii, "So storony," *Odesskie novosti*, 29 October 1910.

15. Ibid.

16. V. Zhabotinskii, "Tochka nad i," *Ukrainskii vestnik*, no. 7 (2 July 1906): 399–404 and "Non multum, sed multa," *Ukrainskii vestnik*, no. 9 (16 July 1906): 645–50.

17. Mikhail Vinnitskii, a leader of the Odesa underworld who operated until 1920, was widely known under the name Mishka Iaponchik. Isaac Babel wrote about him in a series of short stories whose hero, Benia Krik, was based on Mishka Iaponchik.

18. *Ukrainskaia zhizn'*, no. 12 (Moscow, 1912): 1.

19. Saul S. Friedman, *Pogromchik: The Assassination of Simon Petlura* (New York, 1976). The author apparently did not know Russian. He transliterated the Russian word *pogromshchik* as "pogromchik," which in Russian means "a small pogrom."

20. See Solomon Goldelman, *Lysty zhydivs'koho sotsiial-demokrata pro Ukraïnu* (Vienna, 1921); German translation, *Juden und Ukrainer: Briefe eines jüdischen Sozialdemokraten* (Vienna, 1921); idem, *Jewish National Autonomy in Ukraine, 1917–1920* (Chicago, 1968); Arnold Margolin, *Ukraine and Policy of the Entente* (New York, 1977, trans. of Russian edition, *Ukraina i politika Antanty: zapiski evreia i grazhdanina* [Berlin, 1921]); idem, *From a Political Diary: Russia, the Ukraine, and America, 1905–1945* (New York, 1946); idem, *The Jews of Eastern Europe* (New York, 1926); and I. M. Cherikover, *Antisemitizm i pogromy na Ukraine 1917–1918 gg.: k istorii ukrainsko-evreiskikh otnoshenii* (Berlin, 1923).

21. See Introduction, n. 36. One of Beilis's lawyers at the trial, Arnold Margolin, later became a fervent supporter of Jewish-Ukrainian cooperation. See Margolin, *Ukraine and Policy of the Entente*, pp. 14–16.

22. *Ukrainskaia zhizn'* (Moscow), no. 5 (1912): 125–26.

23. Symon Petliura, *Statti, lysty, dokumenty*, 2 vols. (New York, 1956–79), 2: 95, 102.

24. See S. Shchegolev, *Ukrainskoe dvizhenie kak sovremennyi ėtap iuzhnorusskogo separatizma* (Kyiv, 1912); idem, *Sovremennoe ukrainstvo: ego proiskhozhdenie, rost i zadachi* (Kyiv, 1914); *Encyclopedia of Ukraine*, 5: 503–4; *Entsyklopediia ukraïnoznavstva*, part 2, 8: 2974.

25. *Ukrainskii vestnik* (St. Petersburg), no. 6 (25 June 1906): 391. The text of the "resolution" appears in Russian—most likely a translation from the Ukrainian.

26. See chapter 3 of the present work.

27. V. Jabotinsky, *Avtobiografia* (Jerusalem, 1947), p. 88.

28. I. Shekhtman, *Evrei i ukraintsy*, pp. 30–31.

29. V. Zhabotinskii, "Non multum, sed multa," p. 646.

30. *Sbornik materialov ob ėkonomicheskom polozhenii evreev v Rossii*; Maurycy Horn, *Żydzi na Rusi Czerwonej w XVI i pierwszej połowie XVII w.* (Warsaw, 1975); S. Dubnow, *Noveishaia istoriia evreiskogo naroda*, 1: 271–5.

31. V. Zhabotinskii [under the pseudonym Zimri], "Evrei i rusiny," *Evreiskaia mysl'* (Odesa), no. 1 (5 October 1906): 11.

32. V. Zhabotinskii, "Non multum, sed multa," p. 647.

33. D. S. Pasmanik, "Natsional'naia bor'ba evreev v Avstrii," *Evreiskaia zhizn'* (St. Petersburg), no. 4 (1906): 79.
Daniil Pasmanik (1869–1930), Jewish political writer and public activist from Ukraine. He is known for his works on the economic condition of the Jews in Russia and on the nationality question. A Zionist, he wrote for various Jewish and Russian periodicals, particularly *Rassvet* (Paris) while it was under Jabotinsky's editorship after 1924.

34. G. Abramovich, "Genezis natsional'noi idei i sushchnost' natsionalizma," *Evreiskaia zhizn'* (St. Petersburg), no. 11 (October 1904): 100.

35. V. Zhabotinskii, "Non multum, sed multa," pp. 648–49.

36. Ibid., pp. 649–50.

37. Ibid., p. 650.

38. For a detailed discussion, see Goldelman, *Jewish National Autonomy in Ukraine*.

39. Roman Dmowski (1864–1939), Polish political leader. He was one of the founders of the National Democratic Party and leader of the Polish circle in the second and third State Dumas. Dmowski was an extreme anti-Semite. During the existence of the Second Polish Republic between the two world wars, Dmowski held extreme right-wing views that were not far removed from fascism. Hostile to Germany, he called for a rapprochement between Poland and the USSR.

40. Jabotinsky, *Avtobiografia*, pp. 60–62.

41. V. Zhabotinskii, "Poliaki i evrei," in *Fel'etony*, p. 143.
Arnold von Winkelried was the legendary hero of Switzerland who enabled the Swiss Confederation, supported by the Swabian League, to win a great victory over the Habsburg Leopold III of Swabia at the Battle of Sempach in 1386.

42. V. Zhabotinskii, "Non multum, sed multa," p. 650.

43. V. Zhabotinskii, "Homo homini lupus," in *Fel'etony*, pp. 109–10.

44. See especially V. Zhabotinskii, "Poliaki i evrei," in *Fel'etony*, pp. 139–51. In that article, written in 1910, Jabotinsky adapted a verse from Taras Shevchenko's poem "Haidamaky" (1841). In the poem, Polish confederates force the Jew Leib to sing the following verse:

> Before the landlord, Theodore,
> A Jew is dancing on the floor,
> At times retreating,

Then forward fleeting,
Before the landlord, Theodore,
Dancing for all he's worth.

*The Poetical Works of Taras Shevchenko*, trans. C. H. Andrusyshen and Watson Kirkconnell (Toronto, 1964), pp. 73–74.

45. V. Zhabotinskii, "Na lozhnom puti," in *Fel'etony*, pp. 259–60.

46. Ibid., p. 260.

47. M. Slavinskii, "Imperiia narodov," *Ukrainskii vestnik*, no. 1 (21 May 1906).

CHAPTER 2

# Vladimir Jabotinsky, Petr Struve, and the Shevchenko Anniversary: A Discussion of the Ukrainian Question

In the volume *Rebel and Statesman*, written in memory of his mentor, Joseph Schechtman states: "In unpublished, handwritten autobiographical notes, Jabotinsky said that during the years 1910–13 he 'began a systematic press offensive against the last fortresses of assimilationism in South Russia [Ukraine]; all my best work as a Jewish publicist in the Russian language belongs to this period.'"[1] Jabotinsky also referred to the 1910–12 period as follows: "During that period we began our offensive against the Society for the Promotion of Culture among the Jews of Russia—the bastion of Odesa Russifiers. Ahad Ha-Am had launched a war against them a few years earlier, but when he went to England that war ended."[2] Thus Jabotinsky's aim at that time was to attack the process of Jewish assimilation, which by then had progressed so far that a preponderant part of the Jewish intelligentsia, whether in ethnic Russia, Ukraine, Lithuania or Belarus, considered Russian to be its native language.

All Zionists without exception considered the process of Jewish assimilation to be harmful, since denationalization of the Jewish masses threatened the Jewish people's very existence. Preparation for realizing the Zionist idea required the Jewish people in the Diaspora to be kept spiritually healthy and nationally conscious. No Zionist had any doubt on that score. Yet that conviction coexisted paradoxically with the fact that many principled opponents of assimilation spoke and wrote in Russian, gave their children a Russian education, published Russian-language periodicals, and were infatuated with Russian culture. An analogous paradox is evident even today among Diaspora Jews in many countries.

This was hardly the result of hypocrisy. Rather, its roots lie in the practical conditions of life in which a different language and a different national environment give rise to a "categorical imperative." This is not an imperative in the Kantian sense, but an inescapable demand issuing from the external environment and urging adaptation to it. Only at the cost of great sacrifices, which involve breaking the pattern of one's own and one's family's life, can one resist the demands of that imperative. It is a step that few are capable of taking. The categorical imperative does not operate while Jews live in ghettoes, in conditions of rather strict isolation from the non-Jewish world, but leaving the ghetto means entering territory where the categorical imperative imposes its demands.

Jabotinsky wrote a great deal about the conditions under which Jews abandoned their own culture for another. He noted in particular that for many Jews, love of Russian culture came not through their familiarity with the Russian people (since Jews in the Pale of Settlement were in contact with Ukrainians, Poles, Belarusians, Lithuanians or Moldavians rather than Russians), but through contact with the culture itself, with the highest, purest expressions of the Russian spirit.[3] Jabotinsky wrote that Jews were "unconsciously and humiliatingly" infatuated with Russian culture. He considered it degrading that representatives of one of history's oldest cultures, which lay at the basis of the West's entire civilization, should pay slavish homage to a young nation's culture in a country that scarcely treated them as full-fledged human beings. This was only one element in the general state of humiliation besetting the Jewish people within the Russian Empire.

The launching of Jabotinsky's offensive against assimilation was not, in itself, entirely original, since many other Zionists both before and during this time had been engaged in such work, but the way in which he pressed his attack was so striking that it quickly thrust him into the front rank of political writers in tsarist Russia. *Feuilletons*, a collection of most of Jabotinsky's cycle of articles on the subject, "could be found in thousands of Jewish homes. Together with Jabotinsky's translation of Bialik's poems, they [*Feuilletons*] became the most popular present on many festive family occasions, and one could easily discern numerous—often unconscious—quotations from them in conversations and discussions among the Jewish intelligentsia."[4]

What was most striking and attractive in that cycle of articles was originality of thought, subtlety of journalistic form, depth of feeling, clarity of illustration, familiarity with a wide range of social problems, strong convictions, and greatness of spirit. What decisively differentiated Jabotinsky from other writers on that theme, both before and after him, was his fresh and consistent conception. This was no mere exposition of the idea that assimilation is evil—a notion quite familiar to the Jewish reader. Jabotinsky consistently linked the Jewish national problem both with the problems of the peoples among whom Jews in the Diaspora lived and more generally with the problems of contemporary world society. He drew Jewish national thought away from the provincialism of the ghetto and the timorousness of separatism into the broad expanse of the world's sociopolitical problems. He argued that the Jewish people could exist in that expanse, if it wished to survive in dignity, not in isolated groups that were more or less assimilated into various cultures, but as an independent nation within the community of nations. Such a Jewish nation would have its own cultural and national values, its own language, and its own clearly defined national consciousness, that is, its own national profile. The very fact of living among other nations, with their numerous national and international problems, should force the Jewish nation to adhere to its own dignified, principled political line, which would be friendly toward other nations and was the only policy capable of enabling Jewry to engage in dialogue on equal terms with the other nations of the world.

The memoirs of the Ukrainian civic leader Ievhen Chykalenko preserve an interesting recollection of one of Jabotinsky's appearances before a group of nationally conscious Ukrainian social activists in which he emphasized the affinity of national tasks. The speech was delivered in January 1911, and the account is especially significant because Chykalenko provides a detailed explanation of Jabotinsky's attitude toward the Ukrainian people and its national movement:

> Yesterday, the well-known Zionist political writer V. Ie. Jabotinsky arrived from Odesa. He came with the express aim of reaching an understanding with the directors of the Ukrainian press.
>
> At a meeting in the Ukrainian club he made a long and wonderful speech in which he tried to show that the desiderata of Zionist Jews, and nationalist Jews in general, were completely identical to those of the Ukrainians, and that for the time being they had the same tasks and the same enemies. Both for us and for them the question of the day is national education; both they and we will be fighting Russifiers and Polonizers. For these reasons we should be coordinating our activities.
>
> At the moment, when the Poles are trying to curb Jewish rights while introducing self-government in Poland, we must jointly use our press to point out that wherever the Poles have power they oppress all weaker nations; that is how it was in the old Poland, where they oppressed the Ukrainians, Belarusians, and Lithuanians. Now in Galicia they are oppressing Ukrainians and those Jews who wish to remain Jews, as opposed to "Poles of the Mosaic faith."
>
> Jabotinsky promises that the Zionist press, which is produced in argot as well as in the ancient Hebrew and Russian languages, will put forward the idea that Jews must concern themselves with Ukrainians and the Ukrainian movement and should not be Russifiers, because the Ukrainian movement has a future and the day will come when the Jews will be sorry that they linked up with the Russifiers.[5]

In the speech that Chykalenko described, Jabotinsky expressed the ideas that he repeated in various forms in dozens of articles from the beginning of his political career up to 1914. Those ideas permeated the articles collected in *Feuilletons*, and he defended them ardently in the polemic unfolding at that time in the press of the Russian Empire.

Jabotinsky wrote his articles of this period in Russian, not because the categorical imperative so dictated, for he had by then completely liberated himself from it spiritually and was soon to do so practically, but because Russian was the language spoken by the people Jabotinsky was trying to reach—Russified Jews. That was the community from which he had come and which he was trying to draw after him, away from the assimilationist melting pot and toward national dignity.

It was characteristic (and fundamentally important for understanding Jabotinsky's views and ideas) that he linked his offensive against assimilation with an event and debate that, for Jewish circles, bore scarcely any relationship to Jewish problems—the fiftieth anniversary of the death of the greatest Ukrainian national poet, Taras Shevchenko, and the subsequent debate that unfolded on the pages of the Russian and Ukrainian press. The discussion lasted until 1914, when a new Shevchenko anniversary was marked—the centenary of his birth. The anniversary was to be commemorated in 1911, but the Ukrainian press was already printing material dedicated to Shevchenko in 1910, the year in which Jabotinsky began his offensive. The Ukrainian cultural and national circles of the day sought to give this anniversary the greatest possible resonance. At a time when Ukraine did not possess even the shadow of political or cultural autonomy, Shevchenko was, as he remains, the symbolic embodiment of national ideals, a monument to Ukrainian letters and national consciousness, and a prophet of future Ukrainian statehood.

The histories of many nations feature towering cultural and political leaders who decisively influenced the nation's formative process. Theodor Herzl declared at the First Zionist Congress in 1897 that "I created the Jewish state in Basel," although he did so only on paper. So Shevchenko could also have said at the end of his life: "I created the Ukrainian state," even though he only wrote poetry. Shevchenko created the spiritual preconditions for Ukrainian statehood, just as Herzl created certain preconditions for the formation of the Jewish state. Jabotinsky described Shevchenko in just that way: "Shevchenko is a national poet, and therein lies his strength.... He offered his own people and the entire world clear, firm proof that the Ukrainian spirit is capable of the highest flights of original cultural creativity.... Shevchenko [will] remain just as nature shaped him: a dazzling precedent that will not permit Ukrainianism to stray from the path of national renaissance."[6]

In the discussion that developed around the Shevchenko anniversary both sides, Ukrainian and Russian, advanced their views, and the debate remains one of the most interesting and substantial sources for studying the social atmosphere in Russia from the beginning of the twentieth century to the revolution of 1917.

What was Shevchenko's significance for Russian society—both for that part of it normally called progressive and for that part usually called reactionary? More generally, what was the Russian attitude toward the rights and the destinies of colonial nations—a fundamental question in all multinational empires?

The extreme right-wing Russian nationalists, the Black Hundreds and their supporters, considered the empire a Russian state in which the Russian language and culture should rule absolutely, and where there could be no question of national autonomy for the non-Russian peoples. The "Union of 17 October" (the "Octobrists") was a bit more to the left. The party began its activity in 1905 with a moderate liberal program, but quickly moved to the right and soon transformed itself into a party that in practice supported the main points of government policy, including discrimination against the Jews and the unconditional preservation of Russian dominance throughout the empire's entire territory.[7] The strongest position, both in Russian society and in the State Duma, was held by the Constitutional Democrats (Cadets), a liberal party that stood in opposition to the tsarist regime. Russified Jews played a prominent role in its leadership, as did representatives of other non-Russian peoples. Despite this non-Russian participation, the party remained indisputably Russian, indeed it was Russian nationalist.[8]

The nationalism of Russian liberal circles expressed itself first of all in the tendency to identify the military, political and territorial greatness of the Russian Empire with the interests of the Russian people. On the basis of democratic principles and liberal inclinations, Russian liberals theoretically recognized the right of the non-Russian peoples to preserve their national identity and develop their own cultures, or at least they considered the expression of some degree of sympathy for the national aspirations of the non-Russian peoples to be consistent with their stated political positions. This attitude was not easily reconciled with the traditional notions, quite widespread in Russian society (including its liberal section), that the greatness, power, and indivisibility of the Russian Empire were necessary conditions for the preservation of Russian national interests. Such notions were deeply imbedded in the psychology of the Russian popular masses as well as in the state leadership and the nationalist right. Most of the Russian liberal intelligentsia was also inclined toward those notions.

The right-wing press charged those liberal figures who supported autonomy for the non-Russian peoples (cultural rather than administrative autonomy, certainly not separation) with possessing the covert aim of dividing the empire, for cultural autonomy could become the thin end of the wedge of complete emancipation, leading to eventual political independence for the non-Russians. This right-wing pressure was fairly strong, and eventually Russian society was dominated by an atmosphere that threatened any defender of the rights of the non-Russian peoples with accusations of lacking patriotism. Since the liberal intelligentsia considered itself 100 percent patriotic, it was very pained by such charges. If Russian patriotism meant unchallengeable Russian dominance in the cultural as well as in the administrative field, liberal circles were faced with a dilemma. Either they could risk the hazards of joining battle with an important section of Russian society for a different interpretation of patriotism or, for the sake of preserving their influence in society and peace within their own ranks, they could agree with the interpretation forced upon them by the right and backtrack to some extent on the issue of rights for the non-Russian peoples.

The liberals were anything but ready to fight for new definitions of Russian patriotism and Russian national interests as they pertained to the nationality question. They based themselves upon democratic ideals that were not rooted in Russian consciousness or in Russia's public life. To have used such ideals to oppose powerful and deeply rooted imperialist notions would have demanded levels of energy and courage that the liberals scarcely possessed. Moreover, there was no unity on the issue within liberal circles. The right wing of the Cadets held democratic views on civil rights, but an imperialist position on the nationality question. They all finally satisfied themselves with the calculation that when the time came to create a truly democratic order, a democratic parliament would be able to determine how best to satisfy the demands of the non-Russian peoples, while simultaneously preserving the unity of the state.

In general, the idea that democratization automatically resolves all national problems and quells all national conflicts was very widespread among supporters of democracy in Russian society.[9] Jabotinsky decisively opposed such a view. He indicated that the nationality question had to be approached on a completely different plane and that the liberalization or democratization of political life would in no way guarantee a resolution of nationality problems. This is how he described those who thought either that the nationality question was insignificant or that it would be resolved with democratization:

> The charge of being totally ignorant on the nationality question...applies not just to the Jewish part of local society. Many others also share in that sin, living in the blissful belief that the nationality question does not really exist but is deliberately manufactured by people of ill will, since no decent party would take it up seriously and positively. It is particularly fashionable among us to oppose "nationalism" to "democratism." We consider it axiomatic that the more democratic a party is, the more indifferent it will be toward such matters as the preservation and development of national peculiarities, language rights, the proportional representation of nations in parliament, and so on. That is why our average intellectual is deeply convinced that social democrats, for example, do not even want to hear about such questions. Moreover, he is utterly convinced that the whole national complication will be solved readily and easily by democratizing the political order. One should therefore fight, it would seem, only for this "general" principle without any need to worry specifically about the national elements. They will sort themselves out at the same time.

Jabotinsky used the example of the Social Democratic Party of Austria to show that the nationality question was so important and so distinct from other issues that the party had found itself obliged to occupy itself with the matter seriously for a number of years and even split into separate national factions over it. Jabotinsky drew the following conclusion:

> ...Obviously life forced this to happen, life prompted the idea that the way out of national conflicts lies only in delimiting boundaries by mutual agreement.[10]

In Russia, the situation was different than in Austria: none of the all-empire parties wanted to divide into national factions. As far as the Russian liberals were concerned, they would adopt a hurrah-for-the-Fatherland, elevated, patriotic tone as soon as a united, indivisible Russia was called into question. With comparatively few variations, that tone was common to all Russian nationalists, from the extreme right to the liberals. A Cadet leader, the Jew Maksim Vinawer, used that patriotic tone in a speech:

> ...Russia is dear to all the nationalities that inhabit it. They are aware that after irrigating her fields with their blood, after covering her territory with all the paths of the liberation movement, they have the right to consider themselves her sons. I have no doubt that there will come a time when they will all join together, united by ties of love, and defend the common interests of a single fatherland.[11]

In another speech, prompted by the Białystok pogrom, Vinawer said: "There are very few of us [Jews], but we have one enormous strength—the strength of despair, and we have one ally—the whole Russian people, which is filled with genuine compassion."[12]

Although Jabotinsky was by no means an enemy of the Russian people, he in no way shared such enthusiastic notions about it as an ally to the Jews in the struggle for their rights. In a series of articles he argued that the Russian liberal intelligentsia would undoubtedly move to the right, descending into chauvinism and anti-Semitism. Jews, in his opinion, should not count on support from Russians, but should instead rely upon their own forces:

> They have pounded into the heads of the Jewish community the completely unfounded belief that the Jews have a faithful friend and protector in the Russian intelligentsia, one that may be trusted with confidence. Every national initiative on the part of Jewry has been completely subverted by this. The senseless belief in foreign assistance has been the main obstacle on the path of the national idea. The senseless belief in foreign assistance put a brake on the activity of Pinsker, the Zionists, and the Bund. Because of that belief alone, a Jewish parliamentary faction was not formed in the First Russian Duma.... But that belief is an absurdity. The better part of the Russian intelligentsia is indifferent to us, while its mass shares the common folk's antipathy toward us. That is now known to one and all: it is openly spoken of by Russians, Jews, and even baptized Jews. Only in the press ànd in public speeches are lies diligently cultivated on that issue.... The Russian intellectual is no worse and no better than the Polish, German or French intellectual. Do not rely on the first, the second or the third; be vigilant and organize yourselves![13]

Vinawer's position elicited both refutation and derision from Jabotinsky: "Let us permit Mr. Vinawer and other fine people to reach the age of Methuselah while adhering to their curious views, which lead them to stare into the master's eyes and say with tender passion, 'You do love us after all!', while Messrs. Miliukov and Struve reply, 'Mmm...not too much.'"[14]

Another prominent Zionist, Daniil Pasmanik, frankly described the Russian liberals and their views as "national-liberal":

> Everything forces one to bow to the assumption that the Great Russian national-liberal party will behave like the German National Liberals, who are backing the Prussian government in its anti-Polish policy.... It suffices for us to listen to the Constitutional Democratic Party's statements. They begin by distinguishing between nationalities whose autonomy has been "advanced by experience and supported by popular instinct" and nationalities whose autonomy has been more or less invented by the intelligentsia. The whole issue assumes an opportunistic character. We must also remember that this view has been expressed by an opposition party striving for power and therefore in need of support from all who are dissatisfied with their fate. What happens to an opposition that becomes a government party? There is no need for lengthy reflection upon that question. We can state with certainty that the Great Russian bourgeoisie will agree only to oblast decentralization, which is to its own advantage, but will in no way agree to broad national autonomy.[15]

Pasmanik's assumption that once the liberal opposition came to power it would not agree to broad national autonomy was borne out to the letter. In June 1917 the Cadets resigned from the Russian revolutionary Provisional Government in protest at that government's agreement, under pressure of circumstances, to recognize Ukraine's autonomy in severely restricted form. They later rejoined the government, but their consistent opposition to any concessions to the national movements significantly narrowed the government's social base, thereby facilitating the Bolshevik victory.[16]

The Russian liberals' turn to the right, in the direction of great-power chauvinism, was observed not only by Jewish political writers. In Ukrainian circles Dmytro Dontsov, political writer and civic leader, was one of the first to show a true grasp of the meaning of that process, notably in his articles in *Ukrainskaia zhizn'* (Ukrainian Life) titled "Russian Liberalism and the Ukrainian Movement" (1912) and "Russian Imperialism and Ukrainianism" (1913). In these he noted that the clear signs of Russian liberalism's transition to an imperialist stance indicated the need to reorient Ukrainian political thought: "The hopes, widespread in Ukrainian society, for a liberal Russia are greatly exaggerated and are even, in part, simply prejudices.... If that is the case, then do not the usual prescriptions for resolving the Ukrainian question in Russia turn out to be invalid?"[17]

This article of Dontsov's drew a reply from Jabotinsky, "On Russian Liberalism," also published in *Ukrainskaia zhizn'* as a letter to the editors.[18] Jabotinsky agreed in principle with the idea that Russian liberalism would sooner or later become *openly* hostile to the non-Russian national movements, but he expressed the view that this would happen more slowly, at least not until the non-Russian peoples had begun actively to squeeze Russians out of cultural and public life in the non-Russian parts of the empire. Dontsov prophesied:

> In general, as Russian liberalism has become an active force on the political arena in recent years, it has brought great disillusionment to Ukraine.

> ...I think that liberal Russia can hardly expect a brilliant future if the starting point of its national policy has already proved unworkable in Austria, a policy that begins by dividing nations into privileged and "second-class" varieties.[19]

Jabotinsky felt that many years would pass before that could happen. History, however, proved that Dontsov, rather than Jabotinsky, was right, for less than five years later the non-Russian peoples responded to the Petrograd revolution by immediately demanding their right to self-government within their national territories. It rapidly emerged that as the liberal forces moved from opposition to government they were not merely unwilling to grant the non-Russian peoples the unrestricted right to self-determination, but were prepared to fight resolutely against the exercise of that right. Indeed, revolutionary Russia lost its "brilliant future" in 1917 largely because the Provisional Government was unable to work out a modus vivendi with the national movements and therefore did not gain their support.

Although Jabotinsky did not generally agree with Dontsov, he did share one idea—that Russian society was neither politically nor psychologically ready for a peaceful and constructive examination of the empire's nationality problems. It could not comprehend the fact that the nationalism of the non-Russian peoples was not some terrible evil on the order of a cholera epidemic or the invention of a gang of malefactors, but one of the natural and inevitable problems of a multinational state, and one that could be, and had to be, resolved by recognizing the equal rights of all peoples. Ridiculing numerous elements in Russian society under the collective name *Zamoskvorech'e* (Lands beyond the Moscow River), Jabotinsky wrote:

> There are, in this world, some terrible words, like "bugbear" and "sword," words that are feared by some people. Among such terrible words is the word "nationalism." *Zamoskvorech'e* shudders at that fearful sound and imagines that this is what it should be doing, in line with the latest European fashion. Yet in Europe all trace of that fashion has long disappeared.[20]

It was in the pages of *Ukrainskaia zhizn'* that Jabotinsky appealed to the Ukrainian national movement, calling upon it to strengthen the national movements within the empire so that Russian society would grasp the decisive importance of the empire's nationality problems.

> We nonnatives (*inorodtsy*)...have had the responsibility foisted upon us to prove what we have known for ages and what all political parties in Russia will sooner or later be forced to recognize: that the nationality question in this empire is primary, not secondary. Moreover, it is the most important of all problems, much more important than the agrarian or labor questions. For us nonnatives, the entire liberation movement, the whole prospect of Russia's renewal, has meaning and value only to the extent that it brings us national freedom. Except under such conditions, we have no "common cause" nor any stimulus for a united struggle.

> ...We nonnatives, and no one else, must once and for all explain to liberal Russia that we will not agree to divide the united struggle into two stages: first "the constitution," and then "the nationality question." For we know history well and remember that in such instances those satisfied in the first stage leave the scene, while those still hungry are forced to continue to push their way through the ranks.... The nationality problem must, from this day forward, take its place at the top, at the center, at the forefront of Russian political life.[21]

Jabotinsky began his article "On Russian Liberalism" with a polemic against Dontsov, but concluded it with an appeal for the "intensification of the national movements." That was clearly the main idea that he wished to impart to the Ukrainian journal's readers.

A discussion of the attitude of various Russian circles to the nationality question cannot overlook the stand taken by socialist and social-democratic circles and parties. Russian socialists of all persuasions recognized the national and cultural rights of all peoples, but they considered the nationality question to be secondary, subordinate to the primary question, which was, from their point of view, the class struggle. The limits within which socialists were prepared to recognize the national rights of the non-Russian peoples ranged from national-territorial autonomy to the right to complete separation from the empire. The right of nations to self-determination, up to and including separation, was proclaimed in particular by Bolshevik Leninists, especially after 1917. However, the Bolsheviks used the slogan of the right of nations to self-determination in a demagogic manner, with the aim of winning over the national forces of the non-Russian peoples. After the Bolsheviks seized power, they operated contrary to their own slogans and used military force to unite the empire, which had disintegrated as a result of revolutionary events. The Russian social-democratic Mensheviks were not consistent on the nationality question and often leaned toward an imperialist position, as the years of the revolution clearly revealed.[22]

In such conditions, the Shevchenko anniversary took place in 1911. It is not surprising that a majority of the Russian press was not, on the whole, favorably disposed toward those Ukrainian leaders who sought in their speeches to emphasize Shevchenko's significance as a Ukrainian national poet. The Russian press tried, on the whole, to downplay the anniversary's significance, treating it as a third-rate cultural event. By contrast, the Ukrainian press tried to give the anniversary such scope as to make it a factor helping to unite Ukrainian national forces and raising Ukrainian national consciousness. To be sure, the Ukrainian press also tried to draw the Russians out into debate. It succeeded to a significant degree, and the Russian press had to produce a whole series of discussion articles. The general tone of those in the moderate, progressive press was condescendingly indulgent. It may be summarized as follows: "Our younger Ukrainian brothers are playing at having a national poet of their own. He may not even be bad, although he certainly has a long way to go to attain the level of the great Russian poets. We do not interfere with their games, but every cultured and intelligent person knows that a single great Russian culture exists, while so-called Ukrainian culture is merely a second-rate local phenomenon, to some extent a fanciful concoction of a few conceited provincial intellectuals."

The consistent reminders in the Ukrainian press that the rights of nations in the cultural and political fields were just as integral a part of liberal-democratic principles as the rights to freedom of speech, association, demonstrations, and strikes ran up against quite transparent insinuations that the so-called Ukrainians, with their peasant language and primitive culture, had no business trying to push their way into the community of cultured peoples, for whose benefit those "progressive principles" existed.

Such selectiveness in applying "progressive principles" brought some Ukrainian leaders, particularly Dmytro Dontsov, to the brink of despair. For as a rule they believed religiously in liberal-democratic ideals and suffered painfully when their Russian liberal colleagues treated those ideals in a manner that had a great deal in common, as the Ukrainians saw it, with imperialism, not progressive politics. The Ukrainian-Russian discussion developed far beyond the framework of the Shevchenko anniversary and turned into a debate about the fundamental nature of the Russian state, its social order and state policy. This Ukrainian-Russian dispute might have been confined to the subject of relations between Eastern Slavs, but for Jabotinsky's intervention. His participation gave the discussion a different tone and impelled him into the ranks of the most prominent theoreticians on the nationality question.

The immediate occasion for Jabotinsky's involvement was the publication of articles by Petr Berngardovich Struve (1870–1944) that provoked a great storm of polemics in the Russian and Ukrainian press. Like many Russified Germans, Struve was an ardent Russian patriot and a refined representative of the Russian intellectual elite. From every point of view, he was an eminent personality. By the time Struve came to discuss the Ukrainian question, his world-view had undergone a lengthy evolution from Marxism to a moderate, even somewhat conservative, liberalism. As a prominent member of the Cadet Party, he edited a serious Moscow journal, *Russkaia mysl'* (Russian Thought), on whose pages he participated in the polemic. At that time Struve was recognized as one of the most authoritative figures in Russian society, and this was apparent in the style of his articles. They were slow, meditative, and somewhat didactic, with all the trappings of noble magnanimity, but not without a noticeable strain of great-power, imperialist arrogance.

Having entered into debate with such a great Russian "lord," Jabotinsky made use of the occasion to formulate and disseminate a whole series of ideas. They were fundamental to his world-view, but decidedly out of tune with the views put forward by Struve and his circle. Struve took a thoroughly serious attitude toward Jabotinsky in the discussion and published one of Jabotinsky's polemical articles, "Letters on Nationalities and Oblasts: Jewry and its Attitudes," in his journal, even though the article was directed against his own views.[23]

As noted earlier, almost from the outset of Jabotinsky's career as a political writer, he had undertaken a "systematic press offensive" against assimilation. This offensive was not limited to the polemic with Struve, for Jabotinsky simultaneously published many other articles with the same aim. Nevertheless, the polemic with Struve was the central and most significant element of what Jabotinsky called his "offensive." It was, in fact, an entire press campaign, led on the Jewish side by Jabotinsky almost single-handedly. This mighty burst of creativity led to the formulation of an entire systematic world-view that could be termed "Jabotinsky's theory on the nationality question." The Struve polemic's centrality for Jabotinsky is shown, besides all else, by the fact that he referred to Struve countless times in articles written in varied contexts over the ensuing years.

In the polemic Jabotinsky maintained his characteristic gentle, tolerant tone, which did not, however, prevent him from expressing his ideas in a clear, unequivocal way and advancing views that sharply contradicted those of his opponents. Jabotinsky also courteously emphasized Struve's liberalism and progressiveness: "I consider it foolish and improper to attack a liberal author just because he happens to agree with one reactionary or another on some particular questions."[24] However, if Jabotinsky had believed that Struve's views were completely accidental and not characteristic of wider Russian circles (and not just of those called reactionary), he would scarcely have devoted so much attention to this discussion. In the end, Struve's stubborn adherence to his views, despite all the powerful arguments advanced against them by Jabotinsky and other, mainly Ukrainian, political writers, exhausted Jabotinsky's patience and respect. In an article published in the summer of 1912, he referred to Struve in a manner devoid of all courteous civilities: "One should not draw general conclusions about everyone on the basis of such exceptional specimens as Mr. Struve. He is a born theoretician who constructs politics deductively and perceives his abstractions and predictions in the same way as other people perceive facts. Indeed, he does not perceive facts at all...."[25] The fact that Jabotinsky ultimately abandoned his markedly polite tone shows that he took his theme very much to heart—the theme of "the nationality problem, the cardinal issue for Russia's future."

Since Jabotinsky is known for having dedicated his life to the Jewish cause and devoted himself to the Jewish problem, why was he so immersed in problems that were fundamental to Russia? He wrote: "If the dispute over national culture has been restricted to an internal discussion between Russians and Ukrainians, then we outsiders have no business being involved—the question will be settled without us, and they will not need our advice."[26] However, it was obvious that the fate of the Jewish people within the empire would depend to a great extent upon how the empire's nationality problem was resolved. There could be no positive solution to the Jewish problem without some general regularization of the national rights of the more than 100 peoples living within the empire's borders. Since such a regularization necessitated the overall reconstruction of the sociopolitical foundations of the tsarist state, the issue was particularly far-reaching and could not but be at the center of every political activist's attention.

Jabotinsky was very well aware of the wide-ranging significance of this problem:

> This is a dispute about the ethnic nature of the Russian state; about whether one should or should not consider Little Russians and Belarusians to be separate nations; about whether Russia should be a "national state"; about whether it is headed in the direction of a so-called *Nationalitätenstaat*. This dispute deserves the most serious and (if one can put it that way) the most weighty discussion. I am deeply convinced that it will gradually become the subject of such a discussion in all the serious Russian public forums. For the nationality question is fundamental to Russia's future, more important, more basic than all other political and even social problems, including even agrarian reform.... There was a time in Austria when they also thought that the nationality problem was a secondary issue that was humbly leaving the proscenium to make way on stage for the "real," namely the economic, interests, but life showed that the whole existence of the state, so to speak, the entire axis around which it is doomed to revolve, hinged on the problem of the nationalities. In the end even social democracy began to fissure precisely along the seams of national divisions. Austria did not escape its fate, and neither will its neighbors.[27]

History showed that Russia could escape the fate of all multinational empires for a time by adopting a communist dictatorship that was far more ruthless than the former tsarist regime. But that was not yet the end of history.

In January 1911 Jabotinsky's article "Letters on Nationalities and Oblasts: Jewry and its Attitudes" was published in Petr Struve's journal, *Russkaia mysl'*. The article did, of course, move beyond the parameters of the "offensive against assimilation," because it was intended for a Russian readership. Its description of the development and current status of the Jewish community's political and social movements treated matters well known to Jewish readers, but much less familiar to the Russian readers of the "monthly literary and political publication," as Petr Struve's journal described itself on the front cover of every issue. Having detailed the ferment among Jewish social and political forces, Jabotinsky ended with a remarkable conclusion that began: "All of this is contemporary. The question of the future is an entirely different matter." He went on to develop his ideas about Russia's future, on which the future of Jewry within the Russian Empire naturally depended.

It was this concluding section that provoked sharp opposition from Struve and led to the polemic. Jabotinsky expressed his basic idea on the destiny of the peoples of the empire as follows:

> The question of whether Russian Jewry is fated to assimilate or to develop as a separate nationality depends mainly on the answer to the following momentous question: in which direction is Russia developing—toward a nation-state [that is, a unitary nation] or toward a "state of nationalities"? In a unilingual state, an ethnic minority, particularly a dispersed one, will inevitably assimilate sooner or later, but its fate would be completely different in a country where several nationalities and languages were allowed to develop freely.[28]

Thus Jabotinsky established a definite link between the prospects of free cultural and national development within the empire for Jewry and the prospects of similar development for the other peoples.

Jabotinsky's postscript also attacked assimilation, but did so in a way that was bound to annoy the patrician consciousness of Struve, who was proud to belong to the elite of an imperialist nation. The idea that Russia should be a "state of nationalities" in which many peoples and languages would develop freely on the basis of equality rather than a Russian nation-state was certain to provoke Struve's opposition. Furthermore, by referring to the Ukrainians and Belarusians as separate nations, Jabotinsky touched the most sensitive spot in the soul of a Russian nationalist who considered Ukraine to be Russia's most ancient region and saw Kyiv as the "mother of Russian cities."

In his study of Struve, Richard Pipes notes that "Ukraine was always Struve's blind spot,"[29] and that was indeed the case. Struve's uncompromising defense of the empire's cultural unity—on the basis of Russian culture, of course—was much more decisive than the position of the Cadet Party leadership. The latter was not, at that time, in a position completely to disregard the national aspirations of the non-Russian peoples as long as it wished to retain influence in the non-Russian parts of the empire. While the Cadet Party vacillated on the issue, trying to combine imperialism with some consideration for the demands of the non-Russian peoples within the state, Struve allowed no vacillation or compromise. Until the end of his life, he insisted on the unity of the empire founded on the complete cultural hegemony of the Russians. Since Ukraine was the most important non-Russian part of the empire and its Russification would be a decisive victory for Russian imperialism, Ukraine became Struve's "blind spot."[30]

Jabotinsky differed. He considered that Jewish involvement in the forcible Russification of non-Russians was not only unethical, but also shortsighted in view of the likely future course of events within the empire:

> In Russia...the Jews live en masse among the Little Russians, Belarusians, Poles, Lithuanians, and Moldavians; they have the least contact with the Great Russians. Thus, even if they accepted Russification, the Jews would be

> assimilated not by the majority population around them but by a people that constitutes a weaker, scattered minority within the Pale of Settlement and dominates today only thanks to state coercion. In the event of the liquidation of that coercion, the local national cultures would develop and thrive, forcing Jewry also to separate finally into a distinct cultural group. It would be impelled not only by the attraction of example...but also by necessity, born of a sense of political self-preservation.[31]

Thus the Jews living among the non-Russian peoples should not assimilate either to the Russian or to the local cultures, but should remain within the bounds of their own culture. When Jabotinsky put that idea to Jews, they perceived it as a call for national self-preservation. Ukrainian national-democratic circles understood and sympathized, for they were appealing to their own people with a similar message. In a Russian journal, however, that idea could be read as a call for the dismemberment of the empire. It is not difficult to grasp that a multinational empire like Russia depended on state coercion as its principal means of preserving territorial unity. The end of such coercion would mean the liquidation of the empire. Anyone who was aware of Russia's problems would understand the matter in this way, and that was exactly how Struve took it. In fact, Jabotinsky never spoke directly about the desirability of dividing up the empire. Instead, he always stressed only the need for the untrammeled and independent cultural, national and political development of all the peoples of the empire. Yet it is hard to imagine that he had failed to understand that such unrestricted development, especially if state coercion were eliminated, would inevitably lead to the empire's collapse.

Further on in the *Russkaia mysl'* article, Jabotinsky stressed the idea, which he put forward on many occasions (especially in the collection *Feuilletons*), that if Jews were to play the role of Russifiers in the non-Russians lands, they would expose themselves to serious danger:

> In the type of mixed community that exists in every gubernia within the Pale of Settlement, linking up with any of the neighboring cultures would provoke anti-Semitism among the others; adopting the role of being practically the sole bearers of Great Russian culture throughout the entire region would be even more dangerous. It would be equivalent to issuing a direct challenge to the whole local population. Even now the Ukrainian press is protesting sharply against the Russifying role that the assimilated Jewish intelligentsia is unconsciously playing in the towns of the southwestern region. The Poles and Lithuanians blame the Jews directly for the Russification of Vilnius, and there is a good deal of truth in that charge. As soon as all those nationalities gain partial influence over the country's affairs, even the convinced Jewish assimilators, if they can be found, will be forced to change their attitude. Whether out of direct conviction or through the fact of their exclusion, the Jews will be forced to choose the only possible way out—Jewry's separation into a distinct cultural entity.[32]

As if to provoke a reply from Struve, Jabotinsky ended his article by making it clear that he was aware of having completely contradicted the stand of the journal's editor-in-chief. And as if to ensure Struve's irritation, he added a finale:

> The nationality whose language is Russian constitutes only 43 percent of the empire's population, according to the undoubtedly exaggerated statistics of the 1897 census. That is a large number, but not enough to make all the rest, the "nonnatives," willingly accept the role of an ex gratia supplement to the Great Russian nationality. They have the greatest respect for that nationality and for its majestic culture, and they want to continue living in close spiritual intercourse with it. Nevertheless, they consider that the true homeland of that culture is demarcated by the ethnic boundaries of Great Russia. The reason such boundaries do not exist today lies mainly in primordial coercion and injustice. We "nonnatives" foresee only one of two possibilities: either there will never be freedom and justice in Russia or each of us will consciously exploit freedom and justice in order to develop our particular national identity first and foremost and to emancipate ourselves from an alien culture. Either Russia will take the path of national decentralization or else no principles of democracy will be conceivable within its borders, including, for a start, the right of universal suffrage. For Russia, progress and the creation of a *Nationalitätenstaat* are synonymous, and any attempt to skip over this truth and impose strong discipline in the country in opposition to the will and consciousness of three-fifths of the population will end in failure. The "nonnative" nationalists, and not only they, see it that way. Time will tell who is right.[33]

Time would show that the problem of freedom and human rights within the Russian Empire, whatever the name by which it chose to call itself, was indeed inseparable from the problem of the national rights of the non-Russian nations. When Marxists asserted that no nation that oppresses another can itself be free, this was one of the few instances in which they were entirely right. Perhaps they were right because this idea that they were so fond of repeating was never in essence Marxist. It involved national categories rather than those of class or economics. In almost every country in which Marxists came to power, they in fact rejected a policy of national equality, thereby proving it to be an aberration within their ideology.

Jabotinsky's phrase about the greatest respect for the Russian people and its culture is interesting. This was probably not merely a routine courtesy to a Russian journal and its readers. His works show that he paid equal respect to all nations and their cultures, and the Russians were obviously no exception. Jabotinsky's examination of Russia's future did not, for one moment, allow him to abandon his benevolent, friendly attitude toward the Russian people, but in contrast to Struve and other Russian imperialists, he did not equate the interests of the Russian people with those of Russian imperialism. Jabotinsky argued his unequivocal position with such tact and dignity that even the most inveterate supporters of Russian imperialism were unable to attack him for anti-Russian tendencies. Moreover, he was quite a prominent Russian writer of the day and had enriched Russian culture with his literary achievements. Petr Struve also understood Jabotinsky's place and significance in social and cultural life, since he accepted the challenge of publishing Jabotinsky's article with his own reply in the same issue of the journal. True, his reply was very short—four pages of the journal, in comparison with Jabotinsky's twenty—however, since Struve replied not to the whole article but only to its last two pages (the "postscript"), the reply may be considered exhaustive.

Struve expressed the idea—the credo of many Russian nationalist authors—that a single Russian nation and culture united the three East Slavic peoples: the Great Russians, the Ukrainians, and the Belarusians. These three branches of a "single Russian people" together constituted two-thirds of the empire's population. He went on to say that the Ukrainian and Belarusian cultures and languages were simply local dialect branches of Russian culture and that only Great Russian culture embodied the single culture of all the Eastern Slavs. Struve went even further, arguing that there were only two portions of the Russian Empire—the Kingdom of Poland (the part of Poland within the Russian Empire) and Finland—that were entitled to an autonomous cultural existence. All the other peoples, including the Muslims, would ultimately have to embrace Russian culture: "Where in Russia are there cultures that can stand up to Russian culture as forces of objectively equal value, and most importantly as cultures that can stride forward without basing themselves on Russian culture and without thereby submitting, in a certain sense, to its hegemony?"[34]

Thus Struve put all the empire's peoples in their place—in the servants' quarters of the seigniorial nation and its dominant culture. Struve's good political sense cannot be denied. He specified precisely which peoples would be able to slip through the imperialist fingers—the Poles and the Finns. But that good sense was purely political and had nothing to do with the problem of national cultures. Moreover, with due respect to Finland's culture, the cultures of some of the empire's other peoples, for example, the Armenians or Georgians, are much more ancient and developed than Finnish culture, while Ukrainian culture is hardly inferior to Finland's and is more ancient.

Struve also touched on the Jewish question. He indicated that Jewish cultural, national and religious boundaries were too narrow to provide a basis for outstanding cultural creativity and suggested that everything of prominence that the Jews did create had arisen in the Diaspora under the influence of other peoples. It would appear that Struve felt a certain awkwardness about the fact that the Bible, which laid the foundation for the whole of Western civilization, was created by the Jews and was moreover fashioned neither in the Diaspora nor under foreign influence. If some Russian source had profoundly influenced European or world culture, we may be sure that Struve would not have failed to mention it and would even have made it the main proof of his concept of the supranational significance of Russian culture. Yet he managed to "forget" about the Bible.

About Ukrainian culture, Struve wrote:

> I am deeply convinced that, for example, the creation of a secondary and higher education system in the Little Russian language would be artificial and would in no way justify the outlay of the population's mental efforts. For the historical relationship between the Russian [Great Russian] and Little Russian cultures has developed in such a way that the "Russian" [Great Russian] can be a cultured participant in national life and an educated person without understanding any of the Little Russian language, but the "Little Russian" who understands no Russian is simply illiterate in a national and political sense—he has not yet read the national and political primer.
>
> Whatever the attitude we take toward this state of affairs, brought about by Russia's entire history, to deny its existence would mean denying facts that are obvious to everyone.
>
> The elements for resolving the question "What is Russia?" are to be found in those facts.[35]

Such were the words with which Struve ended his reply to Jabotinsky. He had concisely, but quite adequately, spelled out the basis for Russian imperialism. Like all imperialists, he was studiously silent about the fact that the "state of affairs brought about by Russia's entire history" had arisen from several centuries of bloody violence and was unnatural from any point of view.

This was the first round in the polemic that enabled Jabotinsky to put forward in the press an entire system of ideas on Russia's nationality question. The article "Letters on Nationalities and Oblasts: Jewry and Its Attitudes" put forward the main elements of that system in embryonic form, but a little later Jabotinsky formulated them in greater detail in a whole series of articles. Since the Shevchenko anniversary provided an occasion for linking the whole problem with the Ukrainian question and with Jewish-Ukrainian relations (about one-third of world Jewry lived among the Ukrainians at that time), Jabotinsky devoted most of his continuing dialogue with Struve and a significant part of his writings of 1910–14 to the Ukrainian question.

Those writings generally concerned the nationality problem as a whole and the attitude toward the Ukrainian question in particular. Only in his March 1913 article, "Rebuff," did Jabotinsky touch on an issue that was most important to understanding his position, namely the attitude of the leaders of the Ukrainian national movement toward Jews and the Jewish question. The article was significant because it explained Jabotinsky's particular sympathy for the Ukrainian movement. Although it was mainly about Polish-Jewish relations, Jabotinsky treated the attitude of Ukrainian national-patriotic forces toward Jewry as a positive model, in contrast with the negative attitude of Polish national circles:

> I advised and continue to advise Jewry in the South to pay great attention to the fact that pioneering Ukrainians regard Russified Jews as the main Russifiers in urban Ukraine. Why should we be concerned with this? Not at all because the Russified Jew in Poltava has no moral right to speak, read, and watch plays in Russian, but only because the leading parties of national Ukrainianism recognize the right of Jews to a Jewish national culture. Although they protest against the Russification of Jews, they do not demand that we become Little Russians and they welcome every glimmer of Jewry's nationalization. That position is entirely correct. These people—for the moment, at least—regard us as a people of equal value to their own. They are establishing relations with us on the basis of living together as good neighbors. When the issue is good neighborly relations, it is necessary—very necessary indeed—to consider that a good neighbor may find my actions unpleasant or inconvenient, even if I have a complete moral right to engage in them.[36]

This expresses Jabotinsky's basic view that relations between Jewry and the peoples among whom it lived were to be based on good neighborliness and reciprocity, so that both sides would recognize the obligation of respecting each other's national interests and completely reject the assumption that there is a ruling majority and a subjugated minority. Jabotinsky considered the question in a manner that was especially typical of his thought, placing it within the framework of national sovereignty, equal rights, mutual good will, and appropriate behavior. He was undoubtedly both sympathetic to the Ukrainian national-patriotic forces and fully in harmony with their political principles, which embraced the broadest democracy and guaranteed national rights for every people. He hoped that once the national-democratic parties came to power in Ukraine, in future conditions of broad autonomy or even complete independence, they would guarantee the national rights and interests of the Jewish minority. Jabotinsky did not just hope for this. He also sought to prepare the most favorable atmosphere for such a development through his articles on the Ukrainian problem and on Ukrainian-Jewish relations. However, as will be discussed below, he also foresaw possible dangers facing Jewry in the development of events in Ukraine.

Thus "Rebuff" contains a snapshot of the state of Ukrainian-Jewish relations at that time on the level of the national-democratic circles of both peoples. That snapshot ("for the moment, at least," as Jabotinsky stressed) inspired bright hopes of future cooperation between the two peoples and their leading political and cultural forces. While the Russian chauvinist forces were fomenting and inciting a raging anti-Semitism, the nationally conscious Ukrainian intelligentsia was, on the contrary, coming out in defense of the national rights of all the empire's peoples, including the Jews. It seemed that Ukraine would in future become the most loyal ally of the Jewish people in the struggle for its national goals. (The prospect of massive Jewish pogroms in Ukraine did not seem very plausible then, although Jabotinsky anticipated them with foreboding.) Jabotinsky was inspired by a grasp of the closeness of the Ukrainian and Jewish national movements' ideological bases, and his articles unreservedly supported Ukrainian national demands. The logic of a national struggle, in a state that refused to recognize the rights of the non-Russian peoples, inevitably produced an awareness of common interests among the national forces of the various peoples that were prepared to recognize the rights of their neighbors.

Jabotinsky's article "On Languages and Other Matters," already mentioned above, was "a response to a response," that is, a continuation of the discussion with Struve that had begun with "Letters on Nationalities and Oblasts" and Struve's reply. In it Jabotinsky refuted Struve's arguments for the existence of a single culture of the three East Slavic peoples—Russians, Ukrainians, and Belarusians. Jabotinsky dismissed the idea that the dominance of Russian culture in the large cities of Ukraine, Belarus, and some other non-Russian oblasts proved that all the peoples considered that culture to be as high as, or higher than, their own. Instead, he saw that dominance as a consequence of centuries of violence and forcible restrictions on the development of local languages and cultures, that is, of imperialist tyranny. Ukrainians and Belarusians possessed their own national consciousness and did not in any way identify themselves as Russians. For them, embracing Russian culture and adopting the Russian language was an entirely artificial process that could only take place through the direct and indirect intervention of the imperialist rulers with the help of the *uriadnik* (local police official). Jabotinsky's use of the *uriadnik* as a symbol of Russian lawlessness and government high-handedness was quite understandable, as the word was applied in exactly that sense by all progressive political writers. Jabotinsky wrote: "To reiterate Struve's phrase, there is 'some sort of stubborn tradition' that thoroughly conflates under the word 'Russian' three separate peoples that differ from one another in language, history, temperament, physical type, innate individuality, way of life, and social order."[37]

Jabotinsky took it for granted that the empire's fate depended largely on the Ukrainian people's stance, on the extent of its determination to remain itself. He further stated that the imperialists also understood this, despite all their phrase-mongering about a "single Russian people":

> One may boldly assert that the resolution of the dispute about Russia's national character depends almost entirely on the position taken by the 30–million-strong Ukrainian people. If it accepts Russification, Russia will move in one direction, but if it rejects Russification, Russia will be forced to go in another direction. The right-wingers in the State Duma have fully understood this. When there was a debate on the issue of what languages to use in the schools of other peoples, for a laugh they even voted for the *shaitans* and for the "Kazan Greeks." They did not even vote against the Hebrew language, obviously aiming to make the whole bill detestable and unacceptable to the authorities. As

> soon as the discussion turned to the Ukrainian language, however, they abandoned their buffoonery and cunning calculations and simply voted against, because they sensed that this was the most dangerous spot, the decisive step; there could be no more joking or insidious reasoning.[38]

Jabotinsky's "On Languages and Other Matters" completely took over the arguments that the nationally aware Ukrainian political writers normally used to defend their views. He even quoted at length from Mykhailo Hrushevsky on the Russian imperialist rulers' attempts over several centuries to destroy Ukraine's language and culture. He reinforced his quotations from Hrushevsky with a rehearsal of the authorities' anti-Ukrainian measures since the mid-nineteenth century, including the ukases restricting the use of the Ukrainian language (the Valuev Circular of 1863 and the Ems Ukase of 1876), the attempts to suppress "Ukrainomania" and "separatism," etc. That article, and the entire cycle devoted to the polemic with Struve and to the Shevchenko anniversary, showed Jabotinsky maintaining a "united front" with the Ukrainian national-democratic press.

The best passages of Jabotinsky's article soar beyond the political level to attain literary stature. The theme struck a sufficiently deep spiritual chord to evoke a certain literary inspiration within him when he wrote about the fate of Ukrainian culture and about Struve's objections to the development of non-Russian national cultures within the empire:

> The finest and most beautiful thing about world culture is precisely its variety. Every historic nation has made its own particular, inimitable and unique contribution to it. The greatest treasure of human civilization lies in that incalculable wealth of *forms* and not in the number of products. If the small two-million-strong people who live in Norway had listened to Mr. Struve's advice at that time and joined the Germans instead of "wasting" their resources on creating their own culture, then the primer of German literature would have been enlarged by a few names, but the world would not have had the completely original, especially fragrant, and particularly worthy divine bouquet that is known as Norwegian literature.[39]

Jabotinsky's article ended with his fundamental idea that every nation's right to its own endogenous culture is determined not by theories (such as Struve's "theory" of the dominant role of Russian culture), but by the nation's will to exist: "The presence of such a will has been manifested by the Little Russians and the Belarusians and by all the innumerable, countless peoples within the Russian state; time will accomplish the rest."[40]

A thoroughly impartial comparison of Struve's and Jabotinsky's arguments would have to yield the conclusion that Jabotinsky was right. (Perhaps that is how all readers of the summary of this dialogue will assess it, except those hopelessly smitten by a Russian imperialist complex.) The debate might have ended there, but Jabotinsky clearly considered the problem too important to break off the discussion just as it was getting under way. One month after "On Language and Other Matters" appeared in *Odesskie novosti*, another of his articles, "The Lesson of the Shevchenko Anniversary," was published. It became the central event in the discussion of the anniversary.[41]

Jabotinsky argued that the Russian and Jewish communities, which took part in the Shevchenko celebrations or which, in his words, "responded" to it, were utterly inconsistent and did not draw necessary and even self-evident conclusions. While they recognized Shevchenko's poetic genius, most gave absolutely no thought to his previous and current place in the cultural and political situation within the tsarist empire. Why did he write in Ukrainian, and what consequences followed from that fact? Is it possible for a nation that is not distinct to possess its own great national poet and national prophet and yet be part of the Russian nation, as Ukrainians were viewed by Russian nationalists?

Jabotinsky mounted one of his favorite hobbyhorses—the defense of each national culture as a unique and irreplaceable component in the mosaic of world culture. He then gave the article the character of a passionate monologue on behalf of the "powerful brother, second in strength within this empire," that is, the Ukrainian people and its national culture. The Jewish intelligentsia had gone over massively to Russian culture, taking over many characteristically Russian notions and prejudices, so Jabotinsky's decisive stand in favor of Ukrainianism was a shocking event. It shook the confidence of the Jewish proselytes of Russian culture that their choice was the correct and only possible one, given the conditions prevailing in the Russian Empire. The article was also intended to shatter, at least in the linguistic and cultural field, the Russian imperialists' basic notions about the superiority and exceptional significance of Russian culture and about the national unity of the three East Slavic peoples. That did not mean, of course, that Jabotinsky was advising Jews to embrace Ukrainian or any other non-Russian culture. He stressed the political, cultural, and personal advantages of remaining loyal to one's own national culture.

Thus the article lay fully within the mainstream of Jabotinsky's "offensive against assimilation," but it was also one of his most determined attempts to forge a united front with Ukrainian national forces as part of that offensive. From this angle, such a step required decisiveness, for Jabotinsky was threatened with strong resistance both from the Russians and from a significant section of the Jewish community and press. Still, he did not lack decisiveness. Jabotinsky dotted all the "i's":

> Thus we are now honoring the memory of Shevchenko, or at least responding to the celebration. At the same time no conclusions are being drawn. Neither those who listen and read nor those who write appear to have given any deep thought to the responsibility that recognition of the anniversary entails. It must

> therefore mean one of two things: either Shevchenko is a cultural misunderstanding, a philological curiosity and rarity, in which case there is no sense in celebrating his anniversary, or he is a natural, characteristic phenomenon of life in its course of development, a symptom of what is to come in the future. Then each one of us must proceed from statement A to statement B; in other words, after recognizing the anniversary, we must define our attitude toward the vast phenomenon whose inevitability is prophesied by this anniversary.[42]

This "vast phenomenon" entering the European stage was Ukraine, a great nation equal to the greatest nations of Western Europe. The entrance that Jabotinsky prophesied occurred soon afterwards, in 1917, when the Ukrainian People's Republic was formed.

In "The Lesson of the Shevchenko Anniversary" Jabotinsky emphasized, reiterated, and illustrated in various ways this idea of Shevchenko's significance as a symptom of the national awakening of the Ukrainian people. It is interesting to trace the way in which he argues that it was from one's attitude toward the national problems of neighboring peoples that one derived one's attitude toward one's own people, as well as toward world culture and the sociopolitical problems of the Russian Empire:

> We dutifully salute the event of Shevchenko's anniversary, yet it does not even enter our heads that this is an event of enormous symptomatic importance. If we are intelligent and educated and have foresight, the event should lead us to reexamine certain substantial components of our world-view. What is Shevchenko? He must be one of two things: either a comical freak of nature of the same order as an armless painter or a one-legged acrobat, rather like a rare, antique exhibit in an archaeological museum, or else he should be seen as a shining symbol of the national and cultural viability of Ukrainianism, in which case we must open our eyes wider and take a closer look at the conclusions that follow from this.[43]

Such perseverance in repeating the need for conclusions came from Jabotinsky's grasp of the fact that it was a question of surmounting certain ways of thinking, certain prejudices that had already become obsolete. One such prejudice, held by the vast majority of the Jewish community, was the idea that Ukrainianism was culturally second-rate; that Ukrainian culture was incapable of attaining a level comparable to Russian culture. This often led the Jewish community simply to ignore the reality of the Ukrainian factor and to disregard Ukrainianism completely as a political fact. In an effort to break down those stereotypes, Jabotinsky drew attention to the "arithmetical reality" of the existence of a solid Ukrainian mass of 30 million people living their natural lives outside urban centers. They were not submitting to Russification and probably were scarcely aware that Russian nationalists had long since proclaimed them to be part of the Russian people:

> Here in the towns of the South, we ourselves very assiduously and naively spread Russifying influences: our press concerned itself so much with the Russian theater and with the distribution of Russian literature that in the end we completely lost sight of the genuine arithmetical reality as it exists beyond the bounds of our blinkered world-view. Outside those towns there swirls the sea of an almost 30–million-strong Ukrainian mass. Take a look anywhere and not just at its center, look at any Myrhorod or Vasylkiv district, or take a look at its outer fringes in the Kharkiv or Voronezh gubernias, which are just next to the frontier beyond which the Great Russian language begins, and you will be struck by the extent to which this massive Ukrainian sea has remained virgin and pure.[44]

With a certain amount of sarcasm, Jabotinsky went on to advise Petr Struve to visit Ukrainian regions along the Russian-Ukrainian ethnic border where Ukrainians and Russians lived side by side without mixing, shunning each other and not seeking mutual understanding. Jabotinsky asked whether much of Struve's theory of a "transcendent all-Russian nature" would remain after such a visit. Jabotinsky was obviously not speaking here as a supporter of the two peoples' mutual repudiation, of the lack of reciprocal understanding that existed along the Ukrainian-Russian ethnic border. Rather, he raised the matter in order to establish the undeniable ethnic fact of the existence of two separate peoples, Ukrainians and Russians.

Jabotinsky's article also rebutted the Russian imperialists' common assertions about the Ukrainian language's lack of independence. He repeatedly expressed the view that a language is independent and not the dialect of another language only when a given people recognizes it as such.[45] He advanced arguments for that idea in "The Lesson of the Shevchenko Anniversary." This approach to language was properly subsumed within his fundamental principle that a nation is a separate nation and not part of another nation only when it recognizes itself as such, that is, when it develops its own distinct national consciousness. For Jabotinsky, that was precisely why some Italian dialects, though very different from literary Italian, remained merely dialects—those who speak the dialects call themselves Italians and have no separate national consciousness distinct from general Italian consciousness.[46] Jabotinsky concluded that the distinctiveness of one language or another was a sociopolitical rather than a philological question.

He applied that conclusion to the linguistic relationship between Russian and Ukrainian. While recognizing that the Ukrainian language was sufficiently different from Russian to be considered independent on a philological basis, Jabotinsky emphasized that this had no significance when tackling the question of the ethnic independence of the Ukrainian people. Since that people undoubtedly possessed a distinct national consciousness, from a sociopolitical point of view the extent to which the Ukrainian language differed from Russian or from any other language was insignificant. Jabotinsky derided Russian nationalists who stated that Shevchenko's poems could be rewritten in Russian almost without alteration and gave the example of the Italian poet Giuseppe Belli, who wrote in the Roman dialect. Unlike most other Italian dialects, that one differed very little from literary Italian, yet Belli's Roman dialect poems were examples of high poetry, while his works in literary Italian were thoroughly mediocre. Jabotinsky added that the same fate befell Shevchenko, whose Russian-language works were incomparably less valuable from a literary viewpoint than his Ukrainian works.

With the sensitivity of a true poet, Jabotinsky cited a few lines from Shevchenko's poem "Dumy moï, dumy moï..." (My thoughts, my thoughts...) in Ukrainian and in Russian. He deliberately tried to find the Russian words closest to the Ukrainian ones, yet despite the relatively slight difference in the words, one can only feel that the Ukrainian has the ring of poetic genius, while the Russian sounds like an average rhyme. If one were to attempt to communicate the full poetic depth of that tragic poem, one would obviously not attempt to preserve verbal similarities, but would use other words, not necessarily close to the original in sound, to convey the *spirit* of Shevchenko's work. Is there a better proof that the Ukrainian language embodies its own national spirit? Jabotinsky's argument that the Ukrainian language is not Russian and that the Ukrainian people is not part of the Russian people is generally acknowledged today, but matters were entirely different in 1911. Within the Russian Empire, Ukrainians were denied recognition as a separate people on principle, and the jeering at the Ukrainian language that sorely wounded the national pride of Ukrainians was very widespread among both Russians and Russified Jews. Jabotinsky's articles show that his own humanitarian feelings were also painfully hurt by this.

Jabotinsky then passed from the Ukrainian problem to the question of nationality in general and wrote about the absurdity of trying to destroy any people's national consciousness. He pointed out the bloody conflicts that arose from such attempts and caused great harm without benefiting anyone. He referred to the Hungarians' struggle for the Hungarian form of command to be introduced in the Hungarian sections of the Austrian army—a form of command that consisted of about seventy words. He referred to Croatian deputies' stubborn use of their language in the Hungarian parliament, even though they were scarcely understood. He spoke of the Croatians' struggle against Hungarian signs in Zagreb—a struggle that led to bloody clashes with the army. Jabotinsky generalized from this by arguing that such serious conflicts could not derive from a trifle, but involved important, basic matters that should not be ignored:

> Stupidity, a whim, we say, we provincial philistines from a secluded country, speaking from the summit of our political intelligence and experience. Would it not be much more correct to look at the matter from a different angle and understand that there is no point in quarreling with facts? We have a long list

> of striking facts, both mass facts and even more characteristic individual ones. Thus you have virtually entire nations becoming enraged over seventy words or dozens of signs in a foreign language. You have great poets who instantly lose God's gift as soon as their souls retreat into small, shabby, harmless imitation, saying *svet* instead of *svit*, or *buona sera* instead of *bôna sera*. These are all facts, indisputable phenomena of life that will not change in response to our censure or approval. We should neither criticize nor praise. We should not issue grades to the world order and its manifestations, but should humbly learn wisdom from it. We should accept life as it is in its fundamentals and construct our world-view upon those fundamentals.[47]

The rulers of tsarist Russia considered it their right to "recognize" or "not recognize" one nationality or another, to "merge" or "separate" this or that nationality, so that Russians, Ukrainians, and Belarusians were "merged," while Romanians and Moldavians were "separated." Against that background, Jabotinsky's passionate and courageous appeal for every national entity to be recognized and for every national language and culture to be respected must certainly have made a strong impression on his readers.

Jabotinsky then ended his article with three pages at which, as he said himself, "the reader will probably shrug his shoulders." It is true that the significance of those three pages of reflections would scarcely have been grasped by the average, or even above-average, reader of that time. For Jabotinsky achieved a level of political foresight whose significance would be grasped only after the events of the revolution and civil war. He saw that the popular masses in the South (that is, in Ukraine) could take the path of chauvinist, Black Hundred nationalism if they were not won in time to the side of creative, democratic, humanist nationalism:

> The only idealistic slogan that in today's conditions could rouse the philistine urban masses and clarify and refine their world-view is the national slogan. If they are now following the Right, that is not because the Right is preaching the ram's horn or the iron fist, but simply because the Right has managed to strike the nationalist chord within them. This was a chord not of creative, positive nationalism, but of "pushing out" the "nonnatives." There is no bright flag in the world that will turn our southern philistines away from the slogan of hatred except the flag of protest on behalf of their own nation. I am not competent to judge to what extent some Slobidka-Romanivka is prepared to adopt Ukrainian national consciousness. I can state only one thing: either the Ukrainian movement will succeed in supplanting the Unionists [members of the Union of the Russian People] or no one will. I repeat: all this is so far removed from current conditions that the reader will, I know, shrug his shoulders and say, "suppositions, fantasies." But I think that those who actually imagine and fantasize are those who see only what stares them in the face and who ignore statistics, history, and the experience of the intelligent West. We will wait and see. And it may be that, *if our tactics do not change in time, we may feel it as well....*[48]

Beyond any doubt, this is a prophetic anticipation of the later wave of pogroms in Ukraine.

Jabotinsky's precise evaluation of the situation and grasp of its consequences are very striking. In conditions where nationalist sentiments are awakening, nationalist propaganda of any sort will find a large audience. The Black Hundreds' negative, chauvinist propaganda, backed by the empire's political and police apparatus and by a significant section of the Russian press (for example, the Russian paper in Kyiv, *Kievlianin*,)[49] gained a response in the non-Russian parts of the empire precisely because it struck a "nationalist chord." Thus the Black Hundred propaganda had to be fought with propaganda that was democratic and humanist, but also nationalist. This latter type of propaganda was spread by the upper stratum of the Ukrainian intelligentsia, grouped around a few Ukrainian national-democratic and socialist parties. The nationalist chord in the Ukrainian intelligentsia's soul did not respond to the Black Hundreds' chauvinist appeals. It resounded in harmony with the sentiments of generous liberalism, humanism, and educational work. That situation would have offered the brightest prospects if the Ukrainian national parties had been influential enough to achieve hegemony not only over the majority of the nationally conscious Ukrainian intelligentsia but also the majority of Ukrainian peasants and the urban lower-middle class. Those parties did not, however, have that kind of influence, and their propaganda could scarcely prevail against the chauvinist propaganda of the Black Hundreds, especially in the urban communities.

The position of the Ukrainian national-democratic forces was further weakened by the fact that they had no support from either the Russian or, for a long time, the Jewish opposition forces. If the Russian opposition parties, the Jewish intelligentsia, and the press that was influenced by those forces had supported the Ukrainian national-democratic movement, it might have presented a serious obstacle to Black Hundred pogromist nationalism, for it could have channeled the national aspirations of the Ukrainian masses toward healthy political and cultural development. However, the Russian liberal opposition forces tended to lean more toward imperialism, while the idea of supporting the Ukrainian movement gained approval among Jewish activists too late, only in 1917. Only one person among them, Jabotinsky, understood the problem in all its dimensions throughout the pre-revolutionary years: "If our tactics do not change in time, we may feel it as well."

Jabotinsky was aware that Jewry in Ukraine might feel the consequences of ignoring the Ukrainian movement very painfully. Although the tactics did change in the end, when the Jewish national parties began active and close cooperation with the Ukrainian national forces in the summer of 1917, the change came much too late. The unpreparedness of the Ukrainian and Jewish masses, including the lower strata of the intelligentsia, for mutual cooperation and their unfamiliarity with the very notion that such cooperation was possible had the most tragic consequences. The Ukrainian masses as a whole were in no way prepared for well-organized nation-building and state construction, hence in conditions of civil war and general anarchy a wave of pogroms occurred, perpetrated by all the main armed forces involved in the conflict: the Russian Monarchist Volunteer (White) Army, a section of the Ukrainian People's Republic Army, and numerous armed detachments and bands of various ideological tendencies, including some sections of the Bolshevik Red Army.[50]

Jabotinsky realized that most of his readers were not receptive to the need to support the Ukrainian national-democratic movement, yet he still appealed to those who only "shrug their shoulders":

> That is the significance of the Shevchenko anniversary for every person who knows how to think consistently and to look into the future. Unfortunately we are not rich in this talent. We regard the Ukrainian movement that is developing under our very noses as some sort of game. We ignored it in the past, we ignore it now, and we will probably continue to ignore it after the anniversary. Whether our actions are being guided by the blindness of self-satisfaction or by the callousness of human thought, we are making a gross and inexcusable political error. We could be creating conditions in which this movement, whose consequences will be enormous, might develop with the support of the most influential circles of progressive society and could become accustomed to seeing those circles as its base and its natural allies. Instead we oblige it to remain restricted to its own forces; we are putting a brake on its successes through our silence and indifference; we are provoking and pushing it into opposition to the liberal and radical community. That will not halt the movement's growth, but it would not be difficult to distort its growth and drive it in the least desirable direction—something of which we should be wary.[51]

Thus did Jabotinsky warn of the dangerous consequences of ignoring the national movement in Ukraine and of lacking the desire to cooperate with it. He called on non-Ukrainian revolutionary-democratic circles to recognize the Ukrainian movement as their ally, to concur in its aims, and to form a united front with it. Given the overt or covert imperialist platform of the Russian opposition parties, Jabotinsky's call obviously could not find substantial support within the Russian "liberal and radical community." He was also unable, though for somewhat different reasons, to gain a swift and broad response from Jewish national forces.

It is difficult to gauge to what extent Jabotinsky expected an immediate positive response to his appeal. In all likelihood, given his thorough understanding of the situation, he had no illusions on that score. He nevertheless considered it his responsibility to warn the community, which was the most that he could do. As far as Russian society was concerned, its resolve to oppose the Ukrainian movement grew stronger as it came to realize the threat posed by that movement to the unity of the empire. The Jewish community should have been stirred most by Jabotinsky's foresight and warnings, because the "least desirable direction" meant a threat to the Jews' physical existence. The Jewish population's interests should obviously not have been linked in any way to the maintenance of the empire's territorial and political integrity, since the latter entailed defending the interests of an anti-Jewish imperial regime, whatever the name under which it posed.

Jabotinsky's unequivocal foresight and warnings verged on being a judgment: "All of this may produce the direst consequences for future relations in this huge region, South Russia, if we fail to come to our senses in time, if we fail to grasp and take into account the whole vast scope of the mass phenomenon of which the Shevchenko anniversary reminds us, and if we fail to adapt all our positions, all our tactics in local and state affairs to it."[52] However, the tactics of the Jewish political parties changed too late, and even when they began to cooperate with the government of the Ukrainian People's Republic, they altered their political aims only partially and inconsistently, especially on the very question that was most crucial to establishing genuine agreement and cooperation with the Ukrainian national forces—the question of imperial unity. After the Bolshevik coup in Russia, when the Ukrainian political parties and the Central Rada posed the question of Ukraine's complete separation from the empire, the Jewish political parties in the Central Rada did not support that position, but either abstained or voted against it. That was the start of a cooling of relations, of mutual distrust between Ukrainian and Jewish political forces, and it led to the direst consequences. Black Hundred and various other anti-Semitic forces in Ukraine gained a trump card in their anti-Jewish agitation among the peasants and urban lower-middle class.[53] Thus the "Lesson of the Shevchenko Anniversary" was not assimilated, and precisely those "direst consequences" that Jabotinsky had warned about occurred.

Jabotinsky ended "The Lesson of the Shevchenko Anniversary" with a significant conclusion that is worth quoting in full:

> Shevchenko is a national poet, and therein lies his strength. He is also a national poet in a subjective sense, that is, a poet-nationalist, even including all the outbursts of uncontrollable hostility to the Pole, the Jew, and other neighbors.... More important is the fact that he is a national poet in an objective sense. He offered his own people and the entire world clear, firm proof that the Ukrainian spirit is capable of the highest flights of original cultural creativity. That is why he is so beloved by some and so feared by others. That love and fear would in no way have been diminished if Shevchenko had been an aristocrat like Goethe or Pushkin rather than a populist. We could expunge all the democratic affirmations from his works (and censorship did just that for a long time), and Shevchenko would remain just as nature shaped him: a dazzling precedent that will not permit Ukrainianism to stray from the path of national renaissance. Reactionaries understood that significance very well on the eve of the Shevchenko anniversary when they raised lamenta-

> tions against separatism, treason against the state, and the approaching end of the world. We are still a long way from the end of the world and other horrors, but what is true remains true: Shevchenko cannot be honored merely as talented Russian writer number so and so; to honor him involves acknowledging everything that is linked to his name. To honor Shevchenko means that there is not and cannot be a single culture in a country inhabited by more than 100 peoples; it means understanding, acknowledging, and moving aside to make room and give the powerful brother, second in strength within this empire, his rightful place.[54]

An objective reader of such articles as "On Languages and Other Matters" and "The Lesson of the Shevchenko Anniversary" could not help but acknowledge that the views advanced by Petr Struve on the nationality question had been completely demolished, at least in theory, but great-power imperialist practice was not based on theories. On the contrary, the theories were invented to justify the practice. Even if Struve had agreed with Jabotinsky, he could not have changed his views, which reflected the opinions of broad elements of Russian society. Thus Struve and those elements remained unyieldingly convinced of the harmfulness of "Ukrainian particularism" and of the existence of a single culture of the three East Slavic peoples. The debate went on. However, Struve no longer made use of Jabotinsky's articles on that theme, nor did he refer to him, obviously feeling that he was not up to arguing with that political writer. Only indirectly, without naming names, did Struve continue to attack Jabotinsky's views. Jabotinsky, on the other hand, referred more and more often to Struve, and his criticism of Struve's theories became increasingly acerbic.

Struve chose, as the pretext for his next presentation on this theme, a very restrained letter to the editors of the journal *Russkaia mysl'* signed by "A Ukrainian."[55] The journal published that letter in May 1911, and Struve's reply, "All-Russian Culture and Ukrainian Particularism," appeared in January 1912.[56] It was probably no accident that Struve chose to respond to a letter whose author took a very cautious approach. The "Ukrainian" demanded no broader national rights for the Ukrainian people than the right of Ukrainian culture to exist, since "every cultural movement is an expression of the Spirit of God within humanity." Struve's reply rehearsed all the standard arguments in defense of a "single Russian nation" and its "single culture." True, on this occasion Struve did not insist that the "single Russian culture" should encompass the empire's entire population, including the Muslims, Caucasians, and other non-Slavic peoples. He spoke only of the "unity" of the Eastern Slavs. Struve openly called upon Russian public opinion to prepare the groundwork for the preservation of imperial unity after the "downfall of reaction," which could only have meant the downfall of tsarism.

Struve declared that just because the authorities and all the reactionary forces were combating both civil and national rights with equal ruthlessness, this still did not mean that the progressive community should fight with equal vigor both for civil rights and for the "particular" rights of those Ukrainians and Belarusians who did not consider themselves to belong to the "single Russian nation." In his opinion, the fight should be for civil rights, but there should be no support for "particularism." (Such a selective interpretation of human rights was common to many other liberal activists in Russia as well.)[57] Struve's article repeatedly stressed that the future democratization of the social and state order should not lead to the breakup of the "single Russian nation" or of the "single Russian culture," which would mean the breakup of the empire in general. His article ended with this résumé: "I personally consider that after adhering to a tradition of Ukrainophilism...Russian progressive public opinion must cast aside all equivocation and indulgence and rise up energetically for an ideological struggle against 'Ukrainianism,' treating it as a tendency that weakens and partially even annuls one of our great historical achievements—an all-Russian culture."[58] Struve was right in the sense that Russian public opinion was Ukrainophile in its own eyes. Russians love Ukrainian songs and the Ukrainian countryside; they love and value the wealth of the Ukrainian earth; and they even extend their favoritism toward Ukrainians so far as to proclaim them (without their permission, to be sure) part of the Russian people. Struve saw nothing odd about such a stance and, in fact, identified Russian Ukrainophilism with a "struggle against 'Ukrainianism.'"

However much Struve may have preferred arguing with weaker opponents, Jabotinsky would not leave him in peace. In March 1912 Jabotinsky published "Struve and the Ukrainian Question" in *Odesskie novosti*.[59] Just as Struve had repeated and expanded his old arguments for "a single all-Russian culture," so Jabotinsky also repeated and expanded ideas he had expressed on many previous occasions, spelling them out in greater detail—ideas about the essence of national culture and about the determining role of national consciousness in nation-building. Jabotinsky noted the interesting fact that a right-wing nationalist newspaper, *Kievlianin*, had published an article using practically the same arguments Struve used in defense of a "single Russian nation" shortly before Struve's reply to "A Ukrainian" appeared. It was a very doubtful honor for a well-known figure in the liberal Cadet Party that his thinking on such a basic question concurred with the ideas of a newspaper whose orientation differed little from the publications of Black Hundred organizations. This was undoubtedly a further indication of the extent to which the views of Russian liberal circles were tending to approximate those of the extreme right-wing Russian nationalists on the nationality question.

Once again Jabotinsky's argumentation left no doubt about the erroneous character of Struve's arguments. It may appear self-evident that any ethnic group can be considered part of a given nation only when the group itself agrees to be so considered. It may seem equally self-evident that no one can proclaim a given nation to be part of another without asking the former's consent. Russia may be the only country in the world in which such elementary notions have to be argued out in strenuous, protracted debate. Comparison of the argumentation used by Struve and Jabotinsky shows that logical and moral ascendancy belonged to the latter, but the discussion between those two figures was a dispute between two liberals. These two, moreover, held quite similar positions on many other questions at that time, for example, on rejecting socialist ideology. Furthermore, they were both nationalists, one Russian, the other Jewish. Why were there such striking differences between them on the nationality question within the Russian Empire? Primarily because Struve stood for imperialism while Jabotinsky stood for anti-imperialism. Inasmuch as the imperialist character of the state in relation to the colonial peoples was in fact the most important question determining the empire's future, Struve and Jabotinsky ended up on opposite sides of the barricades.

From another angle, it is readily apparent that Struve's imperialist attitude increasingly led him to reject important components of the liberal world-view, for example, recognition of the right of all peoples to free cultural, national and political development, and to move closer to an extreme right-wing, chauvinist world-view. Thus Jabotinsky was a much more consistent liberal than Struve. However, Jabotinsky cared little about proving his own personal moral victory in the dispute with Struve. His thought revolved around the interests and fate of the Jewish people. He was conducting an "offensive against assimilation." His "united front" with the Ukrainian national-democratic movement was first and foremost a means of finding allies to promote the recognition of the national rights of all peoples and to create favorable conditions for Jewish life and cultural maintenance in Ukraine. To that end he both argued that the Jewish people had to remain within the bounds of its own culture and language and presented a brilliant interpretation of the nationality question. Last but not least, he offered a profound analysis of the political processes within the Russian Empire in general and in Ukraine in particular. In another article, "On the Wrong Path," Jabotinsky repeated again and again the most important points of his analysis, as if trying to drive them into the heads of his readers:

> The main mass of Jews live among Ukrainians, Poles, Belarusians, and Lithuanians. Those peoples are beginning to raise their heads in much the same way as the Czechs did sixty years ago. This is taking place before our very eyes, and surely only a short-sighted person could overlook that phenomenon. We need to have a course of action adequate not just for today but also for tomorrow. There is a choice between two options: either Russia will remain within the jaws of the police or else all the nationalities will take advantage of political freedom to transform Russia first of all into a greater Austria. Whether we like it or not, that is what will take place, and neither Struve nor we together with you will prevail against this 30–million-strong mass of Little

> Russians, nor even against the small Lithuanian nation. So how do we define our position on this question? What will be our role in this future Russia, in which 100 peoples all around us will be developing independently, creating their own national values in their own languages? Will we remain in the role that is already being hinted at—that of the sole agents of Russification in the borderlands? Will we travel the path of the Austrian assimilators by changing our nationality with every shift of political forces? Or will we perhaps choose a third path and let Russians be Russians and Poles be Poles while we ourselves establish our own beacons?[60]

When Jabotinsky spoke of transforming Russia into a greater Austria, he had in mind the national-cultural autonomy enjoyed by the peoples of Austria-Hungary, even though it entailed considerable restrictions. At that time, when the great majority of national parties among the non-Russian peoples of the tsarist empire were demanding only cultural autonomy, Jabotinsky could not speak of anything more, but his analysis of national relations and of the political fate of the empire could have led a careful reader to much deeper and more radical conclusions. We should not forget that the Jewish people at least were offered a goal with a much clearer perspective, the creation of their own independent state in Palestine, while national-cultural autonomy for the Jews in Russia, Ukraine or anywhere else was considered only a transitional stage whose goal was to preserve Jewish national identity in the Diaspora.

The end of the "offensive against assimilation" heralded the end of Jabotinsky's activity on the territory of the Russian Empire. In 1914 he traveled to the West and returned only for brief visits to the empire's largest cities in the summer of 1915. While the tragedy of the civil war was taking place in Ukraine, and the Jewish pogroms were creating lasting enmity between the Jewish and Ukrainian peoples and their political circles, Jabotinsky was in England creating a Jewish Legion within the British Army. He then fought as an officer of the Legion against Turkey, and after demobilization, he organized self-defense units against pogroms in Palestine that were then being prepared by Arab extremists. For this a British court-martial sentenced him to fifteen years' hard labor, but was soon obliged to revoke the sentence. His next encounter with the Ukrainian problem took place in 1921 in Prague, where he made an agreement with his old friend Maksym Slavinsky, a representative of the Ukrainian government. The next chapter is devoted to that period of Jabotinsky's activity.

# Notes

1. Joseph Schechtman, *Rebel and Statesman: The Vladimir Jabotinsky Story*, 1: 147.

2. V. Jabotinsky, *Avtobiografia*, p. 84.
   The Society for the Promotion of Culture among the Jews of Russia was a Jewish organization established in St. Petersburg in 1863 to propagate the Russian language and culture among Jews in the empire. The society had a very strong and active section in Odesa. See *Evreiskaia ėntsiklopediia*, 13: 59–62.

3. V. Zhabotinskii, *Evreiskoe vospitanie*, pp. 10–11. For further detail, see the introduction to the present work.

4. Schechtman, *Rebel and Statesman*, 1: 146–47.

5. Ievhen Chykalenko, *Shchodennyk (1907–1917)* (Lviv, 1931), pp. 185–86.

6. V. Zhabotinskii, "Urok iubileia Shevchenko," in *Fel'etony* (St. Petersburg, 1913), pp. 240–41.

7. *Evreiskaia ėntsiklopediia*, 14: 519–20.

8. For discussions of Russian liberalism, see V. Zhabotinskii, "O russkom liberalizme (pis'mo v 'Ukrainskuiu zhizn'')," *Ukrainskaia zhizn'* (Moscow), no. 7–8 (1912): 47–55, as well as his "Chetyre stat'i o 'chirikovskom intsidente,'" "Dezertiry i khoziaeva," "Asemitizm," "Medved' iz berlogi," and "Russkaia laska," in *Fel'etony*, pp. 71–100; Richard Pipes, *Struve: Liberal on the Left, 1870–1905* (Cambridge, MA, 1970) and *Struve: Liberal on the Right, 1905–1944* (Cambridge, MA, 1980); George Fischer, *Russian Liberalism: From Gentry to Intelligentsia* (Cambridge, MA, 1958).

9. Similar views prevailed among Russian liberal-democratic dissidents in the USSR. The negative reaction of many Russian democrats toward the proclamation of independence by the former republics of the Soviet Union demonstrates that no fundamental change has taken place in that respect.

10. V. Zhabotinskii, "Demokratizm i natsionalizm," *Odesskie novosti*, 19 August 1912.

11. *Iz dumskikh otchetov: Rechi M. M. Vinavera (partii narodnoi svobody)* (St. Petersburg, 1907), p. 6.

12. *M. M. Vinaver i russkaia obshchestvennost' nachala XX veka: sbornik statei* (Paris, 1937), p. 70.

13. V. Zhabotinskii, "Nabroski bez zaglaviia," *Rassvet* (7 June 1909): 7.

14. V. Zhabotinskii, "Medved' iz berlogi," in *Fel'etony*, p. 88.

15. D. S. Pasmanik, "Sionizm ili seimizm," *Evreiskaia zhizn'* (St. Petersburg), no. 6 (1906): 98.

16. See William H. Chamberlin, *The Russian Revolution*, 2 vols. (New York, 1965), 1: 169.

17. D. Dontsov, "Russkii liberalizm i ukrainskoe dvizhenie," *Ukrainskaia zhizn'* (Moscow), no. 5 (1912).
At this point Dontsov still held liberal-nationalist views; subsequently he moved to the extreme right.

18. V. Zhabotinskii, "O russkom liberalizme," *Ukrainskaia zhizn'*, nos. 7–8 (1912).

19. D. Dontsov, "Russkii imperializm i ukrainstvo," *Ukrainskaia zhizn'*, no. 2 (1913).

20. V. Zhabotinskii, "Demokratizm i natsionalizm."

21. V. Zhabotinskii, "O russkom liberalizme," pp. 54–55.

22. See especially M. Frenkin, *Russkaia armiia i revoliutsiia, 1917–1918* (Munich, 1978), pp. 213–14, 216–17, 230–31, 242, passim; and Israel Kleiner, "On Lenin's Attitude toward the Right of Nations to Self-Determination," *Crossroads* (Jerusalem), no. 5 (Winter 1980): 177–97.

23. V. Zhabotinskii, "Pis'ma o natsional'nostiakh i oblastiakh. Evreistvo i ego nastroeniia," *Russkaia mysl'* (Moscow), no. 1 (1911): 95–114.

24. V. Zhabotinskii, "Struve i ukrainskii vopros," *Odesskie novosti*, 2 March 1912.

25. V. Zhabotinskii, "O russkom liberalizme," p. 49.

26. V. Zhabotinskii, "Struve i ukrainskii vopros."

27. V. Zhabotinskii, "O iazykakh i prochem," in *Fel'etony*, pp. 218–19. The article was first published in January 1911 in the newspaper *Odesskie novosti*.
The German term *Nationalitätenstaat* (a state of nationalities) was used at the time by political writers to mean a multinational state in which the autonomous rights of all nationalities would be recognized.

28. V. Zhabotinskii, "Pis'ma o natsional'nostiakh i oblastiakh," p. 112.

29. Pipes, *Struve: Liberal on the Right*, p. 210.

30. For the Constitutional Democrats' position on the nationality question, see P. N. Miliukov, "Raschlenenie Rossii pod lozungom samoopredeleniia," in *Istoriia vtoroi russkoi revoliutsii*, 3 vols. (Sofia, 1921–24), 1: 139–65; and Pipes, *Struve: Liberal on the Right*, p. 214.

31. V. Zhabotinskii, "Pis'ma o natsional'nostiakh i oblastiakh," pp. 112–13.

32. Ibid., p. 113.

33. Ibid., pp. 113–14.

34. *Russkaia mysl'*, no. 1 (1911): 186.

35. Ibid., p. 187.

36. V. Zhabotinskii, "Otpor," in *Poliaki i evrei* (St. Petersburg, 1913), pp. 64–65.

37. V. Zhabotinskii, "O iazykakh i prochem," in *Fel'etony*, pp. 222–23.

38. Ibid., pp. 219–20.

    Neither the *shaitans* nor the "Kazan Greeks" existed as nations within the Russian Empire: these names were invented by opponents of national rights for minorities so as to discredit the whole idea of granting such rights. This is apparent from the names themselves: *shaitan* means "devil" in Tatar, and Kazan, which was never inhabited by a Greek colony, is the capital of Tatarstan.

39. Ibid., p. 229.

40. Ibid., p. 230.

41. V. Zhabotinskii, "Urok iubileia Shevchenko," *Odesskie novosti*, 27 February 1911; *Fel'etony* (1913), pp. 231–41; *Fel'etony* (Berlin, 1922), pp. 186–94. The 1913 edition was also reproduced in Tel Aviv in 1971. Another reprint appears in Jabotinsky, *Izbrannoe* (Jerusalem, 1978), pp. 144–53.

42. V. Zhabotinskii, "Urok iubileia Shevchenko," p. 231.

43. Ibid.

44. Ibid., pp. 235–36.

45. For Jabotinsky's most detailed consideration of this idea, see his long article, "Samoupravlenie natsional'nogo men'shinstva," *Vestnik Evropy* (St. Petersburg), September and October 1913. The same idea is presented from various angles in several articles in *Fel'etony*, as well as in other works.

46. Jabotinsky also offered the following observations: the Spanish language, which is closer to literary Italian than some Italian dialects, is without doubt a separate national language because the Spaniards, possessing a distinct national consciousness, regard their language as such. Similarly, parts of Germany near the Dutch border are inhabited by speakers of a language that should, from a philological point of view, be recognized as Dutch. In spite of this, the language is viewed on one side of the border as a German dialect and on the other side as Dutch, because its bearers on one side regard themselves as Germans, and on the other as Dutch. Further examples can be found among the Slavs and many other peoples.

47. V. Zhabotinskii, "Urok iubileia Shevchenko," pp. 234–35.

48. Ibid., pp. 239–40. Emphasis added.

49. *Kievlianin* was a daily Russian newspaper that appeared in Kyiv from 1864 to 1919. Its editorial content was imperialist and anti-Ukrainian, bordering on Black Hundred attitudes. From 1911 to 1919 it was edited by the Russian nationalist Vasilii Shulgin

(1878–1976), who, after World War II, supported the USSR on the grounds that the communist rulers in Moscow were continuing Russian imperialist traditions.

50. See I. M. Cherikover, *Antisemitizm i pogromy na Ukraine 1917–1918 gg.* (Berlin, 1923); I. Shekhtman, *Pogromy Dobrovol'cheskoi armii na Ukraine: k istorii antisemitizma na Ukraine v 1919–1920 g.g.* (Berlin, 1932); I. M. Trotskii, "Evreiskie pogromy na Ukraine i v Belorussii (1918–1920 g.g.)," in *Kniga o russkom evreistve, 1917–1967* (New York, 1968), pp. 59–69; Committee of the Jewish Delegations, *The Pogroms in the Ukraine under the Ukrainian Governments (1917–1920)* (London, 1927).

51. V. Zhabotinskii, "Urok iubileia Shevchenko," p. 238.

52. Ibid., pp. 238–39.

53. S. I. Goldelman, *Jewish National Autonomy in Ukraine,* pp. 47–50; A. Margolin, *Ukraine and Policy of the Entente*, pp. 32–33.

54. V. Zhabotinskii, "Urok iubileia Shevchenko," pp. 240–41.

55. Ukrainets, "K voprosu o samostoiatel'nosti ukrainskoi kul'tury (Pis'mo v redaktsiiu)," *Russkaia mysl'* (Moscow, May 1911): 131–46.

The Ukrainian sociologist and lawyer Bohdan Kistiakivsky usually wrote under this pseudonym.

56. P. Struve, "Obshcherusskaia kul'tura i ukrainskii partikuliarizm. Otvet Ukraintsu," *Russkaia mysl'* (Moscow, January 1912): 65–86.

57. Highly characteristic of this approach is the chapter "Raschlenenie Rossii pod lozungom samoopredeleniia" in Miliukov, *Istoriia vtoroi russkoi revoliutsii.*

58. P. Struve, "Obshcherusskaia kul'tura i ukrainskii partikuliarizm," p. 86.

59. V. Zhabotinskii, "Struve i ukrainskii vopros," *Odesskie novosti*, 2 March 1912.

60. V. Zhabotinskii, "Na lozhnom puti," in *Fel'etony*, pp. 262–63.

This was the last article in the polemic with Struve, but Jabotinsky did make passing, invariably critical, references to Struve in many of his later works.

CHAPTER 3

# The Jabotinsky-Slavinsky Agreement: Act of Courage or Fatal Error?

The year 1921 was a watershed in the attitude of the Entente countries toward Russia's Bolshevik rulers, because they shifted from their previous irreconcilable opposition to the Bolsheviks (more in words than deeds) toward a stance of biding their time. The intention of making peace with the Bolshevik rulers eventually became more marked. The break occurred in the autumn of 1921, when the Western Allies rejected plans to overthrow the Bolsheviks by armed force. Nevertheless, in August-September 1921, when the events described in this chapter took place, the anti-Bolshevik circles were still hoping for a new armed offensive against the Bolsheviks, which was due to begin in the spring of 1922.

A year earlier, in the autumn of 1920, the army of the Ukrainian People's Republic (UNR) had finally retreated from the Eastern Ukrainian territories, leaving them under Bolshevik rule. The Ukrainian territories in Galicia fell under the rule of the newly established independent Poland, and it was on those territories that the remainder of the Ukrainian army and the government of Symon Petliura were interned. The elements of the army that retreated to Polish territories with the Ukrainian government were comparatively small in number, but they were also the most dedicated. Inasmuch as the Western Allies intended to use the Ukrainian army during the projected offensive against Bolshevik Russia, they gave it some aid in Galicia. In 1921 the Ukrainian government army there had 15,000 armed troops ready for battle.[1] Petliura and his government expected that in the event of a new attack on Ukraine, they would be supported by a mass popular uprising that would eventually lead to Ukraine's independence from Bolshevik Russia.

Both Petliura's government and Jewish circles abroad were painfully, fearfully aware that a popular uprising and a new civil war in Ukraine could lead to new anti-Jewish atrocities, which would bode ill not only for the Jewish population but for the cause of Ukrainian liberation as well. The pogroms did not simply strike a blow against the Ukrainian national movement's reputation (although its leadership tried to combat them), but also increased disorder and anarchy. In addition, the pogroms led forces not under the government's control to run riot, produced disintegration in the army, and created conditions in which the government lost control of the situation. Pogroms were also the strongest argument that Bolshevik propaganda could use to win the Jewish population over to the Bolshevik side and to discredit the Ukrainian national movement abroad. Although the Bolshevik army had also carried out many Jewish pogroms during 1917–19,[2] the Bolsheviks, aided by well-organized propaganda, successfully created the impression that they alone were the principled defenders of the national rights and safety of the Jewish population. They were helped in this by the undeniable fact that the Bolshevik commanders and commissars included a considerable number of Jews. This gave the non-Jewish population the impression that all Bolsheviks were Jews and that all Jews were Bolsheviks.

The foundation for that impression had been laid by the old myth of Jewish hegemony within the revolutionary movement, which was born after revolutionaries murdered Alexander II in 1881. Although only two of the twenty-eight members of the Executive Committee (the leading organ) of the People's Will, which carried out the assassination, were Jews,[3] the rumor spread among the people (not without help from certain chauvinist and pro-government circles) that "the Jews killed the tsar." This led to the wave of pogroms in 1881. From then on the tsarist government systematically used anti-Semitism in the struggle against the supposedly Jewish revolutionary movement. That provocative idea sank deep into popular consciousness and was one of the foundations of Russian Black Hundred ideology. During the civil war in Ukraine and afterwards, the idea took the form of the slogan, "All Jews are Bolsheviks."

That view had a negligible relationship to the truth. Jews, in fact, formed a significant percentage only of the Bolshevik leadership, not of the Bolshevik rank and file. At the same time, Jews formed a sizeable proportion of the leadership of *all* the revolutionary parties in Russia. This was a reaction to the Jewish people's lack of rights in the empire and to the tsarist government's anti-Semitic policies. As for the Jewish masses, the majority supported the Zionist movement. The Bolsheviks, however, were always, in principle, enemies of Zionism. They viewed it as a bourgeois movement and did not conceal their extreme hostility toward the theory and practice of Zionism. Thus the millions of Zionist-inclined Jews in the towns within the Pale of Settlement could in no way be dubbed ideological supporters of Bolshevism. If in 1919–20 a significant section of the Jewish masses in Ukraine leaned toward neutrality or even supported the Bolsheviks in their struggle against the Ukrainian People's Republic, the main reason for this was the Jewish masses' hopes for an end to the pogroms. This did not mean that Jews blamed the Ukrainian People's Republic for the pogroms. The Jewish masses could see the weakness of that government and its inability to master the situation in Ukraine. The Bolsheviks were the only power that promised, and seemed capable of establishing, strong law and order.

The insignificant degree of ideological influence exerted by the Bolsheviks, and by the socialists in general, over the Jewish masses in Ukraine at the start of the revolutionary period of 1917–20 can be gauged from the results of various elections that took place in Ukraine in 1917. In the elections to the All-Russian Constituent Assembly, no Jewish socialist party won a single seat, and only the Zionist parties were successful among the Jewish electorate. In the elections to the Ukrainian Constituent Assembly in December 1917, the non-socialist Zionists gained more than 70 percent of the Jewish vote. That was the situation in 1917. However, within the governing bodies of the Ukrainian People's Republic, Jewish representation among the deputies went quite contrary to the will of the electorate. In the Central Rada, almost 80 percent of the fifty Jewish deputies were socialists.[4] This is explained by the general mood in revolutionary circles, both Ukrainian and, to a significant degree, Russian and Jewish. The socialist parties, which had declared themselves representatives of "revolutionary democracy," had a tendency to push the non-socialists out of the political arena.[5] Although the leading position of Ukrainian socialists in the governing bodies of the UNR largely corresponded to the political orientation of the Ukrainian popular masses, the great majority of socialists among the Jewish representatives in the Ukrainian government and parliament in no way corresponded to the balance of political forces among the Jewish masses in Ukraine. Joseph Schechtman stated that the Ukrainian socialist majority used its own judgment in choosing Jewish leaders to invite onto the Central Rada. Socialists were obviously invited first of all. Schechtman expressed his indignation at that undemocratic move, considering that the Rada should have proposed that Jewish political circles choose deputies to the Central Rada from among themselves on behalf of Jewry in Ukraine.[6]

That incident is linked to an event that furthered tragic developments in Ukrainian-Jewish relations. In the autumn of 1917 Jewish pogroms began in Ukraine, as well as in some other parts of the former tsarist empire. It is now difficult to examine in detail and understand the conditions that aroused the pogrom element. (Although a great deal has been written about these events, there are grounds to believe that the historical and socio-psychological research needed to explain adequately and thoroughly the mechanism whereby the pogrom atmosphere emerged and developed has not yet been carried out.) In any event, the Russian Black Hundred organizations, aided by the tsarist government, destroyed the rather thin layer of legal consciousness in Russia that stood guard over human life and dignity. The Black Hundreds attempted to destroy the notion of the inviolability of life only as far as Jews were concerned, but their work led to the destruction of the entire principle of legal order and created an atmosphere in which violence became legitimate. This greatly facilitated the subversive activity of the Bolsheviks, especially within the tsarist army.[7]

When the revolutionary explosion destroyed a strong central power on the empire's territory (a power that, despite its links with the Black Hundreds, was still an obstacle to the uncontrolled ferment of destructive forces), the Bolsheviks, with their calls for people to plunder the property of the "exploitative" classes in society, finally heaved aside society's legal and moral principles. Lenin's call to "plunder the spoils of plunder" led to the start of a chain reaction of boundless violence. It was characteristic that in most cases the wave of violence, including the Jewish pogroms, was started by deserters, who literally flooded the country as the Russian army disintegrated. That disintegration was, to a great extent, the result of the agitation of the Bolsheviks, who acted on the issue in full agreement with the German military command.[8]

The wave of violence could not, of course, omit the Jews. The pogrom tradition established in tsarist times, linked as it was to ancient prejudices and to the defenseless position of the Jewish population, made the Jews the constant object of pogrom activity. A characteristic feature of those events was the way in which a majority of the pogromists either viewed the pogrom as part of their political activity or justified their pogrom activity with some sort of political explanation. In most cases, pogroms were explained by the need to fight Bolshevism, since Jews supposedly gave mass support to the Bolsheviks. Actually, the link between cause and consequence was just the opposite. It was precisely the pogroms that led a significant portion of the Jewish masses to support the Bolsheviks, without sharing their ideology.

It was very characteristic and indicative that each armed force perpetrating pogroms charged the Jews with supporting its enemies. For example, the Russian Volunteer Army blamed the Jews for supporting both the Bolsheviks and the Ukrainian People's Republic, while some Bolshevik sections that carried out pogroms blamed the Jews for supporting counterrevolution or for anti-Bolshevism. There is a documented description of a bloody pogrom carried out by the Bolsheviks in the town of Hlukhiv in February 1918 under the slogan, "Long live the International!"[9]

All of this proves that the political charges brought forward to justify Jewish pogroms were simply a convenient myth that varied with the political orientation of the pogromists. The true reason for the pogroms lay in the atmosphere of limitless violence that engulfed all sides in the civil war.

The worst pogroms, in terms of quantity, ruthlessness, numbers of deaths, and territory involved, were carried out by the Volunteer [White] Army. This has been acknowledged by various sources, including the White movement's apologist I. M. Bikerman.[10] The pogroms carried out by various Bolshevik detachments went unpunished only at the start of the revolutionary period. Later, when Bolshevik rule was strengthened and assumed a stable organizational form, the Bolshevik leadership demonstratively combated pogroms and ruthlessly punished pogromists.[11] Thus the Bolsheviks sought to win the Jewish population to their side and to gain a reputation as defenders of order, and in this they succeeded. A great number of pogroms were also perpetrated by various military and paramilitary formations in the army of the Ukrainian People's Republic and forces that supported it. Those pogroms also inscribed many horrific pages in the history of Jewry in Ukraine.

For more than seven decades, academic and political literature has discussed the question of the extent to which the Ukrainian government, and Symon Petliura in particular, were responsible for the pogroms in Ukraine. Saul Friedman asserts that Petliura was personally responsible, and on the dust jacket of his book Petliura is described as "the Jew-hating leader of a Jew-hating people." Soviet sources and Soviet propaganda usually advanced ideas along very similar lines.[12] Arnold Margolin, a participant in the revolutionary events in Ukraine, held the opposite point of view, maintaining that the Ukrainian government, and Petliura in particular, combated pogroms. Margolin even cited ninety-two cases known to him in which pogromists were shot on the orders of the Ukrainian government. A similar view was held by Solomon Goldelman, another participant in the events.[13]

It is not the purpose of the present work to clarify the issue of the guilt or innocence of Petliura and his government, although it is necessary to touch on that issue in connection with a number of events. For our purposes, the crucial event took place in the autumn of 1917, when the pogroms began in Ukraine. In November 1917 Joseph Schechtman, a member of the Central Rada and the Small Rada, persuaded the Zionist faction in the Ukrainian Central Rada to propose the creation of Jewish military units to defend the Jewish population against pogroms. Those units were to be under the authority of the government of the UNR and to be armed by it. In a written question on pogroms to the Small Rada, the Zionist faction asked the general secretary (minister) for military affairs, Symon Petliura, what his views were on the possibility of creating such Jewish detachments. Petliura said that he agreed with the proposal in principle. However, it could only have been implemented with the agreement of the Jewish parties whose representatives were in the Central Rada. Their decision fatally influenced the further development of events, for the representatives of the Jewish socialist parties judged the plan to be nationalist and counterrevolutionary. Soon afterwards they also defeated a plan to organize Jewish self-defense in Ukraine that was put forward by the Union of Jewish Soldiers. Thus were buried the first plans to create Jewish armed detachments, aided by the UNR government, to defend the Jewish population against pogroms.[14] Both Petliura and some non-socialist Zionist circles remained loyal to the idea of Jewish self-defense until the autumn of 1921, when an agreement to that end was signed by Vladimir Jabotinsky and Maksym Slavinsky, a representative of the Petliura government.

It is interesting to note that in the autumn of 1917, when the idea of creating Jewish armed detachments under the aegis of the Ukrainian government was first broached, the socialist Petliura took a position directly opposed to that of his ideological counterparts in the Jewish movement and identical to that of the Zionists.

The second attempt to form Jewish armed detachments as part of the Ukrainian army was initiated in September 1921 during the Twelfth Zionist Congress held in the Czech city of Karlovy Vary (Karlsbad). Jabotinsky was a delegate to the Congress. The world war had caused a gap of eight years between the Eleventh and Twelfth Zionist Congresses. Thus the Twelfth Congress had to take account of, analyze, and assess the great and tragic events affecting the Jewish people and the Zionist movement as a result of World War I, the radical post-war changes on the political map, and several revolutions in various countries.

It was then that Jabotinsky met his old friend from Odesa, Maksym Slavinsky.[15] By the turn of the century, Slavinsky had developed a reputation as a zealous liberal and friend of the Jews. In 1907 his cooperation with Jabotinsky yielded good results, and the two men ran for the Second Duma as candidates in the same constituency, which had a large Jewish population. Slavinsky, whose wife was Jewish, had such a good reputation among the Jews that they elected him as one of their deputies to the Duma. Jabotinsky remembered this in his autobiography: "I was not elected to the Duma. The Jewish arbiters (the elections were in two stages) elected as candidates the Jew Ratner and the Ukrainian Maksym Slavinsky, the same Slavinsky who fifteen years later became a minister in Petliura's government. He was the person with whom I signed the well-known agreement for which I was widely cursed among Jews, but which I would be prepared to sign again."[16] It is true that maneuvers by the reactionary and anti-Semitic bloc caused the majority of left-liberal and Jewish candidates, including Slavinsky, not to reach the Duma, but the fact remains that he was put forward for the Duma as a candidate of the Jewish electors.

Subsequently Jabotinsky and Slavinsky worked together on the same Ukrainian and Russian publications, such as *Ukrainskaia zhizn'* and *Russkie vedomosti*.

In 1921 Slavinsky was the representative in Czechoslovakia of Petliura's émigré government. In that capacity he sent greetings to the Twelfth Zionist Congress, and his message was presented at the start of the proceedings. (The stenographic record of the congress states that it was Jabotinsky who read the greetings to the gathering.)[17] The message began by expressing satisfaction that "the Jewish people, to whom civilization and all the nations of the world owe so much, has become an important factor in world politics." After emphasizing that the Ukrainian people, like the Jewish people, was still struggling to attain its freedom, the author (who would seem to have been Slavinsky) went on to say:

> I must take the opportunity to stress the role played in the history of Ukraine by the section of the Jewish people living on Ukrainian territory. I must more sorrowfully state that in recent years the Ukrainian Jews have experienced terrible persecution from various quarters. The upheavals that made victims of them wounded the Ukrainian people as severely as they did the Jewish people. That section of the Ukrainian people that is aware of its tasks can in no way be held responsible for this, since it rejects and condemns those criminal attacks, for which irresponsible elements must be blamed.

> We wish to live in brotherhood with the Jewish people and to unite in order to carry out our civilizing work on the territory of Ukraine. We most fervently desire the renewal of peace in our lands, which will enable us to heal the wounds inflicted upon our Jewish fellow citizens in recent years.[18]

Jabotinsky and Slavinsky had met twice before the congress. As Slavinsky reported to his government, those meetings took place in Prague in July 1921, when Jabotinsky arrived to take part in the preparatory meetings for the congress.[19] Slavinsky described the themes of his preliminary discussions with Jabotinsky: "As old friends we discussed the fundamental matter of how to repair the damage within Jewish world opinion concerning Ukrainianism. I gave him all the material I had. Furthermore, we hit upon the idea of creating a Jewish gendarmerie."[20] Unfortunately, no other reliable testimony about those first two discussions has been preserved. Nahum Levin's article,[21] which is most often cited as the source on Jabotinsky's meetings with Slavinsky, recounts later meetings only. Slavinsky's phrase, "we hit upon the idea of creating a Jewish gendarmerie," does not tell us whose idea it was. A stenographic record of those first two meetings would undoubtedly have shed crucial light on the details of Jabotinsky's position at that point on the Ukrainian question in general and on Petliura's government in particular. In any event, it is apparent that the tragic events in Ukraine had not changed Jabotinsky's attitude toward the Ukrainian national-liberation forces to such an extent as to make him reject contact with the Ukrainian government or refuse to make an agreement with it.

From Slavinsky's account it would seem that Jabotinsky, as well as Slavinsky himself, was concerned to "repair the damage within Jewish world opinion concerning Ukrainianism." Jabotinsky's standard position on the Ukrainian question should permit a fairly credible guess as to why he cared about this and why he sought to reach agreement with the Ukrainian government. Jabotinsky always considered that, in their own interests, the Jews in Ukraine had to establish good relations with the Ukrainian people and its national movement, as that was the only way to prevent the emergence of pogrom conditions in Ukraine in the event of another revolutionary explosion. Jabotinsky sought ways to break open that "vicious circle" in which Jewry found itself in Ukraine: every conflict exacerbated alienation and hatred, which in turn produced new conflicts. The highly emotional (and, of course, completely understandable) reaction to the pogroms on the part of world Jewry would not yield any benefit to Jews in Ukraine, for no intelligent policy can issue from emotion. Such a thought was bound to emerge in Jabotinsky's mind, given his views on Jewish national policy. Moreover, the anti-Ukrainian attitude expressed by world Jewry was harmful to Jews in Ukraine, since it further exacerbated tensions in Ukrainian-Jewish relations, and thus could only facilitate the emergence of pogrom conditions in Ukraine in the event of a new war or revolution.

Even without such hypotheses about the pressures that may have guided Jabotinsky at this time (however plausible they may be), there is still no doubt that Jabotinsky maintained his characteristic sympathy for the Ukrainian national-liberation movement. Joseph Schechtman, who worked with Jabotinsky for many years and saw him almost daily, even put forward that sympathy as the primary reason for Jabotinsky's agreement with Slavinsky:

> Its [the agreement's] background was determined by two basic elements of his political credo. The first was his active and friendly interest in Ukrainian national aspirations because of his natural sympathy for a nationalist liberation movement. He was also aware of the necessity of Jewish-Ukrainian cooperation for the attainment of Jewish nationalist demands in Russia and the Austro-Hungarian Monarchy (later, in Poland), where the two nationalities lived side by side. In Russia, Jabotinsky had written often and competently about the Ukrainian problem; he was widely known and appreciated by Ukrainian patriots, many of whom had in the meantime become closely associated with the Ukrainian nationalist government headed by Simon Petliura.[22]

With all due respect to Schechtman's ideas and his familiarity with Jabotinsky's attitude, it seems doubtful that "his active and friendly interest in Ukrainian national aspirations" was Jabotinsky's primary motivation in his discussions with Slavinsky. It would be more natural to assume that he was concerned first and foremost with the interests of the Jewish population in Ukraine, and that his sympathy for the Ukrainian liberation movement simply created a favorable atmosphere that rendered it easier to make common cause with the representatives of the Ukrainian government. Such an interpretation of the motives that guided Jabotinsky is based on all his articles and letters that touch upon the agreement with Slavinsky.[23] Hence it is easy to understand why Jabotinsky once again turned his attention to Ukraine in the summer of 1921: a new military intervention was being prepared, which meant that anti-Jewish sentiments could again explode. Such explosions might not have a purely spontaneous character, for there was the possibility that forces interested in discrediting the Ukrainian national-liberation cause might provoke pogroms and exploit them in their own interests as part of a policy of "divide and rule" so as to foster Ukrainian-Jewish enmity. Such forces included the Soviet regime and the anti-communist apologists for a "great, united, and indivisible" Russia, a cause that still had, though in the underground, fairly significant numbers of supporters on the territory of the Bolshevik state.

In 1921 the interests of the Bolshevik regime and the anti-Bolshevik Russian imperialists, as usual, completely coincided on the issue of fighting against the Ukrainian national movement, and this extended to the possibility of exploiting Ukrainian-Jewish enmity. Jabotinsky knew, for his part, that the Ukrainian émigré government was prepared to take the most radical measures in that situation to prevent a new wave of pogroms in Ukraine. This is shown in a letter that he wrote a short while later, in February 1922: "I...gained the impression from the discussions that the Petliura group now fears pogroms more than we do."[24] Jabotinsky may also have been aware that shortly before, in the spring, Petliura had issued an official proclamation, "To the Population of Ukraine and to the Insurgents," in which he urged a comradely and brotherly attitude toward the Jewish population. That proclamation ended with Petliura's announcement of his imminent return to Ukraine and a threat to all pogromists of "severe punishment under martial law as traitors to our nation and servants of the enemy."[25] The proclamation, transported by supporters from Galicia to the Soviet-controlled part of Ukraine through various channels, was in broad outline a repetition of many proclamations and commands issued by Petliura throughout the period 1917–20 to try to combat the Jewish pogroms.

Lawlessness, lack of discipline, and the disintegration of the Ukrainian army and insurgent detachments supporting the UNR meant that those orders and proclamations remained for the most part empty words. However, there are many documented instances in which some of the more disciplined sections of the UNR army or individual officers and state functionaries halted pogroms and arrested, tried or executed pogromists.[26] Petliura was aware how little influence his threatening proclamations and commands against pogroms exerted. In May 1926, in a letter written a few days before his death, Petliura wrote about the "historical 'sins' and errors of the Ukrainians' disorganization, of their small degree of culture, and of the unfavorable circumstances in the life of the Ukrainian nation."[27] Appreciation of those "unfavorable circumstances" must have led him to the idea that only armed *Jewish* forces could be effective means of preventing pogroms or crushing any wave of pogroms that occurred.

Although Jabotinsky held discussions only with Slavinsky, the latter spoke on behalf of the UNR government, hence Petliura, the head of that government, was the "other party" to the negotiations. Jabotinsky understood Petliura's behavior as a sincere attempt to find some effective method to prevent pogroms, and that gave him a certain trust in the government. Without it, undoubtedly he would not have entered into negotiations with Petliura's government or signed an agreement with it. His trust must have been reinforced by a fact that was almost certainly known to Jabotinsky, namely, that from January to August 1920, when Petliura was defending the last patch of Ukrainian territory that he held in Western Ukraine, his small but most dedicated and disciplined army decisively crushed all attempts to carry out pogroms against Jews.[28]

Information about the later meetings between Jabotinsky and Slavinsky is available in the latter's "Report" to his government and Levin's article. In his "Report," Slavinsky stated that further meetings took place on 30–31 August in Karlsbad. The first meeting was held in the presence of the UNR's ambassador in Berlin, Roman Stotsky. There was then a break in the discussions during which Slavinsky went to Galicia for consultations with his government. During that time Jabotinsky met with some leaders of Ukrainian Jewry who were in Prague because of the congress (including Vladimir Temkin, Izrail Trivus, Iona Machover, and Mikhail Shvartsman).[29] The talks were renewed on 3 September and continued the next day. Also present ("among others," according to Slavinsky) was the English Colonel John Patterson, a firm supporter of Zionism and a commander of the Jewish units of the British army that had been formed during the First World War at Jabotinsky's initiative. Throughout his life, Patterson was a close friend of Jabotinsky.[30]

Levin stated that at one of the meetings Jabotinsky asked Slavinsky: "How could you and Professor Hrushevsky, and Nikovsky, and so many others whom I always knew as honest democrats, how could you tolerate all those pogroms without rebelling against Petliura?"[31] Using the Jewish habit of replying to one question with another, Slavinsky said:

> Why are you Jews so hard on Petliura while you forgive General Allenby and your own Sir Herbert Samuel? Petliura had to deal with 30 million Ukrainians, in a country twice the size of France, and his army consisted of unruly bands! Allenby had 70 thousand well-disciplined troops against a handful of Arabs, and yet he did nothing to stop the pogrom in Jerusalem a year ago, and the organizer of the Jewish self-defense was sentenced to penal servitude; and only a few months ago the Jewish High Commissioner, Samuel, under very much the same conditions, allowed the May pogroms to last almost a week, with about 100 Jewish victims, while the soldiers were ordered to use sticks instead of rifles. Yet you Jews have not "rebelled" against Allenby or Samuel or the British.[32]

This exchange of questions was really an expression of two opposing views. Jabotinsky expressed the view, typical at that time in Jewish circles, that Petliura was to blame for the pogroms, and that those of his co-workers who did not oppose him were thereby also partially responsible. That was hardly Jabotinsky's personal view, and in 1926, a critical time for Ukrainian-Jewish relations after the Jew Schwartzbard assassinated Petliura, Jabotinsky would express a completely different opinion of Petliura. Clearly, during the negotiations Jabotinsky had to take into account the views of the representatives of Ukrainian Jewry whom he consulted, and he was obliged to express the view of Petliura held by them and by most Jews in order to dot all the "i's." Slavinsky's reply reflected the view in Ukrainian circles that Petliura was operating in conditions of anarchy and massive political and criminal banditry; that he was doing everything in his power and could not be blamed for failing to crush the pogroms. Apparently Slavinsky's reply satisfied Jabotinsky, for the negotiations continued and the question of Petliura was not raised again.

In contrast with Jabotinsky, some of the Twelfth Zionist Congress delegates were dissatisfied with Slavinsky's greetings to the Congress. They were also generally dissatisfied with the Ukrainian government's attitude toward the Jews. According to Slavinsky, "during the discussion of the pogroms in Ukraine a large group of East European and Anglo-American Zionists wanted to blame the army and government of the Ukrainian People's Republic for those events."[33]

Jabotinsky's reaction to the views of those delegates is of cardinal importance to the present discussion. According to Slavinsky, "that group's move petered out thanks to the information and explanations given by Jabotinsky and myself."[34] If that were indeed the case (and we have no grounds to disbelieve Slavinsky), then it is further proof that Jabotinsky did not share the view that the UNR government was to blame for the pogroms. Even so, Jabotinsky could not, of course, ignore the views of the majority of the Jewish community and of the Zionist leadership. At that time, as Schechtman points out, Petliura's government was informally regarded as a "moral and political pariah" by Jewish organizations. That is to say, contacts with it were undesirable and could compromise a Jewish leader who attempted to mend fences.[35] With characteristic courage, Jabotinsky would not let himself be swayed by this "pariah status," but he also could not totally ignore Jewish opinion. That was probably what induced him to ask Slavinsky the question blaming Petliura, and it probably explains why Jabotinsky repeatedly emphasized during the negotiations that he was speaking purely as an individual and not on behalf of the World Zionist Organization, although he was a member of its leadership (Executive).

Despite the verbal variance on Petliura, Jabotinsky and Slavinsky agreed about the possibility of pogroms breaking out in the event of a new intervention in Ukraine by the armies of the UNR. The mass popular uprising expected in such circumstances could reawaken the pogrom element. Levin writes:

> Slavinsky then went on to say that the main question was what could be done to improve matters in the future. It was clear that in the next spring the Ukrainian troops would again have to cross the border and would occupy border towns containing Jewish communities. What if those troops would again prove as "unruly" as before? What, he asked, could one advise the Ukrainian nationalists to do to prevent further pogroms? He could swear, he said, that they, the leaders, were willing to do anything to prevent the recurrence of pogroms—anything short of renouncing their hope to reconquer...Ukraine. Should they issue a proclamation to their troops? Should they threaten hanging any offender? They had already tried all this, with no result....[36]

According to Levin, Jabotinsky replied that proclamations and threats should be used, but that they were only a small part of the measures that could be taken to prevent pogroms. The important and most effective step would be to organize a Jewish gendarmerie, composed of Jews and commanded by Jews, with garrisons in all the cities and towns with a significant Jewish population on all the territory occupied by the Ukrainian army. Jabotinsky emphasized that the Jewish gendarmerie would not take part in military operations against the Bolsheviks or anyone else. It would concern itself exclusively with defending a peaceable Jewish population against possible pogroms. Jabotinsky further laid special stress on the fact that he could make such an agreement only in his personal capacity, and not on behalf of any Jewish organization. Levin therefore claimed that the idea of organizing a Jewish gendarmerie was Jabotinsky's. Whoever first hit upon the idea of creating a gendarmerie, one fact, confirmed by all sources, is important: no dispute arose between the two sides, either over organizing a gendarmerie or on the details of the agreement.

On 4 September 1921, in Karlsbad, the agreement was signed by Jabotinsky for the Jewish side and by Slavinsky for the Ukrainians. The main points were as follows:

(1) Alongside the Ukrainian gendarmerie, a Jewish gendarmerie is to be temporarily established, attached to the army of the UNR, with the specific task of defending the Jewish population on the territory occupied by the Ukrainian army.
(2) The Jewish gendarmerie is not to take part in any military operations.
(3) The Jewish gendarmerie is to be recruited by an ad hoc Jewish organization and no communists are to be allowed to join that gendarmerie.
(4) A Jew is to command the Jewish gendarmerie and is to be appointed with the agreement of the ad hoc Jewish organization and of the general staff of the Ukrainian army.
(5) The commander of the Jewish gendarmerie is to be under the jurisdiction of the commander of the Ukrainian gendarmerie on general questions, but on issues concerning the defense of the Jewish population he is to have the right to communicate directly with the army's chief of staff or with others in higher positions.
(6) Members of the Jewish gendarmerie are to have the same rights as members of the Ukrainian gendarmerie and are to be equally responsible before the law.
(7) Like the Ukrainian gendarmerie, the Jewish gendarmerie is to move behind the army's lines and carry out its duties immediately after the Ukrainian army has occupied areas of Jewish population. The Jewish gendarmerie is to act in line with plans worked out by its commander and confirmed by the general staff. Within the framework of those plans, the Jewish gendarmerie is to operate autonomously.[37]

The agreement ended with a supplement stating that the general staff of the Ukrainian army would "repeat the order" prohibiting any violence whatsoever against the Christian or Jewish populations and affirming that any acts of violence would be investigated to the full extent of the law. The guilty would be court-martialed.

Slavinsky's "Report" gave additional information about the creation and maintenance of the Jewish gendarmerie. The Jewish ad hoc organization mentioned in the agreement would assume responsibility for recruiting the gendarmerie and for all further contacts on that matter with the government of the UNR. It would be established outside the framework of the Zionist organization and would concern itself exclusively with the affairs of the Jewish gendarmerie. It would assume responsibility for all preliminary expenses, but from the moment of its entry onto the territory of Ukraine, the Jewish gendarmerie would be financed entirely by the government of the Ukrainian People's Republic.

Today it is difficult to determine how Jabotinsky envisaged the Jewish organization that would have guided the gendarmerie's formation. He probably planned to form it with his own supporters and with prominent Zionists from Ukraine who were then in the emigration. In his "Report," Slavinsky indicated that Temkin might have headed the organization.[38] In any event, the whole affair was really limited to the signing of the agreement, for during that autumn of 1921 the Western nations changed their plans vis-à-vis the Bolshevik regime and the Ukrainian army did not resume operations in Ukraine (apart from the brief Winter Campaign). Soon that force was disarmed and the whole matter of the Jewish gendarmerie came to an end.

There is no doubt that both parties to the agreement intended to make a joint effort to put a stop to Jewish pogroms in Ukraine. It might seem self-evident that these efforts would have been welcomed and supported by the Jewish community throughout the world. It is more than likely that if the Ukrainian army had intervened in Ukraine, and if the agreement had been implemented, there would have been a basic shift toward understanding and cooperation between the Ukrainian and Jewish peoples. The formation and effective functioning of a Jewish gendarmerie financed by the Ukrainian government would have shown the Jewish population in Ukraine and world Jewry that the Ukrainian national-liberation movement and the whole idea of Ukrainian statehood were not, in principle, hostile to the Jewish people. This could have created a new social atmosphere for Ukrainian Jewry in which its safety would have been guaranteed far better than at any other time in the history of Ukraine.

Such positive prospects undoubtedly occurred to the participants in the agreement. By that time Jabotinsky had had experience in the formation of Jewish armed units for the Jewish Legion attached to the British Army. The legion had been established at his initiative and played an enormous role in raising Jewish national consciousness, spreading Zionist ideas, and raising the international prestige of the Zionist cause. Jabotinsky's *Story of the Jewish Legion* contains a noteworthy passage: "...except through the idea of the Legion, it would be impossible to push Zionism into the rank of those questions in which the world might be interested at that extraordinary time."[39]

The same point can be made about the situation in Ukraine, associating it with the idea of creating a Jewish gendarmerie. It is a fact that the tragedy of the Jewish pogroms evoked sympathy mainly from world Jewry, while non-Jewish opinion, though not entirely indifferent, nevertheless showed considerably more indifference than the Jews expected. (The same situation would recur during the Nazi genocide of the Jews.) There is little reason to doubt that if pogroms had taken place again following the planned incursion of the Ukrainian army in 1922, the world would once again have shown little inclination to help the Jews. But if a Jewish armed force had been active in Ukraine (whether it took the form of a Jewish gendarmerie or another organization), events would have assumed quite a different character, attracting keen world attention and demonstrating the effectiveness and vigor of the Jewish national movement. Jewry would have become a potent political and even military factor. In a word, the creation of a Jewish gendarmerie would have "pushed" the problem of Jewry in Ukraine, as well as the national rights and demands of Jewry in general, "into the rank of those questions in which the world might be interested." And if the idea of a Jewish gendarmerie had been realized, what Jabotinsky wrote about the agreement creating the first Jewish regiment in the British Army could have been written about the Slavinsky-Jabotinsky agreement. The Legion agreement was signed by Jabotinsky and a few dozen like-minded men in Alexandria in 1915. Jabotinsky said of it: "Some day our national library in Jerusalem will get the document that was signed that spring night...."[40]

Probably Jabotinsky should have said that the agreement would have become one of the most important events in Jewish history, but he modestly confined himself to the remark about the national library. And although the idea of a Jewish gendarmerie in Ukraine, for reasons beyond the control of its author, remained on paper, who knows whether it too will not one day be inscribed in capital letters in the Jewish historical record.

Nevertheless, the idea of forming a Jewish gendarmerie in Ukraine was intended to serve not only Jewish interests, but undeniably Ukrainian interests as well—the protection of law and order in Ukraine, the suppression of the destructive pogrom element (destructive both for the Jews and for the Ukrainian state), the winning of Jewish sympathy for the Ukrainian national movement, and the establishment of a good international reputation for that movement. Clearly, Jabotinsky did not think that those benefits for the Ukrainian government and the Ukrainian national movement contradicted Jewish interests. On the contrary, as a genuine sympathizer of all peoples fighting for their national rights, he wished the Ukrainian patriots and the Ukrainian people well. (Not for nothing did Schechtman write of Jabotinsky's natural sympathy for every national-liberation movement.)[41] In fact, it may confidently be asserted that he gained some satisfaction from an enterprise offering simultaneous benefits to two nations and two national-liberation movements.

Although Jabotinsky based himself on the interests of the Jewish population in Ukraine and on the world Zionist movement, the World Zionist Organization's leadership was very hostile to the Jabotinsky-Slavinsky agreement. The Zionist leadership had been equally hostile to the idea of creating Jewish units within the British Army during World War I. The originality of Jabotinsky's political thinking clearly induced a negative reaction in the majority of Zionist leaders, and Jabotinsky quickly gained the reputation among them of being an *enfant terrible*. While, to judge from his later letters,[42] Jabotinsky expected the Zionist leadership to resist his actions, the reaction from Zionist circles and the press proved much sharper than he had anticipated.

In *The Story of the Jewish Legion*, Jabotinsky gives an interesting explanation for the behavior of Jewish circles in decisively opposing actions that would logically appear to conform to the needs of the day. Visiting one of the "Fathers of Zionism," Max Nordau,[43] Jabotinsky expressed amazement to Nordau that many leading Zionists failed to understand the benefits to be gained from creating Jewish armed units in the British Army. "The old sage replied to my question with a profound saying: it wasn't until much later that I came to realize how profound it was. He shook his wise head and said, 'This, my young friend, is logic; but logic is a Greek art, and Jews can't stand it. The Jew learns not by way of reason but from catastrophes. He won't buy an umbrella merely because he sees clouds in the sky; he waits until he is drenched and catches pneumonia—then he makes up his mind.'"[44] In the case of the attempt to form a Jewish gendarmerie in Ukraine, Jewish political thought acted under the influence of the terrible catastrophe of the pogroms, which affected Jabotinsky differently than it did the majority of Jews throughout the world. In line with his active nature and combativeness, Jabotinsky tried to prevent a repetition of the catastrophe through the formation of Jewish armed forces. In contrast, most of the Jewish community was left by the pogroms in a state of trauma that paralyzed its ability to think and act decisively. Moreover, modern Jewish political thought, founded forty years earlier by the first discoverers and practitioners of Zionism, was still suffering from youthful immaturity and exaggerated emotionalism. While laden with purist idealism, the political thought of many Jewish circles lacked sufficient psychological preparation to employ new, totally untried, practical methods to accomplish the extraordinary task of gathering together a dispersed nation and creating a new state. That required a deep and fundamentally novel analysis of the world situation and a new Jewish policy differing in essential ways from the political formulae then fashionable in the Western world. (The most fashionable at that time was socialist ideology, which Jabotinsky fundamentally opposed.)

The Jewish philosopher Martin Buber was correct when he wrote: "Despite its political equipment, the modern Zionist movement has been given too little feeling for the world and world history during its progress...."[45] In attempting to recruit Jewish armed forces, Jabotinsky had learned history's repeated lesson that the Jewish people needed self-defense, as he had seen with his own eyes in Odesa. By launching a campaign against Jabotinsky and the idea of a Jewish gendarmerie, the Zionist leadership proved once again that "history teaches only the fact that it teaches nothing at all." That powerful campaign against Jabotinsky involved predominantly socialist-oriented Zionist circles. The campaign went beyond striking notes of exaggerated emotion and disagreement over tactical issues. It also clearly involved an attempt to compromise an ideological opponent and "rebel" who stubbornly pursued his own course and did not wish to swim with the current. In 1921, following the pogroms in Ukraine, when the Jewish community was electrified with anti-Ukrainian sentiment, it was very easy to incite massive indignation against Jabotinsky by depicting him as a collaborator with Ukrainian pogromists. By fanning the campaign against Jabotinsky and attempting to portray his agreement with the Petliura government as the greatest scandal in the history of Zionism, Jabotinsky's political enemies sought to deal a death blow to his reputation as a Jewish social and political leader. The Jabotinsky-Slavinsky agreement therefore became a pretext for attacks that rained down upon Jabotinsky until his death and did not stop even then. This battle against him, provoked by the situation within the Zionist movement, had a direct effect on the external political issue of the Zionist leadership's attitude toward the Ukrainian problem, making bad Jewish-Ukrainian relations even worse.

The very first reaction to the agreement's publication from the majority of the Jewish press was extremely unfavorable to Jabotinsky. A Berlin newspaper, *Die Jüdische Rundschau*, published the text of the agreement and Slavinsky's "Report," but its commentary expressed the deepest sorrow that "such an affair had come to pass."[46] The three main objections to the agreement advanced in that newspaper would be repeated over the years by many other writers:

(1) If Jabotinsky cares about the defense of Ukrainian Jews against pogroms, he should take steps toward creating Jewish self-defense units and not make an agreement with Petliura's government.

The newspaper seems to have forgotten that the idea of creating Jewish self-defense units in Ukraine in 1917 ran up against the opposition of just those Jewish socialist circles that opposed Jabotinsky's agreement with the government of the Ukrainian People's Republic. Also, the newspaper consciously or unconsciously took no account of the simple and obvious fact that it would hardly have been possible to create Jewish armed forces on the territory occupied by the Ukrainian army without the approval of the Ukrainian government and without an appropriate agreement with it. Jabotinsky's agreement with the Ukrainian government was precisely an attempt to gain such approval and create Jewish self-defense units, this time under the name of a Jewish gendarmerie, but otherwise no different in meaning and purpose.[47]

(2) Zionism should remain neutral in the struggle between Bolshevik and anti-Bolshevik forces, whereas the agreement with Petliura's government would be considered by the Bolsheviks to violate that neutrality.

This statement by the newspaper is based on the notion that it was possible for Zionism to maintain some kind of neutrality vis-à-vis the Bolsheviks. Supporters of that idea forget that neutrality is conceivable only when all sides in a conflict recognize it. An attempt by one side, which has sustained an attack, to proclaim its unilateral neutrality is tantamount to capitulation. Since the Bolsheviks, from the very beginning of their movement, proclaimed Zionism to be their enemy (because in their view Zionism was a type of "bourgeois ideology" and a "bourgeois movement"), and waged a constant struggle against it, the attempt by some Zionists to proclaim unilateral neutrality in relation to Bolshevism was devoid of sense.

Moreover, Jabotinsky took every possible step to ensure that it would be difficult to treat his agreement with Petliura's government as a Zionist plan to enter the armed struggle against the Bolsheviks. The agreement stressed that the sole aim and purpose of the Jewish gendarmerie was to defend a peaceable Jewish population and that it would not take part in any military actions. Despite the fact that Soviet propaganda took advantage of Jabotinsky's agreement to fan the flames of an anti-Zionist campaign,[48] there was no basis for it in the agreement's contents.

Clearly, Jabotinsky had no reason to make his political decisions and the destiny of Jewry in Ukraine dependent on what Soviet propaganda might or might not say. Whatever the situation, Soviet propaganda would find the means to use any steps taken by its political opponents to sling mud at them. Jabotinsky certainly understood that the attempts by some Zionist circles to remain neutral toward Bolshevism were doomed to remain one-sided and therefore pointless. In *The Story of the Jewish Legion*, he devoted considerable space to his skirmishes with the Russian Bolshevik Georgii Chicherin between 1915 and 1917. Chicherin, later to become the Soviet People's Commissar for Foreign Affairs, was then a political émigré living in London. Unlike the majority of the Zionist leadership, Chicherin grasped very well the great benefit that the Legion would bring to Zionism and therefore took the most brutal measures to prevent its creation. He organized a press campaign and hired a few gangs of hooligans to try to break up meetings that Jabotinsky organized in support of the Legion.[49] Jabotinsky had by then already lost any illusions about Bolshevism's true nature and its attitude to Zionism.

(3) Jabotinsky, as a member of the leadership (Executive) of the World Zionist Organization, broke its discipline by signing the agreement without prior consultation with the organization's leadership.

This accusation was also without foundation. Nowhere did the agreement state that Jabotinsky was acting on behalf of the World Zionist Organization or that this organization was in any way involved with the agreement. Jabotinsky always emphasized that he was negotiating with Slavinsky in his personal capacity. Furthermore, the Zionist Congress in Karlsbad resolved that all Zionist political work in the countries of the Jewish Diaspora would be under the jurisdiction of the national Jewish organizations (*Landesorganisationen*), and not of the World Zionist Organization. From that point of view Jabotinsky behaved with complete propriety: before signing the agreement, he consulted eleven of the most prominent representatives of the Federation of Russian and Ukrainian Zionists, and the majority of them approved the steps he took. After the agreement was signed, Jabotinsky gave all the relevant materials to that Federation, and his actions were discussed at the Conference of Russian and Ukrainian Zionists held in Berlin on 7–11 September 1922. The Conference approved a resolution that rejected all the accusations made against Jabotinsky.[50]

In a letter to the World Zionist Organization's Executive, Jabotinsky stressed that the campaign against him was being organized by the Zionist movement's socialist wing, which was motivated by ideological considerations: "[It is] characteristic that the only people who seem to be concerned with the whole business are the Po'alei Zion.... [The] Slavinsky government fights the Bolsheviks and the Po'alei Zion are afraid that their socialist competitors [in Soviet Russia—I. K.] might accuse them of friendly contact with the Zionist executive, one member of which is supposed to be in friendly contact with an anti-Bolshevik Government."[51] Here Jabotinsky somewhat understated the number of his opponents by saying that Po'alei Zion was alone in condemning his agreement with the government of the UNR. He was, in fact, opposed by Zionists of various orientations to the left of center, but the main organizers and disseminators of the campaign against him were indeed the socialists.

The *Jüdische Rundschau* criticism of Jabotinsky was still comparatively mild. The attacks against him by the Jewish socialist press and papers that sympathized with the socialists were much sharper. A point was reached where Jabotinsky was practically branded as a criminal for his continual efforts to create Jewish armed forces. David Ben-Gurion's pamphlet *Chaluzischer Zionismus oder Revisionismus* (Pioneering Zionism or Revisionism, 1934) is a clear example of that sort of attack directed against Jabotinsky:

> False prophets who feed off the flotsam and jetsam and the useless riffraff of history, who preach in the name of dark and nefarious forces, have also emerged within Zionism. They are attempting to separate the popular movement from its human ideals, from its aspirations for freedom, and from its cultural heritage and are trying to subordinate it to the rule of blood, dishonor, and slavery. They place all their hopes in the external forces from the past, which has already cut the ground from under their feet.[52]

The injustice and demagogy of such a characterization of Jabotinsky and the Revisionist movement that he led is striking. It would appear that in the heat of the political struggle, Jabotinsky's opponents lost all notion of the acceptable bounds of debate. Jabotinsky never stooped so low in his polemics.

The excerpt from Ben-Gurion's pamphlet demonstrates that Jabotinsky's opponents were ready to use any pretext to compromise their political rival. Nor did they let slip the chance of using such a pretext as an agreement with "pogromists." Moreover, even some of Jabotinsky's supporters considered the agreement to be his fatal error. One such supporter went so far as to state that Jabotinsky had regretted signing the agreement for the rest of his life.[53] Was that really the case? Did Jabotinsky consider the agreement to form a Jewish gendarmerie an error and did he come to regret it? That view does not emerge from Jabotinsky's statements and writings. On the contrary, he repeated many times that he considered the agreement to be, in principle, a correct political decision. Moreover, he never ceased to think that he had to prove its correctness to world Jewry, since he was deeply convinced that his actions in this instance were an example of appropriate behavior, a political line that should be applied in any similar situation.

In March 1922 he wrote to Iona Machover from the United States: "It would seem that the world has forgotten the Slavinsky affair, but I have not. When I return to Europe, I will be the one to make a fight of it and a very important one at that."[54] From America, Jabotinsky probably was not able to follow developments in Europe carefully. Far from forgetting the Slavinsky affair, the Jewish "world" had already begun the fight against Jabotinsky. In another letter to Machover, Jabotinsky wrote:

> I have a clear feeling that very soon things will turn out in such a way that people will say: "Jabotinsky wanted to establish a Jewish gendarmerie and he is completely right; these should always be established even if it means negotiating with the devil...." The commotion will last a month and then what remains will be the idea that a Jewish gendarmerie is the only instrument against pogroms; and after America, I will go to Berlin or Vienna and will get an ovation from the riffraff, as always. You will see that I am right.[55]

Jabotinsky never did get that ovation for the agreement on a Jewish gendarmerie, but he insisted until his death that his political move had been a correct one.

Many of the articles and letters that Jabotinsky wrote in the 1920s leave the impression that a two-way battle of emotions was being fought within his soul—on the one hand, pain and deep sorrow over the pogroms in Ukraine, and on the other, sincere sympathy for the Ukrainian national-liberation movement. The first emotion stemmed from his national patriotism and from his personal humaneness. The second stemmed from another equally characteristic and basic feature of his world-view—a principled attitude toward the free cultural and political development of all nations. As a patriot of his own nation, he could neither forget nor forgive the bloody injustice meted out to his people in Ukraine, but as a supporter of the freedom and independence of all nations, he wished with all his soul for the Ukrainian people to succeed in its liberation struggle.

He could have found an escape from this contradiction by accepting the postulate, propagated by Ukrainian émigrés, that the Ukrainian national-liberation movement was not to blame for the pogroms on the grounds that they had been carried out by uncontrolled forces, while the Ukrainian government had done everything in its power to stop them. Many indisputable facts and documents survive to support that claim, but there are also facts that prevent complete and unreserved acceptance. The Central Rada undeniably passed a law on national-personal autonomy that granted the Jewish minority in Ukraine national rights broader in scope than those previously gained by Jews in any country, but it is also undeniable that in the UNR's second period of existence (the period of the Directory, from November 1918 until the final defeat of the Army of the Ukrainian People's Republic in 1920) there were circles close the military and state leadership that were known for their anti-Jewish sentiments. It is undeniable that Symon Petliura and many other leading figures in the UNR were known for their personal pro-Jewish views, but it is also undeniable that they were unable to implant such views in every supporter and defender of the UNR.[56]

The question of blame for the pogroms and of the mechanism whereby the pogrom wave rose and spread should be the theme of a separate major research project. It has not yet been accomplished, despite the existence of some fairly detailed works on this theme, most notably those of Joseph Schechtman and Elias Tcherikower. There is no doubt that Jabotinsky was acquainted with the events in Ukraine in detail, events that had given Jewish communities throughout the world such a traumatic shock. The Jewish community believed that Jews in Ukraine were annihilated simply because they were Jews, regardless of their political convictions, party affiliation or state orientation. One of the first resounding facts to give rise to such an idea was the murder, on 20 January 1918, of the head of the Union of Jewish Soldiers, Iona Gogol, along with several of his colleagues in the Union. The murder was carried out by Mykhailo Kovenko, the UNR commandant of Kyiv and leader of the Free Cossacks, who was also responsible for other anti-Jewish atrocities in Kyiv at that time. These anti-Jewish actions by the Ukrainian military authorities inaugurated an abrupt cooling of relations between Jewish and Ukrainian national circles. It was then that Moishe Zilberfarb, the first minister for Jewish affairs in the UNR government, resigned as an act of protest.[57] Jews saw the atrocity as motivated by anti-Semitic rather than political factors: Iona Gogol, a very popular figure among the Jews, was killed by a prominent organizer of the Free Cossacks, who was also the military commandant of Kyiv. Gogol was murdered despite the fact that he was a firm supporter of the Ukrainian People's Republic and of Jewish-Ukrainian cooperation.

Gogol and several other Jews were killed in the headquarters of the Kyiv military command when they went to request that the military authorities protect the Jewish population from a pogrom. At about that time, Levko Chykalenko, a well-known Ukrainian political activist and sincere Semitophile, uttered the prophetic words: "They [anti-Semites in the Ukrainian military] will drown Ukrainian freedom in Jewish blood."[58] An ardent Jewish supporter of the Ukrainian People's Republic, Arnold Margolin, focused on the pogroms' destructiveness to the Ukrainian cause in a letter to Symon Petliura:

> As you know, I have no doubts with regard to the absolute democratism and freedom from anti-Semitism on the part of those who stand at the head of our entire governmental apparatus.
>
> Unfortunately, the same cannot be said about many of our officials and persons in public life, some of whom occupy high offices in Ukraine as well as abroad. The stigma of anti-Semitism was imposed on the entire population of former Russia by the old Russian school, but that poison was always imposed even more in the so-called "Pale of Settlement." Only time and persistent work against that phenomenon may cure the organism of Ukraine of that disease.
>
> However, you are very well aware of all this yourself, dear Symon Vasyliovych. I am returning to this subject here because of the disastrous consequences of anti-Semitism in relation to our struggle for the existence of Ukraine as a state.[59]

Another event that made a particularly horrifying impression upon the Jewish community in Ukraine, Russia, and abroad was the bloody pogrom of 1919 in the town of Proskuriv, which was carried out by a Ukrainian military detachment under the command of Otaman Semesenko.[60] In "More on the History of the Proskuriv Pogrom" (1927), Jabotinsky returned to the question of what had provoked the pogrom, arguing that it was not a response to an uprising by Jewish Bolsheviks in Proskuriv against the Ukrainian authorities, as some Ukrainians had claimed. That uprising was organized by Russian and Ukrainian Bolsheviks and Socialist Revolutionaries. Very few Jews were involved, hence the pogrom was simply an anti-Jewish action for which political reasons were invented to justify the pogromists.[61]

Without entering into a detailed analysis of the pogroms in Ukraine, it must be said that they poisoned relations between the Jewish and Ukrainian peoples very deeply and continue to do so. As his articles and letters show, Jabotinsky did not endorse Jewish opinion in placing the blame for the pogroms on the entire Ukrainian people and on the Ukrainian national movement, but many of his articles, letters, and speeches were marked by his spiritual division between sympathy for the Ukrainian national movement and solidarity with Jewish public opinion. That is apparent in the course of his negotiations with Slavinsky and emerges even more clearly in his response to the trial of Petliura's assassin,

Schwartzbard (see chapter 4). On several occasions he bowed to Jewish "street" opinion, for as a political activist and leader of the Zionist Revisionist movement, he could not and did not have the right to ignore it. He bowed to such pressures, for example, at the start of his negotiations with Slavinsky, when he asked, "How could you...tolerate all those pogroms without rebelling against Petliura?" and also when he wrote that to create a Jewish gendarmerie it would be worthwhile even "negotiating with the devil" (which can be interpreted as an indirect comparison between Petliura and the devil). Yet even while he sharply condemned the pogroms in Ukraine and those responsible for them, Jabotinsky never forgot to add that he did not identify the pogromists with the Ukrainian national movement and that he remained the latter's ally: "I remain a friend of the Ukrainian movement.... I will continue to aspire to agreement with the Ukrainian movement—as I did, inter alia, in the agreement with M. A. Slavinsky—despite that movement's grave sin against the Jews."[62]

Although there is a certain ambivalence in Jabotinsky's attitude to the pogroms in Ukraine, and in particular to Petliura, on one issue he never wavered in the slightest—his positive evaluation of the agreement with Slavinsky, his unbending certainty that the agreement exemplified correct Jewish policy. In that connection, it is interesting to trace Jabotinsky's attitude toward an event that occurred soon after the agreement with Slavinsky was signed—the Winter (or Ice) March by units of the UNR army into Soviet-occupied Ukraine in November 1921.[63] Three comparatively small military units (400 or 800 men in each) crossed the Polish-Soviet border and fought their way a few hundred kilometers into the Ukrainian territories under Bolshevik rule. The smallest of those groups, the Podilian, successfully returned to Poland a month later, but the largest group, the Volhynian, was dealt a mortal blow by Soviet cavalry under the command of Hryhorii Kotovsky, a prominent military leader. Only a small remnant of it returned to Polish territory. The third group did not engage in military action and left Ukraine for Romanian territory after a few days. None of the three raiding groups managed to awaken the mass popular uprising in Ukraine for which their commanders had hoped. Also, the Winter March was a rehearsal for the planned large UNR military campaign in Ukraine scheduled for the spring of 1922. The failure of the march hastened the Western nations' decision to cut off aid to Petliura's government and disarm his forces.

There were rumors that new anti-Jewish atrocities had been committed by the Ukrainian raiding groups. No reliable information has yet come to light to corroborate such allegations, and the very conditions of the march—incessant, exhausting battles, with no possibility of escaping from combat for even a short breathing space in one spot—were by no means conducive to pogroms. However, the rumors reached Jabotinsky, who paid close attention to the matter:

> One aspect of Petliura's latest expedition interests me. I have heard that more pogroms occurred. But, in the first place, was this wave of pogroms larger or

> smaller than the previous one (in proportion to the territory occupied)? We obviously cannot have exact figures, but still.... And in particular, in the second place: were the pogroms carried out by Petliura's soldiers this time or did they occur before their arrival? That, I think, could be clarified. It is clear why this should interest me. I am, of course, prepared to reach agreement on self-defense even with Zalizniak himself, of blessed memory. I nevertheless gained the impression from the discussions that the Petliura group now fears pogroms more than we do and that they have issued strict orders to their boys. If it turns out that the boys obey, it would be advantageous for the Jews to know that, and especially advantageous for me. Collect the information. This will help me greatly in the future.[64]

Of greatest interest in this letter is the point to which reference has already been made, namely Jabotinsky's surmise that Petliura's government "fears pogroms more than we do." It was also no accident that Jabotinsky was interested to know the extent of the Ukrainian army's discipline and obedience to orders banning pogroms. All this obviously had significance for the organization of a Jewish gendarmerie and for a prognosis of possible future developments in Ukraine.

Three days later Jabotinsky wrote that he was sending someone to Galicia and Bessarabia to collect information on the "Petliura Affair."[65] It seems likely that Jabotinsky was interested in the UNR army's state of preparedness for a new offensive in Ukraine, in conditions in the army, and in the consequences of the Winter March. Unfortunately, it is not known whether the trip by Jabotinsky's messenger took place, and if it did, what resulted. Despite the campaign by many Jewish political circles against him over the Slavinsky agreement, Jabotinsky remained totally convinced of the correctness of his actions and determined to maintain contacts with the Ukrainian national movement. Despite all the bitterness that engulfed Jabotinsky over the pogroms in Ukraine, Joseph Schechtman's conclusion remains correct: "One of the chief motives which prompted Jabotinsky to negotiate with Slavinsky was his acute realization of the necessity of restoring some understanding and cooperation between the Ukrainian and the Jewish peoples."[66]

Jabotinsky stood by that view to the end of his life. In 1925 he explained once again that the attempt to organize a Jewish gendarmerie was the sole means for Jews to influence the course of events during the UNR army's incursion into regions of Ukraine with a significant Jewish population. Only in that way, he argued, could the Jewish national movement avoid being distanced from events that could have a fatal influence on the destiny of Jewry in Ukraine:

> The agreement with M. A. Slavinsky was built on this cold logic, the logic not of people but of the force of circumstances. I shall remind you of its basic points: a Jewish gendarmerie is created at the expense, and under the command, of Jews; it does not participate in military actions; it follows in the rear in the event of an intervention; immediately after the capture of a town with a Jewish popula-

> tion, the defense of order is handed over to the Jewish gendarmerie. I still stand my ground today on those basic points and I vigorously recommend them to all who on the one hand do not wish the slaughter of the Jews and who on the other know how to draw conclusions from the actual state of affairs—in other words, to all those who have a heart within them and a head on their shoulders.[67]

In light of the facts, the attacks on Jabotinsky for his agreement with the UNR government appear completely groundless. Moreover, the affair touched the fundamental issue of the basis of Jewish national policy. On the issue of relations between the Jewish and Ukrainian peoples, the same concept that guided Jabotinsky's opponents during his lifetime is still present within Jewish circles to this very day. Jabotinsky replied to them:

> This is the origin of that hourly split between ourselves and the ordinary movement of Jewish public opinion.... Jewish politics organically fears active foresight. It does not like taking account of unpleasant possibilities, and when those arrive on the scene, it particularly dislikes using real means to tackle them. It gives pride of place to "faith" that nothing, God willing, will happen. At the same time, it refers to last season, in which, God be praised, nothing happened, and with, of course, complete sincerity, it considers that chatter to be argumentation. We, on the other hand, view this incapacity to foresee as a slovenly and destructive malady, and we insist on the need to take account of tomorrow's possibilities and even more on the need to put up lightning rods, even if we expect that the storm will pass.[68]

Of course, for those who continued to follow a "slovenly and destructive" policy, the Jabotinsky-Slavinsky agreement, and more generally Jabotinsky's whole position on the Ukrainian question, was a fatal error or even the consequence of a position that was fundamentally wrong and destructive for Jewry. That was how David Ben-Gurion, in particular, treated Jabotinsky's ideas, even though he borrowed many of them and put them into practice.[69] But those who base their thinking on objective facts and actual circumstances cannot but acknowledge that Jabotinsky showed great public courage and political sagacity by daring to swim persistently against the stream and laying the basis for a new orientation in Jewish national policy. Many of Jabotinsky's other political ideas (for example, the principle of relying upon one's own military strength) were accepted and assimilated into Israeli politics, but his attempt to steer a course toward relations with the Ukrainian national-liberation movement was not. He clearly realized that this course might be grasped and valued only after his death when he stated: "I am proud of the Legion, proud of the part I played in the defense of Jerusalem. But I am even more proud of the Petliura agreement, even though ultimately nothing came of it, and when I die you can write as my epitaph: 'This was the man who made the agreement with Petliura.'"[70]

# Notes

1. J. Schechtman, "The Jabotinsky-Slavinsky Agreement," *Jewish Social Studies* 17, no. 4 (1955): 290–91.
2. I. M. Cherikover, *Antisemitizm i pogromy na Ukraine,* pp. 103, 143–53, 284–302; I. M. Bikerman, "Rossiia i russkoe evreistvo," in *Rossiia i evrei* (Berlin, 1923), pp. 63–64.
3. D. Shub, "Evrei v russkoi revoliutsii," in *Politicheskie deiateli Rossii, 1850–1920* (New York, 1969), p. 358.
4. I. Shekhtman, "Evreiskaia obshchestvennost' na Ukraine (1917–1919 g.g.)," in *Kniga o russkom evreistve, 1917–1967* (New York, 1968), pp. 24–25.
5. S. Goldelman, *Jewish National Autonomy in Ukraine,* pp. 57–58.
6. I. Shekhtman, *Evrei i ukraintsy* (Odesa, 1917), pp. 26–27.
7. Mikhail Frenkin's books *Russkaia armiia i revoliutsiia, 1917–1918* (Munich, 1978) and *Zakhvat vlasti bol'shevikami v Rossii* (Jerusalem, 1982) contain a wealth of information on the subversive activity of the Bolsheviks both in the army and in the country generally. They also provide a great deal of reliable data on the Ukrainian and Jewish national movements during the revolution and civil war.
8. Frenkin, *Russkaia armiia i revoliutsiia*, chapter 4, and *Zakhvat vlasti bol'shevikami v Rossii*, chapters 3 and 10; D. Shub, "Parvus, Lenin i Vil'gel'm II (Germano-bol'shevistskii zagovor 1917 g.)," in *Politicheskie deiateli Rossii*, pp. 180–243.
9. Cherikover, *Antisemitizm i pogromy na Ukraine*, pp. 146–47, 286–91.
10. Bikerman, "Rossiia i russkoe evreistvo," p. 66. Interestingly, Bikerman explains that the pogroms carried out by the Volunteer Army were more ruthless and massive than those carried out by Ukrainian military units, because the Volunteer Army had larger forces and occupied more territory (p. 66). Can one then conclude that if the Volunteer Army had had even larger forces and had occupied all the territory of the empire, it would have slaughtered all the Jews?
11. I. M. Trotskii, "Evreiskie pogromy na Ukraine i v Belorussii (1918–1920 g.g.)," in *Kniga o russkom evreistve, 1917–1967*, pp. 67–68; Bikerman, "Rossiia i russkoe evreistvo," pp. 63–64.
12. Hundreds of titles of propaganda literature were published in the Soviet Union against the "Petliurivtsi," including some that were given an academic appearance. Two typical articles: Taras Myhal', "Iuvilei han'by," *Literaturna Ukraïna* (21 August 1979), characterizes Petliura in virtually the same terms as Saul Friedman, favorably refers to Friedman's book, and even quotes from it; L. Iu. Berenshtein, "Krytyka sionists'kykh fal'syfikatsii istoriï Velykoï Zhovtnevoï sotsialistychnoï revoliutsiï," *Ukraïns'kyi istorychnyi zhurnal*, no. 1 (January 1978): 128–34.

13. Cf. the works of these two authors cited above. For information on the execution of pogromists by the Ukrainian forces, see Arnold Margolin, *Ukraine and Policy of the Entente*, p. 201.

Arnold Margolin (1877–1956), prominent Jewish-Ukrainian leader, born in Kyiv. As a lawyer, he defended Beilis at his trial. He was one of the leaders of the organization of territorialists of Russia. (Territorialists, as opposed to the Zionists, considered that the future Jewish state need not necessarily be in Palestine.) During the existence of the Ukrainian People's Republic, he served as deputy minister of foreign affairs, and later as ambassador in London. From 1922 he lived in the United States. He wrote several books on the Ukrainian problem and on Ukrainian-Jewish relations.

Solomon Goldelman (1885–1974), Jewish-Ukrainian leader, sociologist, and economist. During the existence of the UNR he was a member of the Central and Small Radas, minister of labor, deputy minister of trade and industry, etc. In the emigration he was occupied with academic and political work. He wrote several books. Until his death, Goldelman, like Margolin, remained sympathetic to the cause of Jewish-Ukrainian understanding and cooperation.

14. Shekhtman, "Evreiskaia obshchestvennost' na Ukraine," pp. 31–32; Cherikover, *Antisemitizm i pogromy na Ukraine*, pp. 84–92, 211–21; Schechtman, "The Jabotinsky-Slavinsky Agreement," p. 294; Goldelman, *Jewish National Autonomy in Ukraine*, pp. 51–52.

15. Schechtman, "The Jabotinsky-Slavinsky Agreement," p. 290. Two different spellings exist in the literature: Slavyns'kyi and Slavins'kyi. He used the first spelling when he signed the report about his agreement with Jabotinsky. See "Znosyny z sionistamy," 16 September 1921 (Archives of the Jabotinsky Institute in Tel Aviv, henceforth Jabotinsky Archives).

16. V. Zhabotinskii, *Avtobiografia*, p. 73. Jabotinsky is in error here: Slavinsky became a minister in the UNR government in 1918, that is, eleven years after the elections to the Second State Duma, not fifteen. *Entsyklopediia ukraïnoznavstva*, part 2, 8: 3877–78.

17. *Stenographisches Protokoll der Verhandlungen des XII Zionisten-Kongresses in Karlsbad vom 1 bis 14 September 1921* (Berlin, 1922), p. 36.

18. Ibid., p. 37. The greeting was written in French but printed in German in the *Protokoll*. This version is translated from the German.

19. Slavinsky, "Znosyny z sionistamy."

20. Ibid.

21. N. Levin, "Jabotinsky and the Petliura Agreement," *Jewish Standard* (London), 16 August 1940.

22. Schechtman, "The Jabotinsky-Slavinsky Agreement," p. 289.

23. This book comments on those works of Jabotinsky that touch on the agreement with Slavinsky. There are also approximately twenty letters written by Jabotinsky in 1921–22, now held in the Jabotinsky Archives, that refer to the agreement. See also *Igerot Ze'ev Zhabotinski: reshima u-mafteakh* (Ze'ev Jabotinsky's Letters: Summaries and Index), 1 (Tel Aviv, 1972), which lists eleven letters on this subject (nos. 427, 432–34, 436–38, 440–41, 445, 457). Other letters pertaining to the agreement were discovered after the publication of that volume. Jabotinsky also referred to it in later works and letters.

24. Jabotinsky (New York) to I. Trivus, 9 February 1922, Jabotinsky Archives. In *Igerot Ze'ev Zhabotinski*, vol. 1, it is letter no. 441, p. 112.

25. The declaration "To the Population of Ukraine," 12 March 1921, signed by Petliura, is in the Archives of the Symon Petliura Library, Paris. The text, in Russian, is in A. Margolin, *Ukraina i politika Antanty* (Berlin, 1921), pp. 290–93; cf. Margolin, *Ukraine and Policy of the Entente*, pp. 208–10. A translation from Russian into Ukrainian is in Symon Petliura, *Statti, lysty, dokumenty* (New York, 1956–79), 1: 287–88.

26. Margolin, *Ukraine and Policy of the Entente*, pp. 201, 224–25, passim; S. Goldelman, *Lysty zhydivs'koho sotsiial-demokrata pro Ukraïnu*, pp. 8, 54–55, passim; idem, *Jewish National Autonomy in Ukraine*, p. 116, passim; Committee of the Jewish Delegations, *The Pogroms in the Ukraine under the Ukrainian Governments (1917–1920)* (London, 1927), pp. 96–102.

27. Petliura, *Statti, lysty, dokumenty*, 1: 453.

28. *The Pogroms in the Ukraine under the Ukrainian Governments*, pp. 98–102.

29. Levin notes this break, which is not mentioned in Slavinsky's "Report." Levin writes that his article was based on a private discussion between Jabotinsky, a few friends, and Levin himself. Joseph Schechtman confirms that Levin's notes were checked and approved by Jabotinsky. Schechtman, "The Jabotinsky-Slavinsky Agreement," p. 291.

30. John Henry Patterson (1867–1947), English officer and friend of Jabotinsky. He commanded the Jewish units of the British army, and throughout his life had the deepest sympathy for the Zionist movement. He wrote several books on the events in Palestine and the Jewish units of the British army. In *Slovo o polku* (Paris, 1928), Jabotinsky referred to him as "one of the most wonderful Christian people who ever came across our path in all the centuries of dispersal" (p. 24).

31. Levin, "Jabotinsky and the Petliura Agreement." Andrii Nikovsky (1885–1942), Ukrainian social and political leader, literary scholar, and journalist. He was known for his sympathy toward Jewry. From 1920 he was minister of foreign affairs in the UNR government-in-exile. In 1924 he returned to the Soviet Union. A few years later he was arrested and died in prison.

32. Ibid.

33. Slavinsky, "Znosyny z sionistamy."

34. Ibid.

35. Schechtman, "The Jabotinsky-Slavinsky Agreement," p. 290.

36. Levin, "Jabotinsky and the Petliura Agreement."

37. *Jüdische Rundschau* (Berlin), 23 December 1921.

38. Vladimir Temkin (1861–1927), Zionist leader of Ukrainian origin; leader of the Zionist movement in the Russian Empire. From 1920 he lived in Paris. He was a member of the editorial board of *Rassvet* and first president of the World Zionist Revisionist Organization.

39. V. Jabotinsky, *The Story of the Jewish Legion* (New York, 1945), p. 46.

40. Ibid., p. 40.

41. Schechtman, "The Jabotinsky-Slavinsky Agreement," p. 289.

42. Jabotinsky to the Executive of the World Zionist Organization, 19 October 1921, 20 November 1921, and 3 December 1921. In another interesting letter of 9 February 1922, Jabotinsky clearly explained that he was concerned with the organization of Jewish self-defense, and a Jewish gendarmerie was, from his point of view, a way to organize such self-defense.

43. Max Nordau (1849–1923), Zionist leader born in Hungary. He was an eminent leader and ideologue of political Zionism and author of many political and literary works. During the last years of his life, however, he was in opposition to the leadership of the World Zionist Organization.

44. Jabotinsky, *Story of the Jewish Legion*, p. 32.

45. M. Buber, "The Pressing Demand of the Hour (On Leo Pinsker and Theodore Herzl" in *On Zion: The History of an Idea*, trans. Stanley Godman (New York, 1973), p. 123. In the German original this is particularly colorful: "Trotz ihrer politischen Ausrüstung hat die moderne zionistische Bewegung zu wenig 'Welt,' zu wenig Gefühl von Welt und Weltgeschichte auf ihren Weg mitbekommen." M. Buber, "Die drängende Stunde (über Leo Pinsker und Theodor Herzl)," in M. Buber, *Israel und Palästina* (Zurich, 1950), p. 156.

46. *Jüdische Rundschau*, 23 December 1921. From 1902 to 1938 the newspaper was the organ of the Zionist Organization of Germany.

47. It is interesting that the Bolsheviks had a better understanding of the Jabotinsky-Slavinsky agreement than did many Jewish circles. In the first edition of *Bol'shaia sovetskaia èntsiklopediia*, vol. 24 (Moscow, 1932): 600, it is explained that

Jabotinsky made an agreement with Petliura on the organization of Jewish self-defense.

48. Yitzhak Rabinovich, "Heskem Zhabotinski-Slavinski bifnei mishpat ha-bolshevikim" (The Jabotinsky-Slavinsky Agreement on Trial by the Bolsheviks), *Ha-olam* (London), 5 August 1943.

49. Jabotinsky, *Story of the Jewish Legion*, p. 68ff.

50. *Rassvet* (Berlin) 41, no. 4 (28 January 1923): 15, interview with Jabotinsky. See also Schechtman, "The Jabotinsky-Slavinsky Agreement," pp. 298–99.

51. Schechtman, "The Jabotinsky-Slavinsky Agreement," pp. 294–95.

52. David Ben-Gurion, *Chaluzischer Zionismus oder Revisionismus* (Berlin, 1934), p. 79. The Hebrew word *chaluz* means "pioneer."

    David Ben-Gurion (1886–1973), Jewish political leader and first prime minister of Israel. He was a leader of the Palestinian workers' movement for many years, although his political views were more right-wing than those of most other prominent Zionist socialists. He was a consistent opponent of Jabotinsky and the Zionist Revisionist movement, although in practice he often adopted the ideas and methods of the Revisionists. He played a major role in the creation of the Jewish state.

53. "Interv'iu s Israėlem Ėl'dadom," *22* (Tel Aviv) (December 1980): 121.

54. Jabotinsky (New York) to I. Makhover, 9 March 1922 (letter no. 457, p. 117 in *Igerot Ze'ev Zhabotinski*).

55. Jabotinsky (New York) to I. Makhover, 18 December 1921 (letter no. 436, p. 110 in *Igerot Ze'ev Zhabotinski*).

56. Numerous facts pertaining to both aspects of the problem are to be found in Cherikover, *Antisemitizm i pogromy na Ukraine*, as well as in the works by Margolin and Goldelman cited above.

57. Cherikover, *Antisemitizm i pogromy na Ukraine*, pp. 74–78; *Mysl'*, 28 February 1918; *Evreiskoe slovo*, 11 (24) February 1918; and *Rassvet*, no. 5 (11 [24] February 1918).

58. M. G. Rafes, *Oifn shvel fun der kontrrevoliutsie* (On the Threshold of Counterrevolution), (Kyiv, 1918), p. 93.

59. Margolin, *Ukraina i politika Antanty* (Berlin, 1921), pp. 391–92. Cf. English translation in Margolin, *Ukraine and Policy of the Entente*, pp. 160–61.

60. A detailed description of the pogrom in Proskuriv and a series of documents pertaining to it are to be found in *The Pogroms in the Ukraine under the Ukrainian Governments*, pp. 58–61, 176–91. See also "Proskurov," *Encyclopedia Judaica*, 13: 1194–95.

61. Iust (pseud. V. Jabotinsky), "K istorii proskurovskovo pogroma," *Rassvet* (Paris, 29 May 1927): 11–12.

62. V. Zhabotinskii, "Petliura i pogromy (Pis'mo v redaktsiiu)," *Poslednie novosti* (Paris, 11 October 1927).

63. *Encyclopedia of Ukraine*, 5: 700–701; *Entsyklopediia ukraïnoznavstva*, part 1, 3: 828–30.

64. Jabotinsky (New York) to I. Trivus, 9 February 1922. Jabotinsky Archive (letter no. 112 in *Igerot Ze'ev Zhabotinski*).

    Maksym Zalizniak was one of the leaders of the *koliïvshchyna*. For details, see the introduction to the present work.

65. Jabotinsky (New York) to I. Makhover, 12 February 1922 (letter no. 113 in *Igerot Ze'ev Zhabotinski*).

66. Schechtman, "The Jabotinsky-Slavinsky Agreement," p. 305.

67. V. Zhabotinskii, "Vopros o Petliure," *Rassvet* (Paris, 8 March 1925): 5–6. In this article Jabotinsky stated that the Jewish gendarmerie would be financed by Jews, but did not add that once military action began, financing would be assumed by the government of the UNR.

68. Ibid., p. 5.

69. "Interv'iu s Israėlem Ėl'dadom," pp. 115–16.

70. Levin, "Jabotinsky and the Petliura Agreement."

CHAPTER 4

# Jabotinsky and the Schwartzbard Trial: Pogrom Trauma and a Voice of Moderation

On 25 May 1926, on the rue Racine in Paris, seven shots rang out. Shalom Schwartzbard, a Jew, had assassinated Symon Petliura.[1] This was the opening scene of the next act in the Jewish-Ukrainian tragedy, an act during which anti-Ukrainian sentiments at times reached virtual hysteria, and cooperation and mutual understanding between Jewish and Ukrainian national-liberation forces were cast aside for many years. The prologue to the scene had been short but very eventful.

After the Winter (or Ice) March of 1921 the Bolshevik government in Moscow and the Ukrainian Bolshevik government in Kharkiv applied strong diplomatic pressure on the Polish government to make the Poles legally ban Petliura and his government from Polish territory. At the end of 1923, following an attempt on his life by the Soviet secret service, Petliura left Poland. He spent some time in Hungary and Switzerland, then settled in Paris in the autumn of 1924.[2] In early 1925 he founded the journal *Tryzub* (The Trident), which often found itself polemicizing with the Russian journal *Rassvet* (Dawn), headed by Jabotinsky, who was also in Paris at that time.

This was not the first parallel experience for Jabotinsky and Petliura. One had taken place at the beginning of the century, when they had fought along parallel lines against the Black Hundreds and reaction, sometimes even cooperating on the same journals. Another had occurred when Jabotinsky made his agreement with the UNR government in 1921. Later, Jabotinsky and Petliura moved to live permanently in Paris at more or less the same time and headed two nationalist journals there, one Jewish, the other Ukrainian. (Petliura was not formally the editor of *Tryzub*, but he was undeniably its ideological leader and driving force.)

In January 1923, Jabotinsky had left the World Zionist Organization. His resignation was largely precipitated by the poisonous atmosphere created by his opponents following the agreement with Slavinsky.[3] In October 1924 he began building the organization of Zionist Revisionists, whose first conference took place in Paris in April 1925.[4] *Rassvet*, which had been published in St. Petersburg until 1918 and had then moved to Berlin, began to appear in Paris under Jabotinsky's editorship as the organ of the new organization that united Zionists opposed to the political direction of the World Zionist Organization.

Although "a black cat crossed the path" of the Jewish and Ukrainian national movements after the pogroms in Ukraine, and many important figures in various Jewish circles and organizations spoke out against all contacts with Ukrainian national circles, there were still some remnants of the former understanding and sympathy. For example, two Jewish supporters of Ukrainian independence, Arnold Margolin and Solomon Goldelman, wanted close contacts to be maintained with Ukrainian émigré political and academic circles and made great efforts to repair the extremely strained relations between the two peoples and their national movements.

Joseph Schechtman, earlier an enthusiastic supporter of the Ukrainian cause and Ukrainian-Jewish cooperation, became one of the most active editors and authors at *Rassvet*. He denounced pogromists in the journal's pages, but always simultaneously stressed that Jews should not confuse pogromists with fighters for the Ukrainian national cause. He emphasized that the idealistic goals of the Ukrainian national-liberation movement—the attainment of freedom and the untrammeled cultural and national development of the Ukrainian people—remained understandable and dear to the Jewish national movement. That this attitude was still, to some extent, present among the Jewish masses was shown by a meeting of Jewish workers in New York. It was held after Petliura's assassination and tended, on the whole, to support Schwartzbard. According to *Rassvet*, the meeting passed a resolution that: "...despite all the violence that the dark Ukrainian masses have inflicted upon innocent Jewish women and children, the participants at this meeting do not condemn the Ukrainian people as a whole. We continue to sympathize with its struggle for an independent national existence."[5]

However, against this background of basic sympathy for the Ukrainian national movement, uncontrollable and very powerful feelings of anger and hatred toward pogromists emerged and grew steadily stronger, especially during the Schwartzbard trial. Fanned by the propaganda campaign that swirled around the trial, such feelings destroyed the seedlings of political wisdom within the Jewish masses in a general conflagration of fury that very easily allowed popular consciousness to place an equal sign between such words as pogromist and Ukrainian. At the trial Petliura's assassin, Shalom Schwartzbard, and his defenders worked out a line of defense whose main theme was to blame Petliura for the pogroms. In that version of the story, Schwartzbard's action was provoked exclusively by his desire to avenge the pogroms in Ukraine. The Jewish press, and much of the non-Jewish press in Western countries as well (especially the left-wing press), fully supported Schwartzbard's line of defense.

The huge explosions of emotion thereby produced among Jews throughout the world were so powerful and unanimous that Jewish political circles of all persuasions quickly realized there was no point in trying to contest that phenomenon. In the popular imagination the small, pitiful figure of Schwartzbard attained the proportions of a legendary folk hero, and in such circumstances any Jewish political leader who dared to oppose Schwartzbard would immediately have been banished from Jewish political life. The reasons for the emergence of that phenomenon are clear enough. They were specified in the resolution at the above-mentioned New York Jewish workers' meeting: "Without wishing to prejudge the Paris court's ruling on Petliura's role in the Jewish pogroms in Ukraine, we state that we view Schwartzbard's action as a protest against that silence with which the whole world responded to our overwhelming, excruciating misfortune...."[6] The laconic phrases of this very characteristic quotation offer a thorough explanation of the extremely emotional Jewish reaction to the Schwartzbard affair and of the attitude of Jews to the assassin's trial.

Jews did not view Schwartzbard's trial as a judicial investigation meant to punish an assassin. Rather, they saw it as a trial of all the enemies and persecutors who were ranged against the Jewish people, symbolized by the figure of Petliura. In the imagination of Jews, this was a trial of Petliura. By reversing the case in that way, Schwartzbard's defense gained a brilliant psychological victory that led to the assassin's acquittal.

The resolution of the New York meeting underlined another source of the Jewish reaction to the Schwartzbard trial: the intolerable spiritual anguish left by the pogroms, which grew more intense as Jews observed the rest of the world's apparent lack of interest in their national tragedy. In the Jewish tradition, human life has a supreme, uniquely high value. When this is linked with the Jews' very strong family ties, it means that the death of people who are close inflicts a terrible, irremediable wound. If the Jewish soul did not demand revenge, it required at least symbolic compensation for the injustice that had been meted out to the nation. That compensation took the form of the assassination of Petliura, who was, in those circumstances, easily transformed in the national consciousness into the villain in the Jewish tragedy. In actual fact, he was its scapegoat.

If someone were seeking the best means to exacerbate Jewish-Ukrainian enmity and compromise the Ukrainian national movement, then no step could have been more subtle and cunning in its psychological calculation than the assassination of Petliura by a Jew. That very point struck Ukrainian émigré political circles and the Ukrainian press, hence from the day of the assassination until the end of the Schwartzbard trial they blamed Soviet agents for plotting the murder. By contrast, the Jewish press throughout the world campaigned with enormous vigor in Schwartzbard's defense from the day of the assassination, 25 May 1926, until sentence was pronounced on 26 October 1927. Jabotinsky's journal, *Rassvet*, participated in that campaign, but consistently emphasized that pogromists should not be equated with the Ukrainian national movement. In "Our Court Action," Joseph Schechtman comprehensively expressed the journal's position:

> It is clear to everyone that what is being talked about is not Schwartzbard and his action, and that we are defending not Schwartzbard but ourselves, the blood

> of those who perished, and justice and honor for the living. When the defense demands Schwartzbard's complete acquittal, it is not a matter of saving him from responsibility or punishment, but of establishing the guilt of others: those who murdered, or allowed the murder, not of one person, but many, many thousands of defenseless and innocent Jewish citizens of Ukraine.[7]

Schechtman went on to stress that responsibility for pogroms must lie not only with the pogromists among the Ukrainian forces, but also with "White" pogromists (Russian Monarchist forces) and "Red" pogromists (Bolsheviks). He stated that it was mere accident that Petliura happened to be the first to be called to account by fate.

The Ukrainian press, and *Tryzub* in particular, expressed the conviction that the assassination of Petliura was no accident at all. Ukrainian periodicals, indicating openly that in their opinion Moscow was the culprit in that assassination, offered fairly credible conjectures and some interesting evidence. The French court ignored that evidence, shirking its duty to note such facts as the constant meetings between Schwartzbard and a Soviet agent, Mikhail Volodin; proof that Schwartzbard and Volodin had followed Petliura; information sent by pneumatic post indicating that Schwartzbard had accomplices; and, finally, some discrepancies in Schwartzbard's testimony.[8] However, all these surmises remain, to this day, nothing more than that, since no criminological or academic historical investigation of an impartial and comprehensive character has yet been carried out. Although it is not possible to state categorically that Schwartzbard was acting as a Soviet agent, there are serious grounds for suspicion. If one applies the principle of "cui bono?" (for whose benefit?), then Moscow was undoubtedly the exclusive beneficiary of Petliura's assassination, of the compromising of the Ukrainian movement, and of the kindling of Jewish-Ukrainian hostility.

Schechtman's article ended with words that sounded utterly sincere, although they included advice to the Ukrainian movement that was, and still remains, completely unacceptable to it. That conclusion is sufficiently interesting and characteristic to be worth quoting in full:

> We wish to establish the truth at Schwartzbard's trial. That alone. An immense gulf separates us from the desire that the Ukrainian press demagogically accuses us of possessing, namely, "to put the entire Ukrainian people in the dock and to discredit the entire Ukrainian movement through the person of its national hero, Petliura." We maintain a better opinion of Ukrainianism than those of its defenders who are full of zeal, but not wisdom. We do not equate the Ukrainian people with pogromists and we continue to be sincere and faithful friends of the Ukrainian national renaissance.
>
> Precisely for that reason, we want to establish the truth of the terrible and shameful "pogrom affair," giving everyone his due, separating the wheat from the chaff. If a person who has worked with the Ukrainian national movement

> over the years and has been a member of the Central and Small Radas may be permitted to offer some unsolicited, disinterested advice to the Ukrainian leaders, then that advice would be the following: do not identify Petliura and those surrounding him with the entire Ukrainian cause. Their hands are stained with innocent blood, while a pure cause must be led by those with clean hands. Petliura and all those who created the vile affair of the pogroms and tolerated the pogroms are not the sum total of Ukrainianism. They have been forsaken long ago not only by us but also by many of the best Ukrainian leaders. By exposing those pogrom heroes to pillory, we Jews are not breaking contact with national Ukrainianism. We still have a great distance to travel alongside the Ukrainian people, so we must clear away the fog of bloody pogroms that blinds us to mutual understanding. Let the trial of Schwartzbard become that purifying storm after which the turbid legacy of the pogrom years will recede. You must understand this: do not allow yourselves to become the captives of a misconceived national pride. Join us in the search for truth—the whole truth. The rest will take care of itself.[9]

Thus, the circles close to Jabotinsky sincerely believed that the Jewish and Ukrainian national movements should continue to cooperate, that Jews "still have a great distance to travel alongside the Ukrainian people," and that the Schwartzbard trial was to be only a brief episode, a "purifying storm" that would, in the end, ameliorate Jewish-Ukrainian relations. *Rassvet* reiterated in many different ways the need to maintain friendship and cooperation between the national movements of both peoples. It emphasized that "the two peoples will still have to live together and build together"; that "none of the Jews intends to, or wishes to, dishonor the Ukrainian national idea as such."[10]

Despite the good intentions that undoubtedly guided Schechtman and *Rassvet*, his article and the whole polemic of the Jewish side in this affair were far from realistic. In the first place, it was totally unrealistic to advise Ukrainian national circles to repudiate Petliura and to condemn him as one who tolerated pogroms. For Ukrainian national forces, Petliura was, and remains, a symbol of their entire cause, of all their aspirations. His name resounded, and still resounds, as a synonym for Ukrainian independence, just as the name of Garibaldi does for Italians. (During and after the trial, the Ukrainian press frequently compared Petliura with Garibaldi.) Among Ukrainian national leaders, Petliura had the reputation of an inveterate Semitophile, and his attempts to combat pogroms, his anti-pogrom proclamations and orders, were well known to them.[11] Even if Petliura, finding himself in great difficulty and lacking the means to combat those *otamans* who were formally subordinate to him, but were in fact independent, had to turn a blind eye to their pogromist anti-Semitism (such a view was shared by many Jews, although it cannot be considered proven), Ukrainians were aware of those constraints on his conduct and were in no way prepared to find him guilty.

Equally unrealistic was the statement that the Jews did not wish "to put the entire Ukrainian people in the dock and to discredit the entire Ukrainian movement." There is no doubt that Jabotinsky's circles and *Rassvet* truly did not wish to do so, but there were also influential Jewish and non-Jewish forces that did indeed harbor such intentions. The whole furious propaganda campaign surrounding the Schwartzbard trial was patently designed to compromise the Ukrainian national movement definitively. It suffices to examine the Jewish (and some non-Jewish) newspapers of that time to become fully convinced of this. Soviet propaganda took the lead against the "Petliurites," and that was one of the rare occasions on which the tone and content of the Soviet and the Jewish press throughout the world were quite similar. Moreover, they either omitted altogether or made only passing reference to the Russian monarchist White Guards, the organizers and perpetrators of by far the most numerous and bloody pogroms in Ukraine. (We have already noted the consensus among researchers, including supporters of the Whites, that the most terrible pogroms were those carried out by the White Army). The Soviet predilection for "selective outrage" was clearly designed to discredit the Ukrainian movement, which, unlike Russian émigré circles, presented the gravest threat to the unity of the empire that had been reunited under the name of the USSR. Thus, if one were to surmise that the whole affair was inspired by Moscow, then Moscow's victory was total. It was the start of a process. At the beginning, calls for cooperation with Ukrainianism could still be heard; by the end, the characterizations of Petliura and the Ukrainian people in Friedman's book prevailed—"Jew-hating leader of a Jew-hating people," "architect of the pogroms," "like Adolf Eichmann."[12]

*Rassvet* differed from most of the Jewish press in consistently stating that Petliura was neither the organizer nor the inspirer of pogroms. His guilt lay only in tolerating them, that is, he lacked the desire or the courage to protest against the wave of pogroms with the full weight of his authority. (Many authors at various times have offered evidence both for and against that thesis, but the purpose of the present work is not to prove Petliura's guilt or innocence. That problem still awaits research.) During the first days of the court hearing, *Rassvet* once again expressed that idea: "We view the sin of Petliura and of his loyal comrades as just that—a sin of great indulgence, but we do not believe that the leading stratum of the Ukrainian national intelligentsia wants pogroms, and we do not identify the Ukrainian movement with the thirst for pogroms. We continue to extend a hand, if it is needed and requested, to all that is honest in the Ukrainian movement."[13] That passage appeared in an editorial published in the column "Dnevnik" (Diary). It also contained a warning by *Rassvet* that could have been called prophetic if the sad consequences of the Schwartzbard case had not been obvious from the very start: "We will deeply regret it if our fears are justified and an acquittal verdict causes Jewry to fall out for a long time with the best elements of the Ukrainian movement. We would hope that this will not happen."[14]

Elsewhere the journal expressed certainty that the assassination of Petliura and the trial of Schwartzbard would soon recede into the past and fall into oblivion without damaging Ukrainian-Jewish relations: "When a short time has passed, passions will cool, and it will then turn out that there is no argument between the two peoples or their national movements."[15] Here the journal was expressing its fervent desire that the trial produce no sharp deterioration in relations between the two peoples. As subsequent developments showed, the hope expressed by the journal's editorial writer was not fulfilled.

Although Jabotinsky's journal followed the example of the entire Jewish press and defended Schwartzbard, it also voiced the totally original idea, which differed fundamentally from the line taken by most Jewish periodicals, that Schwartzbard's choice of action ran counter to Jewish tradition, which rejected assassination: "That is not the Jewish way, and let it be closed forever."[16] Here *Rassvet* stressed that Schwartzbard was not, and could not be, a national hero of any kind because of the nature of his action; he was instead a "colorless figure" who should be "placed in the hands of God and forgotten."[17] That advice was not followed, and Schwartzbard was soon recognized semi-officially as a national hero. His remains were transferred to Israel after his death.[18]

*Rassvet*'s entire stance during Schwartzbard's investigation and trial indicated an effort to calm passions and to limit, in any way that it could, the damage to relations between the two peoples. However, the journal was not able to jeopardize its standing within the Jewish community to such an extent as to come out completely openly against Schwartzbard.

At the same time *Tryzub*, which Petliura had founded, took a position that was in some ways analogous to that of *Rassvet*. True, in common with the rest of the Ukrainian émigré press and in contrast with the Jewish press, it demanded Schwartzbard's conviction and resolutely denied Petliura's guilt, but both *Tryzub* and *Rassvet* continually stressed the need for Ukrainian-Jewish dialogue and declared that Schwartzbard's guilt should not be transferred to the whole Jewish people. In line with the rest of the Ukrainian press, *Tryzub* voiced the conviction that Petliura's assassination had been organized by Moscow.

The Ukrainian civic leader Levko Chykalenko, who was known for his pro-Jewish views, wrote in *Tryzub*:

> Ukrainian democratic circles have viewed the assassination of Chief Otaman S. Petliura by someone called Schwartzbard not as a Jewish act but as a Bolshevik act, directed against Ukrainian democracy in the person of the leader whom it produced in the armed struggle for Ukrainian statehood. We have judged the fact that Schwartzbard is a Jew to be a terrible provocation by the Soviet authorities.... The Soviet authorities currently in power have understood very well the complications of Jewish-Ukrainian relations. Being anti-Semitic in their essence, they chose such an assassin in order to divert the masses' hatred away from political struggle and revenge against themselves and toward national

> relations, complicated both by the historical past and by the recent practices of the autocratic Muscovite regime.[19]

Chykalenko also indicated that Ukrainian circles did include extremists of "the school of Krushevan and Semesenko" who were attempting to incite the Ukrainian people to anti-Semitism on the grounds that "the Jews assassinated Symon Petliura." He went on to say that Ukrainian and Jewish democrats should join forces to fight such tendencies, but instead the Jewish press was supporting Schwartzbard and portraying him as the expression of the entire Jewish nation's popular will, thus lending support to anti-Semitic efforts to spread the false version of events: "Our Black Hundred, Jew-fighting circles found unexpected and unlooked-for support for their statements from almost the entire Jewish press."[20] There was obviously a certain logic in that train of thought. In any case, those forces that tried to use the uproar surrounding the trial to intensify Jewish-Ukrainian hostilities achieved a degree of success that almost certainly surpassed their expectations.

Not only the Ukrainian press, but also the official leadership of all the major Ukrainian political parties in the emigration issued statements and appeals that blamed Moscow for Petliura's murder and called upon the Ukrainian people not to blame the Jews for it or to succumb to the influence of those seeking to inflame Ukrainian-Jewish hostilities. In the "Appeal to Peasants and Workers" issued by the Ukrainian Social Democratic Workers' Party, to which Petliura had belonged, that point was emphasized:

> By assassinating Petliura, Moscow's communist rulers are following in the footsteps of the accursed tsarist regime, which ruled by inciting one people against another, which organized the Jewish pogroms and the Armenian-Tatar massacre...
>
> Workers and peasants of Ukraine!
>
> Do not succumb to this provocation by the Moscow communists, who again wish to incite Jewish pogroms and the blood and conflagration of civil war in our land....[21]

This was the stance of the larger part of the Ukrainian emigration during the investigation and trial of Schwartzbard.

It is not difficult to see that this position was pro-Jewish and bore some resemblance to the stance of the Jewish press. The principal difference lay only in the attitude toward two figures: Symon Petliura, whom the Ukrainian press justified, while the Jewish press blamed him for tolerating the pogroms; and Shalom Schwartzbard, whom the Ukrainian press saw as guilty, while the Jewish press justified him. In the opinion of the political groupings around the journals *Rassvet* and *Tryzub*, this contrasting attitude toward the two protagonists was not to be permitted to cloud a principled mutual understanding between the Jewish and Ukrainian national movements, based on the fundamental interests of each of them. As Chykalenko wrote, "...the knot in Jewish-Ukrainian relations that is being criminally tightened on both sides is equally terrible for us [both national movements]."[22]

Did the stance of *Rassvet*, whose ideological leader, director, and editor-in-chief at that time was Jabotinsky, fully reflect Jabotinsky's own reaction to Petliura's assassination? All the quotations from the journal given above were written not by Jabotinsky but by his co-workers. A more detailed analysis of the materials of that time indicates that, paradoxically, Jabotinsky's personal position differed significantly from the opinions of Schechtman and others on the journal who were constantly commenting on the Schwartzbard case. For more than a year—from 25 May 1926, when Petliura was assassinated, until 5 June 1927, when *Rassvet* published "French Anti-Semites and the Schwartzbard Case"[23]—the journal did not publish a single article relating to the case signed by Jabotinsky or appearing under one of his pseudonyms. What prevented Jabotinsky from expressing his views in his own journal? After all, he usually responded immediately to all the problems agitating Jewry, even those far less sensational and painful than the Schwartzbard case. The only possible answer is that his position was not fully in accord with the views of the other members of the journal's editorial board. Two facts support this. In the first place, a few days after Petliura's death, Jabotinsky expressed his views on Petliura and the leadership of the Ukrainian national movement, not in *Rassvet* but in the American-Jewish periodical *Der Morgen Zhornal* (The Jewish Morning Journal), and they were substantially different from what appeared in *Rassvet*.[24] In the second place, articles by Jabotinsky published in *Rassvet* beginning in June 1927 ("French Anti-Semites and the Schwartzbard Case," "H. Torrès," and "V. E. Jabotinsky on the Torrès Interview") touched on the Schwartzbard case but carefully omitted any reference to Petliura.

The views that Jabotinsky advanced on Petliura and the Ukrainian national movement in *Der Morgen Zhornal* are of fundamental importance and deserve to be examined in somewhat more detail. They were expressed in an article devoted to an entirely different matter—the urgent, topical question of Jewish colonization in Ukraine and the Crimea. Both before and after Petliura's death, Jabotinsky, *Rassvet*, and the entire Ukrainian press held similar views on that issue, contrary to the views of a significant section of the Jewish press throughout the world. It is symptomatic and noteworthy that Jabotinsky's views on the question coincided with those of Ukrainian émigré circles and not with the position of the majority of the Jewish press.

It is thus necessary to move some distance away from the Schwartzbard case and turn to another question on which Jabotinsky's views were similar to those of Ukrainian national circles, and in connection with which he expressed his opinion of Petliura and other leaders of the Ukrainian national movement. After the Bolshevik victory in most of the territory of the former tsarist empire (apart from Poland, Finland, and the three small Baltic republics of Estonia, Latvia, and Lithuania, which gained independence from Moscow), there began the persecution of the Zionist movement.[25] The foundations for that process were laid in typical Bolshevik spirit on 1 September 1919, when a group of agents from the Bolshevik political police, the Cheka, stormed and plundered the headquarters of the Central Committee of the Zionist Organization in Petrograd. The newspaper *Khronika evreiskoi zhizni* (Chronicle of Jewish Life) was simultaneously closed down and many Zionists in Petrograd, Moscow, Vitsebsk, Saratov, and other cities were arrested.[26] However, Zionism's great popularity among the Jewish masses and the Bolsheviks' policy of flirting to some extent with the Jews, as they did during the civil war and up to the early 1930s, obliged the authorities to apply a tactic of carrot and stick: crushing the Zionist movement and destroying Zionist organizations on the one hand while pretending solicitude for the interests of the Jewish people on the other.

In order to turn Jews away from Zionism while simultaneously making a propagandistic impact on world Jewry and attracting Jewish capital from abroad, a project was worked out in the USSR in 1924 for Jewish agricultural colonization in southern Ukraine and the Crimea. In January 1925 the Bolshevik government in Moscow formed a special organization to "regulate the distribution of land for toiling Jews in the USSR" that was known by its Yiddish abbreviation, Gezard, and its Russian abbreviation, OZET.[27] In addition, there were so-called Jewish sections (Evsektsii), constituting a network of communist groups that the authorities created to work among the Jewish population. Leaders of the Jewish section were coopted onto the leadership of OZET, as were a few non-Jewish Bolshevik leaders, including the director of the All-Union Central Executive Committee (VTsIK in Russian), Mikhail Kalinin. As director of VTsIK, Kalinin was the nominal president of the Soviet state. The People's Commissar for Foreign Affairs, Georgii Chicherin—who, as we have seen, had organized hooligans in London to interfere with Jabotinsky's formation of the Jewish Legion—was also coopted onto OZET's leadership.

Also in 1925, during a stay in Berlin, Chicherin received a delegation of Jewish leaders from abroad, led by Albert Einstein. The delegation asked that the persecution of Zionists in the USSR be halted, but Chicherin replied that he was not aware of any persecution,[28] although this was shortly after more than 3,000 Zionists had been arrested on 2 September 1924 in 150 different locations within the USSR. The persecution and arrests continued throughout 1925 and did not stop thereafter. It is completely impossible that Chicherin, a prominent member of the Soviet government and a member of the Central Committee of the All-Union Communist Party, knew nothing of this. Moreover, since the persecution of Zionists entailed international repercussions, the action could not have been approved without the participation of the People's Commissar for Foreign Affairs. Against such a background, Chicherin entered the leadership of OZET in order to "concern himself with the distribution of land for toiling Jews," and the USSR's entire propaganda machine started noisily promoting the plan to settle Jews on land in southern Ukraine and in the Crimea.

The propaganda campaign was successful. Large Jewish organizations, Joint and Agro-Joint, paid out sizeable sums of money to assist Jewish colonizers in the USSR.[29] Thus the attention of the Jewish public abroad was largely distracted from the persecution of Zionists in the communist state; the USSR's prestige in the world was raised; and the Bolsheviks gained many supporters within the Jewish community abroad. At the same time, a significant section of the Jewish masses within the USSR turned their thoughts away from Palestine and toward Soviet Jewish agricultural communes. OZET kept publishing batches of brochures with large print runs in Yiddish and Russian that were designed to appeal to the widest readership. They promoted the advantages of Jewish colonization in Ukraine and in the Crimea, and later in Birobidzhan in the Far East.[30] Indeed, the openly anti-Zionist slant of those brochures indicates the true purpose of the whole campaign. Jewish colonization in Ukraine and in the Crimea provoked dissatisfaction among the local peasants, who were then facing a very difficult economic situation. They suffered from a scarcity of land, livestock, and agricultural equipment, so they naturally watched with anger while land, livestock, and equipment were handed over to Jewish settlers who had never previously had anything to do with agricultural work.

Jabotinsky and his supporters, along with some other Zionist circles, followed the campaign to establish Jews on land in the USSR with great anxiety. The growth of anti-Semitism among the local population as a result of the campaign could ultimately have had fatal consequences for Jewry in Ukraine. Jabotinsky could not remain indifferent to that, nor to the obvious anti-Zionist tendency of the campaign. The Ukrainian émigré press also opposed Jewish colonization in Ukraine for similar reasons. Jabotinsky put forward his detailed analysis of the colonization plan, along with his objections to it, in "The 'Crimean' Colonization." He depicted the short-term danger represented by the Soviet rulers' colonization plan in the words of a "letter from one of his friends":

> For the Ukrainian peasantry this whole business appears to be some wild provocation. Not only is their own principle of landownership violated, but every detail of the actual procedure is a new blow to their hearts. Imagine the psychology of a peasant from Kherson today who is not even able to cultivate his own *desiatyna* [2.7 acres] as he had done under Nicholas II, because he cannot repair his broken plough, he cannot buy livestock, etc.; and then he suddenly sees a freight car at the railway station containing a couple of steel ploughs, or a truck with heads of strong oxen sticking out of it, and he asks: who is to get all this? He receives the reply: Jewish colonizers whom the

> government wants to settle on our land. I have never in my life seen anything so well calculated to awaken hatred as this procedure.[31]

The editorial board at *Tryzub* was so enthusiastic about this article of Jabotinsky's that they published it without cuts, despite the difficulties that the journal's contributors must have had in translating it from the Yiddish. At the same time, in an editorial comment on the article, *Tryzub*'s editors pointed out that Jabotinsky's personal views on the Ukrainian question did not always coincide with those put forward by his journal.[32] Arnold Margolin, among others, also expressed anxiety about the possibly dangerous consequences of the colonization plan in the USSR, and *Tryzub* published a translation of his article as well.[33] Thus, on the issue of Jewish colonization in Ukraine and in the Crimea, there was complete agreement among Jabotinsky, some Jewish leaders in Ukraine, *Tryzub*, and a majority of the Ukrainian emigration.

Jabotinsky's "The 'Crimean' Colonization" also presented his view of Petliura and other leaders of the Ukrainian national movement, although that issue bore no strict relationship to the rest of the text. The only justification for such a digression could have been that the article was written immediately after Petliura's death and published on 4 June, ten days after the assassination. One paragraph has been quoted and commented upon dozens of times both by Jabotinsky's supporters and by his opponents:

> I never met Petliura. My negotiations of 1921 were conducted not with him but with Slavinsky, his representative in Prague. On this occasion I would like to state briefly but clearly that even today I stand firmly by the essence of my agreement with Slavinsky, and I consider that the only way to decrease the danger of pogroms during an anti-communist invasion of Russia is by forming a neutral Jewish gendarmerie, but that is not relevant to the present article. What is relevant is the fact that neither Petliura nor Vynnychenko nor the other prominent members of that Ukrainian government were ever what one could call pogromists. Although I did not know them personally, I am nevertheless well acquainted with that type of Ukrainian intellectual nationalist holding socialist views. I grew up with them and conducted a joint struggle with them against anti-Semites and Russifiers, both Jewish and Ukrainian. Neither I nor other thinking Zionists from southern Russia can be convinced that people of that type can be considered anti-Semites. This is important, because it leads us to the main point, a profound truth that we forget at our peril: that the cause lies not in the subjective anti-Semitism of individuals, but in the objective "anti-Semitism of circumstances."[34]

Jabotinsky's characterization of the leaders of the Ukrainian national movement corresponded, of course, to his experience of cooperation with them gained up to 1915 on the territory of the Russian Empire and to his later contacts with them, in particular with Slavinsky. Jabotinsky thus categorically stated here that the leaders of the national-liberation circles, including Petliura, could not be charged either with anti-Semitism or with organizing pogroms. Jabotinsky considered that pogroms occurred not because of the anti-Semitism of individuals but because of the "anti-Semitism of circumstances." This concept of the "anti-Semitism of circumstances" was one of his most fundamental ideas.[35] If formulated briefly, it comes down to the idea that anti-Semitism arises throughout the historical process as a result of many factors, but essentially because of the Jews' unequal legal status in the countries of the Diaspora. This forced Jews to fulfill auxiliary or intermediary roles in society, that is, to serve the interests of certain social strata or classes, playing a role that placed them "between the hammer and the anvil." Jabotinsky considered that the way out of this situation was, in the first place, to create a Jewish state, and in the second place, to work out a proper and balanced national policy. Thus he often repeated the phrase about the "anti-Semitism of circumstances" within a complex of arguments designed to prove the need for a new national policy and the futility of blaming individuals or even whole nations.

Jabotinsky's article described the "objective circumstances" in Ukraine:

> In Ukraine, circumstances are against us. They were formed historically and will remain as they are. It is futile to search for who was responsible for that in the seventeenth century—whether it was we Jews, the Poles or the Ukrainians. If we face the situation as it is today, we find anti-Semitic poison being carried in the wind there, and any disturbance, whether it be an uprising or colonization, would suffice to stir that atmosphere and make the poison spill over into active hatred.[36]

Although the words he used to describe the anti-Jewish circumstances in Ukraine are rather caustic, the Ukrainian emigration generally employed the same idea, expressed in milder terms, to oppose Jewish colonization. When *Tryzub* published its translation of "The 'Crimean' Colonization," it in no way distanced itself from that sharp characterization of the situation in Ukraine. *Tryzub*'s editorial comment noted that Jabotinsky "may well be the first person to approach the Ukrainian cause in the way that this cause demands."[37]

In fact, "The 'Crimean' Colonization" expressed Jabotinsky's own particular view that the Jews in Ukraine (as in every other country) had, in their own interests, to take into account the condition, peculiarities, and moods of the local population (even its prejudices and fantasies) in order to establish relations with it and to develop their local and general national policy on the basis of peace among nations. (This should not, of course, be taken to mean that Jews should approve of all the prejudices and fantasies of the non-Jewish population, but rather that they should take account of them, insofar as such fantasies actually exist, and show understanding and restraint in the face of them.) He considered the enthusiastic reception that many Jews, both within and outside the USSR, gave to the Bolshevik plan for Jewish colonization a gross error. This was an instance of Jews playing the role of tools of the policies of the Bolshevik rulers, policies that the Ukrainian peasants thought were directed against their interests. During the period 1903–14, Jabotinsky had opposed the use of Jews as tools of Russification in the non-Russian territories of the empire, hence in 1926 he maintained the same attitude toward Jewish colonization in Ukraine and in the Crimea.

Later events showed that the Soviet authorities had no intention of genuinely caring for the interests of the Jewish population in the USSR. The actual volume of Jewish colonization was far more modest than the volume of propaganda that surrounded it. Once it had achieved the desired propaganda effect, the Soviet government embarked upon another project for Jewish colonization in 1928, in Birobidzhan in the Far East, which was much less favorable to the Jews, but that project also was discontinued after several years. All that it produced was the formal announcement of a Jewish autonomous oblast centered on the town of Birobidzhan, where the Jewish population reached scarcely 30,000 when the project was "flourishing." Beginning in the 1950s the Jewish population there began decreasing sharply, falling to 8,887 by 1989 (4.15 percent of the oblast's population).[38] Despite the fact that many individuals truly devoted to the interests of the Jewish people took part in the campaign for Jewish agricultural colonization in the USSR, the Bolshevik authorities used the entire campaign to cover up the steady destruction of the Zionist movement, followed somewhat later by the complete destruction of Jewish culture in the USSR.[39] Today, the story of Jewish colonization in Ukraine and in the Crimea is almost forgotten, but what remains and still provokes discussion is Jabotinsky's view of Petliura and other leaders of the Ukrainian national movement as expressed in "The 'Crimean' Colonization."

Given the noisy and almost unanimous campaign in the Jewish press against Petliura and on behalf of Schwartzbard, it took extraordinary courage to express a view flatly contradicting the mainstream. As we have seen, Jabotinsky either did not wish or was not able to express that view in his own journal. It would seem probable that he did not want his journal, which represented the views of the Zionist-Revisionist movement, to bear responsibility for ideas that could provoke disapproval in diverse Jewish circles. He therefore took full responsibility upon himself. It is highly likely that Jabotinsky considered the campaign to inflame Ukrainian-Jewish enmity through the Schwartzbard trial sufficiently menacing for Jewry as a whole, and particularly for the 1.5 million Jews[40] who lived in Ukraine at that time, to exercise his authority, but only his own, not that of the Revisionist movement. There was an uproar in the press as a heavily traumatized Jewry poured forth its anguished feelings of burning injustice that had encountered the world's indifference. There also were the covert forces that were seeking political and propaganda effects favorable to them. Against such a background, there rang out the moderating voice of an individual who adhered to the truth and was guided by political and ethical impulses rather than emotional ones.

On the whole, the Jewish side reacted negatively to the characterization of Petliura and other leaders of the Ukrainian movement that Jabotinsky expressed. The Ukrainian émigré press, on the contrary, ardently welcomed that stand. Ukrainians and other supporters of the Ukrainian national movement such as Solomon Goldelman even expected Jabotinsky to make a statement about Petliura's innocence of the pogroms at Schwartzbard's trial—a statement similar to the one in "The 'Crimean' Colonization." Goldelman visited Jabotinsky in Paris and asked him to appear at the trial. Long afterwards, he described the meeting in a letter to his friend and biographer in the United States:

> Concerning my stay in Paris in 1926, you may add the following. I visited Vladimir Jabotinsky at his home and had a long talk about the trial. I wished to clarify whether he would appear as a witness once he was convinced that no involvement in the pogroms could be attributed to Petliura. He explained to me that to his great sorrow national ethical motives prevented him from flouting the Jewish community's clear will to gain the assassin's acquittal. As for myself, I let Ukrainian as well as Jewish leaders concerned with the affair know that I considered myself the only objective witness able to explain to the court that tragic tangle of events in Ukraine and the tragically impotent position of Petliura in that situation.[41]

Thus, Jabotinsky's explanation meant that he acknowledged his capitulation to Jewish public opinion, despite his disagreement with it. While Jabotinsky's surrender to public opinion was not total, it would seem undeniable that he was obliged to refrain from his usual aggressive posture and to operate with great caution. It would be easy to make that reflect unfavorably upon Jabotinsky, but one can understand the considerations that guided him. He was at the time the leader of the recently formed Zionist Revisionist movement. His political opponents were trying to isolate that movement from the Jewish masses by depicting it as extremist, "bourgeois," and directed against the workers. In other words, they sought to turn Revisionism into something odious to the broadest Jewish strata. In such conditions, any tactical error that Jabotinsky made would have been used to compromise the Revisionist movement. A stand against "the Jewish community's clear will" on such a sensitive issue as Petliura and the Schwartzbard trial would have given the opponents of Revisionism the weapon they needed to destroy utterly the credibility of both Revisionism and Jabotinsky. Those were more than likely the considerations that forced Jabotinsky to express his personal views in a periodical other than *Rassvet*, the official organ of the Revisionists. The same considerations prevented him from appearing at the trial as Goldelman had requested.

In a survey of the course of Jabotinsky's life, it is difficult to find even one other incident in which he stepped back in the face of hostile public opinion, the thinking of well-known authorities, or difficult circumstances. Chaim Weizmann underscored Jabotinsky's natural bent toward "working in an atmosphere where everyone is angry with him and no one can abide him."[42] Weizmann, who was not a supporter of Jabotinsky (although in some instances, notably during the formation of Jewish units in the British army, Weizmann supported him), may have expressed himself too harshly, but in essence he correctly characterized Jabotinsky's innate courage in swimming against the stream. In the specific instance of the Schwartzbard trial, however, the current turned out to be stronger than Jabotinsky, as he acknowledged quite frankly in his discussion with Goldelman.

During the twelve months after "The 'Crimean' Colonization," Jabotinsky did not broach the subject again. However, on 5 June 1927 *Rassvet* carried an article titled "French Anti-Semites and the Schwartzbard Case," signed by "Iust," one of Jabotinsky's pseudonyms. That article was directed against the owner of the newspaper *Le Figaro*, François Coty, who had published an article on the Schwartzbard trial in his paper that struck anti-Semitic notes. Iust used this as an opportunity to come out in support of Schwartzbard and to express the conviction that Petliura's assassination had been prompted solely by a desire to avenge the pogroms in Ukraine. At the same time he rejected the version of events advanced by Ukrainian émigrés, which implicated Soviet agents. Iust's article thus fully accorded with the spirit of the majority of the Jewish press. All this prompts profound amazement, for the article's tone, content, and language contrast starkly with the tone and content of "The 'Crimean' Colonization," and more generally with Jabotinsky's personal tone and style.

The phraseology in the "French Anti-Semites" article was utterly uncharacteristic of Jabotinsky. It mentioned, for example, that "a section of the French press has proclaimed a crusade against communism, ready to see a Bolshevik menace where it does not exist"; moreover, the author clearly condemned that "section." Such a stance is totally atypical of Jabotinsky, who never sympathized with communism. Indeed, shortly after the publication of the "French Anti-Semites" article, he wrote "H. Torrès," in which he warned of the existence of a certain danger connected with the Schwartzbard trial and provoked by the Bolsheviks and their French fellow travelers. Also surprising is the use of the stock Soviet propaganda phrase, "a crusade against communism." It appears to be the only example of a trite Soviet expression in any text that was ever published under Jabotinsky's name or under one of his pseudonyms. Also, though only in passing, the article made approving mention of Schwartzbard's lawyer, yet in "H. Torrès" Jabotinsky took a strongly negative attitude toward Torrès. "French Anti-Semites" also lacks Jabotinsky's characteristic and unique style, such as his typical phraseology, his stylistic methods, and his long sentences divided into sections by semi-colons. Anyone well acquainted with Jabotinsky's writings who reads the article gains the definite impression that this is not Jabotinsky. It is reasonable to assume that the article was not Jabotinsky's, but was published under the pseudonym of Iust for reasons unknown. Yet even that article, geared to supporting Schwartzbard at the trial, included no authorial condemnation of Petliura personally or of the Ukrainian national movement.

"H. Torrès" differs glaringly from "French Anti-Semites." The former appeared in *Rassvet* on 7 August 1927, two months after the latter's appearance, and was signed "V. Zhabotinsky."[43] It concerned Schwartzbard's defense lawyer at the trial, Henri Torrès. It is apparent even from the opening paragraph that Jabotinsky held an opinion of Petliura and the Schwartzbard trial that did not always coincide with the views of *Rassvet*. The article also indicated that he drew a conscious distinction between himself and the journal on the question and did not wish criticism directed at him to harm the journal and the Revisionist movement, whose mouthpiece it was:

> I am writing this note in my personal capacity, as the particular view of a private individual, and I am availing myself of *Rassvet*'s hospitality for that purpose only because *Rassvet* is a Jewish organ in the Russian language appearing in Paris, while the Schwartzbard case will be examined in Paris and pertains mainly to Russian Jewry.
>
> Writing thus in my personal and private capacity with a particular view for which no one save the undersigned is responsible, I consider it my responsibility to say that Mr. Torrès's participation in the Schwartzbard case in the role of lawyer for the defendant is undesirable and harmful to Mr. Schwartzbard and to Jewry as a whole.[44]

Jabotinsky was making an obvious effort to avoid ruining the journal's reputation by publishing his own personal view of the Schwartzbard trial in its pages, but why did Jabotinsky's article oppose Henri Torrès? Clearly, in writing about Torrès, Jabotinsky was putting his finger on one of the basic problems that stemmed from the ferment of diverse forces and interests surrounding the Schwartzbard trial. It was Henri Torrès who held the key to many of the circumstances surrounding the trial. Torrès, the lawyer Schwartzbard himself had chosen for his defense, was an outspoken communist and Sovietophile. Although he asserted that he had left the Communist Party,[45] his public speeches on various occasions were emphatically and even combatively pro-Soviet and pro-communist. Torrès's assistant, Lecache, was an open supporter of the Bolsheviks and made a trip to the USSR during the Schwartzbard investigative hearings. He collected material there on the pogroms and used it as the basis for a book that was soon translated into Russian in the USSR. Torrès himself visited the USSR during the investigation and also published a book in which he presented the history of the pogroms according to the accepted Soviet version of events.[46] The Soviet political police (then changing its name from the Cheka and Vecheka—the All-Russian Extraordinary Commission for Combating Counterrevolution and Sabotage—to the GPU or Main Political Administration) "helped" Torrès and

Lecache to collect information on the pogroms. It would have been quite easy to find many witnesses to the pogroms even without the GPU's assistance, but the GPU of course had enough witnesses willing to give the matter a slant convenient for Soviet policy, in other words, defaming Petliura and the entire Ukrainian national-liberation movement.

The Soviet press, especially the newspaper *Izvestiia* (The News), gave broad coverage to Schwartzbard's trial and came out in his defense. It gave equally broad coverage to the visits of Torrès and Lecache to the USSR and made no secret of the fact that Soviet agencies helped them to collect information on the pogroms. The Paris-based Russian émigré journal *Golos minuvshego* (Voice of the Past) commented on that aspect of the matter:

> ...Sober conclusions about a grim page in the life of the Jewish people, which has truly suffered greatly, do not require the collection of new material, especially with the help of the Bolsheviks, who tend to forget their own bloody deeds and are always prepared to blacken their opponents in every possible way so as to enhance their own prestige in the countries of the European-American world. There was no need for Schwartzbard's defense lawyers to travel to the Soviet Union for information. There was no need for French journalists to travel in the name of clarifying the "truth" to the places where pogroms occurred, travel that was given such extensive coverage in the Moscow *Izvestiia*....[47]

As a Russian émigré journal, *Golos minuvshego* was by no means favorable to the Ukrainian national movement and Petliura, yet it was impartial in stating a fact obvious to any emigrant from the territory of the former tsarist empire—that information gathered with the help of the Soviet authorities could hardly be objective.

Also symptomatic was the fact that the Soviet minister of foreign affairs, Georgii Chicherin, and the Soviet ambassador to France, Khristian Rakovsky (head of the Cheka on Bolshevik-controlled Ukrainian territory in 1918 and of the Ukrainian Bolshevik government from 1919 to 1923), had met Torrès on the Riviera a few months before the start of the Schwartzbard trial, and Torrès had laid on a sumptuous breakfast for them.[48] Whatever the degree of Soviet influence on the course of the trial, the very fact that a pro-Soviet individual was acting as Schwartzbard's lawyer was, in Jabotinsky's opinion, highly unfavorable and dangerous, in view of the likely negative consequences. That was what Jabotinsky expressed with his usual clarity in "H. Torrès." Jabotinsky's train of thought ran as follows: the Schwartzbard case had acquired a pan-Jewish character, with the result that the interests not only of Schwartzbard personally but of the Jewish people itself were involved. On the other hand, Torrès, as Schwartzbard's lawyer, had gained extraordinary popularity among Jews and had even acquired a halo as the defender of pan-Jewish interests, thus greatly strengthening his influence on Jewish public opinion. In such circumstances there arose the danger that Torrès, an active Sovietophile, could present the case in such a way that Ukrainian nationalists, active enemies of the Soviet regime, would also be seen as enemies of the Jewish people. The conclusion to be drawn would be that the interests of the Soviet rulers and of the Jewish people coincided. In "H. Torrès," Jabotinsky decisively rejected such an interpretation of the Schwartzbard case.

Interestingly, Jabotinsky questioned the notion that the case had been turned into a pan-Jewish affair: "Matters have been complicated by the fact that the Schwartzbard case has now taken on a pan-Jewish character. There are various opinions on whether that should have been done. I shall not explore the question. We are faced with the fact that the case has been given a general national dimension."[49] After expressing, in this cautious way, his doubts about the wisdom of the Jewish community's imputation of general national significance to the trial, Jabotinsky asked:

> The Jewish community in all countries has morally taken up arms in defense of Mr. Schwartzbard. That is undeniable, but a very important question arises: why has it taken up arms? Because it sees Schwartzbard's act as an instinctive revenge for thousands of abuses, or is it because Schwartzbard killed an enemy of the Soviet regime? ...The Jewish community decidedly does not want its belief in Schwartzbard's innocence to be treated as a collective endorsement or condemnation of any regime, ideal or movement. It is precisely on that basis, and none other, that the defense of Mr. Schwartzbard should have been established.[50]

During the Schwartzbard affair the question of real or imaginary guilt was posed only in relation to the Ukrainian movement, and none other. Jabotinsky's words were thus a warning against the use of the trial to condemn that movement and its ideals. From another angle, this was a trial at which the Jewish community sought to aid in exculpating a person who had assassinated a principled enemy of the Soviet regime. Jabotinsky also warned against the trial and the expected acquittal of the assassin being treated as proof of the justice of the Soviet regime and of the criminality of its enemies. Thus, despite his caution and his desire to "let sleeping dogs lie," Jabotinsky still managed to demonstrate his opposition to those forces that sought to politicize the trial and exploit it for the advantage of Bolshevism or to the detriment of the Ukrainian national movement.

Jabotinsky then proceeded directly to the person of Henri Torrès, stating unequivocally that there were serious doubts as to whether Torrès would remain within the framework of juridical procedure and would not utilize the trial for political purposes. Jabotinsky drew attention to the fact that Torrès was an outspoken Sovietophile and had expressed such views in all his speeches, not only in political or community circles, but also in courtrooms when the opportunity arose. For example, at one of the Jewish meetings he had "praised the 'Crimean colonization' and the magnanimity of the Soviet regime." At a trial where Torrès had appeared for the defense, according to Jabotinsky, "In practically every appearance [Torrès] sought to whitewash the Soviet regime as such and to blacken the opponents of the Soviet regime as such."[51] Jabotinsky concluded as follows:

> Let us be allowed to express ourselves clearly: Mr. Torrès's participation could transform Schwartzbard's defense not only into a denunciation of pogromists (which is perfectly legitimate), but also into a hymn to the Bolsheviks and the Soviet regime. That threatens first of all to have negative repercussions for the interests of the accused himself, but it also threatens utterly to distort the picture that the whole educated world gains of the interest that Jewry in all countries is expressing in this trial. Jewry considered the assassinated person to be guilty of pogroms, and that is why it thinks Schwartzbard should be acquitted, but Mr. Torrès's case for the defense is obviously going to give the entire case a character whereby its importance lies in the fact that Petliura was an enemy of the Soviet regime and that Jewry sympathizes with Mr. Schwartzbard because of this. Thank you kindly![52]

Such considerations led Jabotinsky to propose that Torrès not remain Schwartzbard's only lawyer, but that he be given another lawyer as an assistant, someone free of blatant political sympathies.

Henri Torrès replied to this in an interview with the Jewish newspaper *Pariser Haynt* (The Parisian Daily). A summary was published in *Rassvet*.[53] Torrès stated that he had no intention of conducting his defense on a political basis. Jabotinsky responded that "Mr. Torrès's monopolization of appearances at this trial, no matter how excellent he may prove, will be interpreted by society instinctively in a particular political sense." He protested against the choice of a lawyer "with such a clear and one-sided political reputation" as Schwartzbard's sole defender at the trial. Jabotinsky again insisted that another, politically neutral, lawyer be added to the defense.[54]

The politicization of the Schwartzbard trial that Jabotinsky unequivocally opposed had three main interlinked aspects: (1) using the trial to attract the sympathy of world Jewry (and also non-Jewish circles to some extent) for Bolshevism as the alleged enemy of all anti-Semites and pogromists; (2) discrediting the Ukrainian national movement and Petliura in particular; (3) inflaming hostility between the Jewish and Ukrainian peoples and their national movements. In the final analysis, all those aspects held out the promise of significant political, psychological, and propagandistic gains for the Bolsheviks. Did Jabotinsky understand his opposition to the trial's politicization to mean an attempt to oppose the inflaming of Jewish-Ukrainian hostility and the discrediting of the Ukrainian movement? Although he did not stress that in "H. Torrès" (probably because of his desire to "let sleeping dogs lie"), as an experienced politician he must have understood it. He must also have known that the Ukrainian press in the emigration was taking a similar stand, hence his own position, in a certain sense, placed him in the camp of the Ukrainian nationalists in the emigration. His phrase opposing the exploitation of the Schwartzbard case for the "endorsement or condemnation of any regime, ideal or movement" undoubtedly applied also, or even first and foremost, to the Ukrainian movement. If it had just been a question of endorsing or condemning the Bolshevik rulers in the USSR, "regime" would have sufficed. Can the "H. Torrès" article be taken to signify Jabotinsky's agreement with the view of the Ukrainian press that Petliura's assassination was the work of Moscow? He rejected that view in "French Anti-Semites," but there are grounds for doubting that the article was actually written by Jabotinsky. It is not clearly apparent from "H. Torrès" that Jabotinsky agreed with the view of the Ukrainian press, but he was undoubtedly very well aware of that view, since *Rassvet* often commented on the contents of the Ukrainian press, and the French press carried a lively discussion of Moscow's possible involvement in the assassination. Against that background, Jabotinsky's stand against Torrès appears to associate him indirectly with the view of the Ukrainian press. If he did not accept the hypothesis of Moscow's direct organization of Petliura's assassination, then at least he outspokenly recognized that with help from the Schwartzbard case Moscow hoped to exploit Jewry for its own ends.

In any event, Jabotinsky's voice rang out once again as a call for political sobriety intended to prevent emotions from diverting Jewry from its appropriate political course into senseless rage and pointless ethnic hatred, which would only serve the purposes of the enemies of the Jewish people. Jabotinsky's stand was a courageous attempt to prevent the negative consequences that the Schwartzbard trial could (and did in fact) produce. It was courageous because Jabotinsky stood alone against the general drift of opinion. Although on this issue he did not dare to be uncompromising and consistent to the very end, nor to call on the Revisionist movement that he led to support his position, he nevertheless demonstrated a political maturity and grasp of the political situation far surpassing that of the great majority of Jewish political leaders.

Jabotinsky's distinctive stand during Schwartzbard's investigation and trial, as well as his characterization of Petliura and the leaders of the Ukrainian movement in "The 'Crimean' Colonization," aroused dissatisfaction in many Jewish circles. Indeed, the pressure was so great that Jabotinsky was forced to return to "The 'Crimean' Colonization" and publicly explain his stand in favor of Petliura. His consistent refusal to involve *Rassvet* and the Revisionist movement in this "delicate" issue led him to put forward his explanation in the Russian émigré newspaper *Poslednie novosti* (The Latest News) in the form of a "letter to the editor" titled "Petliura and the Pogroms." The newspaper was edited in Paris by the historian and former Cadet party leader Pavel Miliukov.

Pointing out that some Ukrainian journals had interpreted his stand in "The 'Crimean' Colonization" and his agreement with Slavinsky in 1921 as a sign that he did not consider Petliura responsible for the pogroms in Ukraine, Jabotinsky decisively refuted that view. Without renouncing what he had written about Petliura in "The 'Crimean' Colonization," he stressed that this did not mean Petliura was morally and juridically free from responsibility for what had happened in Ukraine while he was head of the Ukrainian government. Although Petliura was, in all likelihood, not an anti-Semite, as head of state and commander-in-chief he had not put a stop to the pogroms and punished the pogromists, argued Jabotinsky. Petliura should either have stopped the pogroms or resigned. Since he did not do so, "this means that he took responsibility for every drop of Jewish blood that was shed.... Such a head of government, such a leader of an army, is guilty, in his official capacity, of an unheard-of and unforgivable crime against the Jewish people, the Ukrainian people, and all humanity."[55] As proof of guilt Jabotinsky pointed to Petliura's failure to organize Jewish self-defense detachments in Ukraine to combat pogroms. That charge was less than justified: as noted in the preceding chapter, Petliura supported the creation of such self-defense units, but the Jewish socialist parties blocked the plan, mainly on ideological grounds. The plan's author, Joseph Schechtman, was Jabotinsky's close collaborator in the Revisionist movement and on *Rassvet*; moreover, the episode had been discussed in detail in publications issued before 1927 (notably in Tcherikower's book *Anti-Semitism and the Pogroms in Ukraine, 1917–19*, published in 1923 and widely discussed in the press during the Schwartzbard trial).[56] It is therefore difficult to imagine that Jabotinsky knew nothing about it. In all likelihood, the pressure of circumstances forced Jabotinsky to align himself more closely with prevailing Jewish public opinion.

Despite the rather acerbic tone of "Petliura and the Pogroms," which contrasted sharply with the tone of "The 'Crimean' Colonization," and despite its attack on Petliura, Jabotinsky remained loyal even in this instance to his principal tenets concerning the Ukrainian problem. In the first place, he did not state that he considered Petliura and the leaders of the Ukrainian movement to be anti-Semites, let alone instigators or organizers of the pogroms. On the contrary, he stressed that his positive assertion about them in "The 'Crimean' Colonization" was very likely correct. In Jabotinsky's opinion, Petliura was guilty only of criminal neglect of his duty to guarantee the sanctity of the life, property, and dignity of all citizens of the state. Jabotinsky ended the article with a reassertion of his fundamental desire for cooperation with the Ukrainian national movement:

> If a section of Ukrainian society concludes from this explanation that I have become an enemy of the Ukrainian national movement, this will simply be another piece of nonsense as foolish as the assumption that I consider Petliura

> to be "innocent." I remain a friend of the Ukrainian movement. I will continue as before to try to calm the righteous anger that has accumulated in Jewish souls, even if that obliges me to refer to the philosophy of history [his theory of the "anti-Semitism of individuals" and the "anti-Semitism of circumstances"] or to construct hypotheses about the psychology of leaders unknown to me. Over and above that, I will continue to aspire to agreement with the Ukrainian movement—as I did, inter alia, in the agreement with M. A. Slavinsky—despite that movement's grave sin against the Jews. But I consider it impermissible to deny that transgression or to treat it as a trifle. If there are individuals or groups within the Ukrainian movement who consider the pogroms to be pardonable trifles, who consider that one can permit the systematic slaughter of Jews and remain heroic and pure, then I am not their friend but their enemy. I warn the Ukrainian community that such individuals or groups are not its friends either, but enemies.[57]

Whether Jabotinsky was right or wrong about Petliura, his attitude toward those responsible for the pogroms and those who carried them out would appear to be completely justified. There have been and there still remain individuals and groups in the Ukrainian diaspora, and now in Ukraine, who attempt to deny, or at least to belittle, the participation of Ukrainians in the pogroms, or seek justification for them, as if there could be any excuse for the mass murder of innocent men, women, and children.[58] To be sure, the reasons for the pogroms, the mechanisms that set them off, and their psychological background are all comprehensible, but the actions of pogromists can in no way be justified. If anyone understood Jabotinsky's stand as a justification of the pogromists, then it certainly required clarification.

It is worth noting Jabotinsky's idea that those who tried to deny Ukrainian participation in the pogroms or to depict them as pardonable trifles were enemies of Ukrainian society. This view, of course, implies that the pogroms had already dealt an enormous blow to the prestige and reputation of the Ukrainian movement, and that those who tried to conceal or belittle irrefutable facts were simply spoiling their own case and further harming the reputation of their movement. The mark of any political movement's maturity and responsibility is not engaging in a children's game of hide-and-seek but frankly analyzing events and the reasons for them. This is the idea that emerges from Jabotinsky's "Petliura and the Pogroms."

Even though the article in no way marked a basic change in Jabotinsky's attitude toward the Ukrainian national movement and contained some undeniably correct statements, its emphatically acerbic tone sounded discordant in comparison with his usually heartfelt and fraternal sympathy for everything connected with the Ukrainian national-liberation movement. Before "Petliura and the Pogroms" appeared, the Ukrainian press had included Jabotinsky among the supporters of the Ukrainian movement, but after its publication the press criticized him. It charged him with shifting his position under pressure from the "Jewish street" (that is, from the Jewish masses). A prominent Ukrainian leader, Oleksander Shulhyn, who had been one of the main initiators of the law on national-personal autonomy in Ukraine and was widely known as a committed supporter of Jewry, published an article in *Tryzub* titled "A Reply to Jabotinsky."[59] The article was highly characteristic of the attitude of Ukrainian circles close to Petliura during the Schwartzbard trial. At the outset, Shulhyn stated that:

> Among the entire Jewish press throughout the world, only Jabotinsky...clearly and unequivocally told the truth in the article, "The 'Crimean' Colonization."... [In "Petliura and the Pogroms," Jabotinsky] is steering a different course. It is difficult for Jabotinsky no. 2 to correct Jabotinsky no. 1, but he must do so, for the sake of...the street, the "Jewish street," as their leaders like to call it.... This letter [i.e., the "letter to the editor" "Petliura and the Pogroms"] will undoubtedly make a great impression on Ukrainian circles. We referred to him, Jabotinsky, in our struggle against the hatred that has been growing among Ukrainians over the last year in connection with the infamous assassination and trial. Alongside the names of L. Marshall, A. Margolin, and S. Goldelman, his name gave us the right to ward off the sentiment of national hatred that was growing spontaneously. Now Jabotinsky has unexpectedly destroyed what he said earlier.[60]

Shulhyn thus acknowledged that Petliura's assassination and the Schwartzbard trial had already aroused growing hatred for Jews among the Ukrainian masses and that the Ukrainian movement's leadership had tried to restrain those negative sentiments by citing Jews who were favorably disposed toward the Ukrainian cause and did not identify Schwartzbard's action as an expression of the feelings of the entire Jewish people. Although Shulhyn's article was full of bitterness over Jewry's anti-Ukrainian attitude, he continued, as always, to appeal for Ukrainian-Jewish understanding. He did not, however, recoil from making critical comments on Jewish policies:

> I belong least of all to those who, according to you, consider the pogroms to be "pardonable trifles" [the words Jabotinsky used in "Petliura and the Pogroms"]. I fought them, fight them now, and will continue to fight them. I wish to establish normal Ukrainian-Jewish relations, but does all this uproar in Jewish circles over the Schwartzbard case promote that? Why do the Jews take upon themselves a sin they did not commit, a Bolshevik crime carried out by a corrupt degenerate? Why are they arousing this hatred among Ukrainians toward themselves, a hatred that will not be easy to restrain? Why are they trying, in spite of everything, to transform S. V. Petliura almost into a pogromist, when he so openly, so clearly, and so sincerely took a stand in defense of the Jews?!
>
> S. V. Petliura did not succeed in preventing the pogroms in 1919, but his honest words in defense of Jewry remain. His fame grew boundlessly, and the Ukrainian masses have no higher authority than Petliura. We will use his

> appeals and his words to fight new pogroms in Ukraine that may unfortunately still threaten Jewry because of the special circumstances of Bolshevik rule.
>
> When I consider the Jews' entire policy in the Schwartzbard case, I conclude that they, despite their deserved reputation for practicality, are dreamers in politics. More than that, they are children, but children with a colossal energy for the attainment of their goal. In the name of the "new Maccabee" (let them take a good look at that Maccabee in court), they are neglecting their own true interests.[61]

Shulhyn was, of course, completely correct on one point. By establishing almost unanimous solidarity with Schwartzbard, Jewry aroused the wholehearted hatred of the Ukrainian masses against itself, a hatred that the Ukrainian national movement's leaders were trying to channel against Schwartzbard as an individual and against the Bolshevik regime, which they believed Schwartzbard was serving. Paradoxically, the situation was such that the leaders of the Ukrainian movement were trying to protect Jewry from the wrath of the Ukrainian masses provoked by Petliura's assassination, while Jewry was stubbornly arousing this hatred by standing like a stone wall in defense of Schwartzbard and identifying his action with Jewish interests. Jewry's position contained a great deal of emotionalism and romanticism, but very little common sense. This gave Shulhyn grounds for speaking of Jewish dreaming and childishness. Shulhyn also drew some conclusions about Jabotinsky:

> I used to consider you, Mr. Jabotinsky, to be above all this, but your last article in its entirety—there can be no doubt on this score—was written by you against yourself, in the name of the street, in the name of your popularity. Because of the truth that you uttered [the article "The 'Crimean' Colonization"—I. K.], it had been somewhat undermined.
>
> ...Returning to Jabotinsky, I must repeat: I seek an understanding with the Jews, I desire peaceful coexistence with them in Ukraine, but whereas Jabotinsky's first article made this seem more tangible and possible, his recent letter makes it harder to achieve and puts it off to some distant future. He has introduced yet another complication into the already difficult relations between Ukrainians and Jews.[62]

Shulhyn also pointed out that the Jewish pogroms were carried out at a time when they were only a small part of the enormous pogrom sustained by Ukraine owing to the intervention of several foreign armies. For Petliura to have resigned at such a terrible moment for the Ukrainian nation would have amounted to desertion and betrayal. This was the view not only of Shulhyn, but of the majority of the Ukrainian emigration, as expressed in the Ukrainian press of the time. However, after the Parisian court had acquitted Schwartzbard, the Ukrainian press proved incapable of restraining its disillusionment and pain: it began to stray into anti-Semitism, although such articles still alternated with others that were loyal to Jewry or even pro-Jewish. It could be said that the

Ukrainian press, including *Tryzub*, was also unable to withstand the pressure of "the street." This was another negative aspect of Petliura's assassination and of the attitude that Jewry adopted toward Petliura and Schwartzbard. For example, *Tryzub* made a survey of the Ukrainian press in November 1927, citing the following statements:

> The Jews pounce only upon the weak, on those lying on the ground, and that is why they have chosen Petliura. [*Novyi chas* (New Times), Lviv]
>
> The Jews have dealt a heavy blow to the cause of restoring good relations between the large Ukrainian majority and the small Jewish minority on Ukrainian territory.... This must be stated openly and clearly. The Jews have blackened the name of Ukraine in the eyes of the world without foundation and without reason. [*Dilo* (The Deed), the leading Ukrainian newspaper in Lviv]
>
> A great injustice has been meted out to the Ukrainian people, one that cannot be hidden away in our pocket.... To bridge this abyss that is opening up between Ukrainians and Jews, the latter must give satisfaction to the Ukrainian people. [*Dilo*]
>
> Throughout the entire course of the Paris trial all the Jewish newspapers and politicians bayed like hyenas against our nation. That brazen little Jew Torrès, Schwartzbard's lawyer, hurled insults at our nation at every opportunity in the courtroom, but Jews who were once ministers in Petliura's government have now gone over to serve the Bolsheviks and are themselves tearing into both Petliura and the Ukrainian people. [*Ukraïns'kyi holos* (Ukrainian Voice), Przemyśl]
>
> People arriving from Russia and Ukraine state categorically that when Bolshevik rule falls, the people will take their revenge on the Jews first of all, for during the period of Bolshevik rule the Jews have behaved so insolently and unjustly toward the people that they are arousing hatred against themselves.... [*Ukraïns'kyi holos*][63]

These quotations signified a catastrophic worsening, even a complete break in relations between the two peoples and a rising wave of hatred that was mortally dangerous for Jewry in Ukraine. Nothing of the kind could have appeared in the Ukrainian press outside the Ukrainian SSR before Petliura's assassination and the Schwartzbard trial. The tone and content of those excerpts were highly typical of the attitudes in the Ukrainian press after Schwartzbard's trial. They demonstrate that Ukrainians in the emigration and in Western Ukraine (i.e., not under Soviet rule) had suffered a shock that their former moderation and political sobriety were unable to withstand. Outbursts of extreme emotion that bordered on incitements to pogroms in no way helped to improve the reputation of Ukrainians outside the USSR; they showed that after suffering a shock, the Ukrainians lost their political sense and succumbed to emotionalism just as easily as the Jews. If someone was planning to exploit the pogrom trauma to compromise the Ukrainian national movement and push Ukrainian-Jewish hostility to the brink of almost insane loathing, then the plan succeeded brilliantly.

As for Jabotinsky's role during the Schwartzbard trial, it was neither simple nor straightforward. Since he was under the pressure of his responsibilities as leader of the Zionist Revisionist movement and editor of *Rassvet*, he was obliged to maneuver so as to avoid an open confrontation with Jewish public opinion on the issue of Petliura. If we put to one side his attitude toward Petliura personally (an attitude that was quite contradictory), Jabotinsky's position during the Schwartzbard trial may be summed up as follows: (1) devotion to the idea of Jewish-Ukrainian understanding and cooperation, despite the tragic past and regardless of the Schwartzbard case; (2) reaffirmation of support for the goals of the Ukrainian national-liberation movement and sympathy for it; (3) a warning to Jewry that the Schwartzbard case was being exploited for a political objective that was hostile to its interests—to win Jewry's sympathy for the USSR, to compromise the enemies of Bolshevism, and to create an irrevocable breach between the Jews and anti-communist national-liberation forces.

Despite his enforced restraint and inconsistency, Jabotinsky was one of the very few moderate voices on the Jewish side during the Schwartzbard trial, a voice free from the consequences of the pogrom trauma. As always, Jabotinsky was primarily concerned with establishing an effective political line for the Jews and not with the noisy voicing of their offended feelings that was so characteristic of that situation, even if expressing such feelings brought them some relief. His attitude was that Jews should not appeal hysterically to the world and to one another, displaying their bloody wounds openly, but should instead work out an intelligent and balanced national policy. That was his basic position, and so it remained in principle, despite all the enforced oscillations, during this new act of the Jewish-Ukrainian tragedy that entered history as the Schwartzbard case.

Jabotinsky's articles on the Ukrainian theme practically stopped after the Schwartzbard trial (excluding a few later references to certain aspects of the Ukrainian problem in letters and in his autobiography), but those brief references testify that, to the end of his life, his attitude toward the Ukrainian problem did not change. A positive and tolerant attitude toward the national aspirations and interests of the Ukrainian people, combined with a desire to coordinate these with the interests of the Jewish people, remains an important part of Jabotinsky's political legacy, although one that is not always understood.

# Notes

1. Shalom (Samuel) Schwartzbard (1886–1938), born in Russia, brought up in Ukraine. In 1908 he was sentenced to four months at hard labor for robbing a store in Vienna. In 1909, after another robbery, he was deported from Austria-Hungary. During World War I he volunteered for the French Foreign Legion and was wounded in battle. In the autumn of 1917 he took a boat to Russia, disseminating Bolshevik propaganda during the trip. In Russia he joined the Bolshevik army, serving until 1920. Subsequently he lived in Paris and was involved in anarchist activity. He died in South Africa.

2. For a brief biography of Symon Petliura, see S. Petliura, *Statti, lysty, dokumenty*, 1: 459–62. See also Iurii Kul'chyts'kyi, "Symon Petliura i pohromy," *Symon Petliura: Zbirnyk studiino-naukovoï konferentsiï v Paryzhi*, ed. Volodymyr Kosyk (Munich and Paris, 1980), pp. 137–39; and Jean de Tokary Tokarzewski, *Simon Petliura* (Paris, 1926).

   Concerning Bolshevik pressure on the Polish government about Petliura, see Khristian Rakovsky (head of the Council of People's Commissars and People's Commissar for Foreign Affairs of Ukraine) to the Polish minister of foreign affairs, 28 September 1921, *Visti*, no. 106 (June 1962): 53.

3. Yehuda Benari, *Zeev Vladimir Jabotinsky: A Biographical Sketch* (Tel Aviv, 1977), pp. 20–23; idem, *Zeev Zhabotinskii: Kratkii biograficheskii ocherk*, 2d ed. (Tel Aviv, 1974), pp. 29–30, 33–35; Joseph Schechtman, "The Jabotinsky-Slavinsky Agreement," pp. 295–301.

   Jabotinsky denied that he left the World Zionist Organization because of his agreement with Slavinsky. However, all of his biographers agree that such a causal link existed.

4. Benari, *Zeev Zhabotinskii*, p. 36.

5. *Rassvet*, no. 28 (11 July 1926): 9.

6. Ibid.

7. Iosif [Joseph] Shekhtman, "Nash isk," *Rassvet*, no. 37 (12 September 1926): 4.

8. See *Zbirnyk pamiaty Symona Petliury (1879–1926)* (Prague, 1930); *Dokument sudovoï pomylky: protses Shvartsbarda* (Paris, 1958); Andrii Iakovliv, "Paryz'ka trahediia" in *Zbirnyk pamiaty Symona Petliury* (Prague, 1930), pp. 228–58; Iurii Kul'chyts'kyi, "Symon Petliura i pohromy," pp. 137–59.

9. Shekhtman, "Nash isk," p. 5.

10. *Rassvet* (23 October 1927): 1.

11. M. Koval's'kyi, "Tvortsi antysemityzmu," *Tryzub* (24 October 1926): 4–8. According to the author, the Jewish circles that depicted Schwartzbard as a national hero and identified the murder of Petliura with the Jewish national cause were those most responsible for stirring up anti-Semitism.

12. Friedman, *Pogromchik*, pp. 289, 374; dust-jacket text.

13. *Rassvet*, no. 43 (30 October 1927): 2.

14. Ibid., p. 1.

15. *Rassvet* (23 October 1927): 1.

16. *Rassvet* (30 October 1927): 2.

17. Ibid.

18. In Jewish sources, Schwartzbard is generally depicted as a national hero. For example, in Max Raisin, *Great Jews I Have Known* (New York, 1952), both Schwartzbard and Jabotinsky appear among the great leaders of Jewish history. Certainly Jabotinsky would have been offended to see his name placed alongside Schwartzbard's in such a context.

    See also: *In Memory of Sholem Schwarzbard* (Johannesburg, 1938); Henry Torrès, *Le procès des pogromes* (Paris, 1928); Bernard Lecache, *Au pays des pogromes: quand Israël meurt* (Paris, 1927).

19. *Tryzub*, no. 49 (17 October 1926): 2–3.

20. Ibid., 3.

21. *Tryzub*, no. 41 (22 August 1926): 24–27.

22. *Tryzub*, no. 49 (17 October 1926): 6.

23. Iust [pseud. of Jabotinsky], "Frantsuzskie antisemity i delo Shvartsbarda," *Rassvet* (5 June 1927): 9–10.

    On 29 May 1927, the article "K istorii proskurovskogo pogroma" was published under the name Iust, but it had no direct bearing on the Schwartzbard case. Even counting from the day of Petliura's assassination to the appearance of that article, a whole year passed without a single article by Jabotinsky in the journal on the Schwartzbard case.

24. V. Jabotinsky, "Di 'Krim' kolonizatsie," *Der Morgen Zhornal* (New York), 4 June 1926.

25. The formal union of the Bolshevik empire took place in 1922 with the creation of the USSR, but in practice from October 1917 the Bolshevik rulers centralized their power over all the territories under their control, in Russian as well as non-Russian lands.

26. For more on the repression of the Zionist movement, which began immediately after the victory of the Bolsheviks in Russia, see I. Shekhtman, "Sovetskaia Rossiia, sionizm i Izrail'," in *Kniga o russkom evreistve, 1917–1967*, pp. 315–43; I. B. Margolin, *Kak bylo likvidirovano sionistskoe dvizhenie v Sovetskoi Rossii* (Jerusalem, 1968); S. Abramskii, "Birobidzhanskii proekt, 1927–1959," in *Evrei v Sovetskoi Rossii (1917–1967)* ([Jerusalem, 1975]), pp. 107–25; I. Maor, *Gatnua gatsionit berusiia* (Jerusalem, 1973), pp. 490–537; J. Schechtman, *Zionism and Zionists in Soviet Russia: Greatness and Drama* (New York, 1966); S. K. Gepshtein, "Russkie sionisty v bor'be za Palestinu," in *Kniga o russkom evreistve, 1917–1967* (New York, 1968), pp. 386–98; and S. Gol'del'man, "K voprosu ob assimiliatsii i denatsionalizatsii evreev v Sovetskom soiuze," *XII Konferentsiia Instituta po izucheniiu SSSR* (Munich, 1960), pp. 125–51.

27. Abramskii, "Birobidzhanskii proekt, 1927–1959"; S. M. Shvarts, "Birobidzhan," in *Kniga o russkom evreistve*, pp. 160–203; Oleksander Mytsiuk, *Agraryzatsiia zhydivstva Ukraïny* (Prague, 1933).

28. Maor, *Gatnua gatsionit berusiia*, p. 535; *Rassvet*, no. 42 (18 October 1925): 10.

29. By 1929 Jewish organizations abroad had donated 16.7 million rubles in gold for the resettlement of Jews in the USSR. According to Soviet statistics, this constituted 75 percent of all the money spent on the project at that time. D. A. Baturinskii, *Zemel'noe ustroenie evreiskoi bednoty* (Moscow, 1929), p. 17.

30. See especially I. Kantor, *Evreiskoe zemleustroenie na Ukraine* (Moscow, 1929); M. I. Kalinin and P. G. Smidovich, *O zemel'nom ustroistve trudiashchikhsia evreev v SSSR* (Moscow, 1927); P. S. Korshunov, *Pereselenie evreev v Krym: mogut li evrei rabotat' na zemle?* 2d ed. (Moscow, 1930); I. Sudarskii, *Birobidzhan* (Kharkiv, 1933). See also Mordechai Altshuler, ed., *Russian Publications on Jews and Judaism in the Soviet Union, 1917–1967: A Bibliography* (Jerusalem, 1970), pp. 183–201.

31. Jabotinsky, "Di 'Krim' kolonizatsie." Similar ideas were expressed by the Zionist leader I. Trivus, "Evreiskaia kolonizatsiia v SSSR," *Rassvet*, no. 42 (18 October 1925): 3–5.

32. *Tryzub*, no. 3 (16 January 1927): 7–12.

33. A. Margolin, "Derzhava Kalinina chy respublika Bragina," *Tryzub*, no. 14 (3 April 1927): 11–15, with references to *The New Palestine* (17 December 1926): 438–40.

34. Jabotinsky, "Di 'Krim' kolonizatsie."

35. In many of his works Jabotinsky referred to the idea of the "anti-Semitism of people" and the "anti-Semitism of circumstances." This is argued in more detail in V. Jabotinsky, "The Antisemitism of 'Men' and 'Things,'" in *Nation and Society: Selected Articles* (Tel Aviv, 1961), pp. 50–55 and *The Jewish War Front* (London, 1940), pp. 55–60, passim.

36. Jabotinsky, "Di 'Krim' kolonizatsie."

37. *Tryzub*, no. 3 (16 January 1927): 7.

38. *Itogi vsesoiuznoi perepisi naseleniia 1989 g.* (Minneapolis, 1993), vol. 7, part 2, p. 310; Shvarts, "Birobidzhan," pp. 160–203.

39. Propaganda campaigns aimed at diverting domestic and international public attention were frequently employed by the Soviet authorities. Many researchers, notably Robert Conquest, have drawn attention to the Soviet regime's use of this tactic. Conquest particularly noted the propagandistic airplane flights across the North Pole to the United States. The furious propaganda campaign around those flights was meant to divert the attention of world public opinion from the bloody wave of mass terror in the USSR in 1936–38. Robert Conquest, *The Great Terror: A Reassessment* (New York, 1990), pp. 93, 238.

40. "Materialy i issledovaniia," *Evrei v SSSR*, no. 4 (Moscow, 1929), p. 5.

41. Solomon Goldelman to Lev Bykovsky, 24 December 1964 (Bykovsky's personal archive). In the same letter, Goldelman went on to explain that he did not appear at the trial because the lawyer representing Petliura's family withdrew his witnesses.

42. V. Zhabotinskii, *Slovo o polku*, p. 47.
Chaim Weizmann (1874–1952)—Zionist leader and scholar; head of the World Zionist Organization in 1920–31 and 1935–46. From the creation of the state of Israel in 1948 until his death he served as its first president.

43. V. Zhabotinskii, "H. Torrès," *Rassvet* (7 August 1927): 3–4.

44. Ibid., p. 3.

45. This statement comes from Torrès's interview with the Parisian Jewish newspaper *Pariser Haynt*, and was reprinted in *Rassvet*, nos. 33–34 (28 August 1927): 24.

46. B. Lecache, *Au pays des pogromes: quand Israël meurt* (Paris, 1927) [B. Lekash, *Kogda Izrail' umiraet* (Leningrad, 1928)]; H. Torrès, *Le procès des pogromes* (Paris, 1928).

47. *Golos minuvshego* (Paris), no. 5/18 (1927): 231.

48. *Tryzub* (5 June 1927): 23, based on *Le Journal* (25 May 1927).

49. V. Zhabotinskii, "H. Torrès," p. 3.

50. Ibid.

51. Ibid.

52. Ibid., p. 4.

53. *Rassvet*, nos. 33–34 (28 August 1927): 24.

54. "V. E. Zhabotinskii ob interv'iu g. Torresa," *Rassvet*, nos. 33–34 (28 August 1927): 24.

55. V. Zhabotinskii, "Petliura i pogromy," *Poslednie novosti* (Paris, 11 October 1927).

56. Cherikover, *Antisemitizm i pogromy na Ukraine*, pp. 211–13.

57. V. Zhabotinskii, "Petliura i pogromy."

58. Solomon Goldelman strongly criticized the stand taken by the Ukrainian émigré press on the Jewish question in a letter of 11 May 1964 to the president of the executive organ of the UNR in the emigration, Mykola Livytsky. Lev Bykovs'kyi, *Solomon Izraïlevych Gol'del'man, 1885–1974* (Denver, 1976), pp. 197–217.

59. "Odpovid' Zhabotyns'komu," *Tryzub* (16 October 1927): 15–18.

60. Ibid., p. 16. Louis Marshall (1859–1929), American-Jewish leader, founder and long-time president of the American Jewish Committee. He was opposed to communism and sympathetic to the Ukrainian national movement.

61. Ibid., p. 18.

62. Ibid.

63. *Tryzub* (20 November 1927): 18–20.

CHAPTER 5

# Jabotinsky, the Ukrainian Question, and Jewish National Policy

The Ukrainian question occupied a prominent place in Jabotinsky's life and creative work. It did not constitute either a unique episode or a series of isolated incidents in his biography. Rather, it was a problem that preoccupied him throughout his years of political and practical activity. Judging by the number of articles that he devoted to the Ukrainian question, in his creative efforts it was second only to immediate problems of Zionist theory and practice such as preserving Jewish national identity, resettlement in Palestine, the political struggle to create a Jewish state, the ideology and organization of the Revisionist movement, the situation in Palestine, and relations with the Arabs. This prominence of the Ukrainian question cannot be accidental, and it demands research and clarification if we are to understand Jabotinsky's place and significance in the history both of Zionism specifically and modern times generally. Although this prominence can easily be established by counting Jabotinsky's articles and letters devoted to particular aspects of the Ukrainian question, researchers as a rule either mention in passing or even totally ignore his interest in the Ukrainian theme. The question continues to rankle, but the lesson that Jabotinsky expounded to Jewry over the years, using the Ukrainian problem as his example, remains unassimilated and, on the whole, simply ignored. Thus, a large and important part of Jabotinsky's legacy remains inaccessible and unstudied. This book is a preliminary attempt to study that legacy and arrive at some general conclusions about Jabotinsky's attitude to the Ukrainian problem insofar as he touched upon it throughout all the phases of his life and creative work.

Was he really the first Jewish figure to grasp the significance of the Ukrainian problem? Among his generation of Zionists he was indeed the first, but there was, at the very least, one other Zionist of the older generation who showed an understanding of the Ukrainian question and expressed sympathy for the Ukrainian national movement. This was none other than Theodor Herzl. In Vienna, Herzl met one of the most prominent Ukrainian cultural and social figures, Ivan Franko. More than forty years after that meeting, Franko's friend Vasyl Shchurat related the discussion between Herzl and Franko in detail.[1] Shchurat wrote that it took place "most probably in February 1893." However, since the discussion, according to Shchurat, concerned Herzl's idea of creating a Jewish state, it appears that Shchurat was mistaken about the date. Herzl's biographers state that he did not conceive the idea of a Jewish state earlier than the beginning of 1895.[2]

Despite the probable error in the dating of this event, there is no reason to doubt the veracity of Shchurat's memoirs and the discussion he recreated:

> "I find your idea of reconstructing a Jewish state very appealing," said Franko. "It interests me a great deal, because this idea is like a sister of our Ukrainian idea of rebuilding the Ukrainian state. Are both these ideas realizable today?"
>
> "Why not?" replied Herzl. "Anything on earth that emerges from a human head is possible."
>
> "From an intelligent head!" Franko added.
>
> "Yes, precisely, an intelligent head, because that is the only one worth talking about to people who wish to be considered intelligent," Herzl said. "Even the strangest idea issuing from an intelligent or sensible head becomes realizable once it fires the enthusiasm of the popular masses, who will produce from their ranks chosen representatives prepared for martyrdom. If during Moses' time we succeeded in throwing off the Egyptian yoke and regaining Palestine, then why should it not be possible today?"
>
> Franko replied: "You had a Moses at that time and only one yoke, the Egyptian, to throw off. Today, we Ukrainians have three, but you have ten times more, for you are dispersed all over the world."
>
> "It is true that a Moses is not born every day. He appears under the influence of external oppression," replied Herzl. "This oppression is ten times greater for us than for you. If you ever come to experience the same, then you also will begin to seek your Moses and you will certainly find him, although today you might possibly stone him. In the end, only time can help."
>
> "I think you are entirely right," Franko replied after brief reflection, and warmly shook Herzl's hand.[3]

Herzl's personality and his idea of creating a Jewish state made a great impression on Franko. In 1896, he published an especially favorable review of Herzl's *The Jewish State*.[4] Shchurat also notes in his memoirs that it was under the influence of the discussion with Herzl that Franko later wrote his monumental poem *Moisei* (Moses, 1905), which is one of the masterpieces of Ukrainian literature.

I mention these events only to emphasize that the idea of an affinity of interests between the Jewish people and the Ukrainian movement, or any other movement striving for its liberation and national statehood, was evident to others besides Jabotinsky.[5] Herzl, who had never lived in Ukraine, probably was not well acquainted with the Ukrainian problem (and therefore lacked preconceptions about it). Accordingly, Franko's statement that the idea of creating a Jewish state "is like a sister of our Ukrainian idea of rebuilding the Ukrainian state" struck him as quite natural, and he saw nothing untoward in the notion of mutual understanding and parallelism in the ideas and goals of the two national movements.

Acknowledged as the "father of political Zionism," Herzl nevertheless established no developed political school and did not formulate any comprehensive system of political principles. His merit lies in the fact that he proclaimed the value of a Jewish state. His voice was heard and it led to the creation of a worldwide Zionist movement. Of course, he promoted the idea of the state at a propitious time. Similar appeals had been floated earlier, but had received no mass support.[6] Herzl's proposal that a future Jewish state adopt communal institutions and his ideas on the organizational forms of the movement for emigration to Palestine were not free of utopianism and in some respects more closely resemble the dreams of a rosy idealist than realistic political postulates.[7]

Following Herzl, the Zionist movement developed increasingly in the direction of socialist ideology, and socialist parties finally gained ascendancy within Zionism. From Jabotinsky's standpoint, this path was incorrect in principle.[8] Although he retained the deepest, purest respect for Herzl throughout his life,[9] Jabotinsky understood the inadequacy and lack of elaboration of Herzl's political legacy. He grasped that developments in Europe (first the social explosions in Eastern and Central Europe and later German Nazism) posed terrible dangers for the Jewish people. He saw the creation of a Jewish state and the resettlement of large numbers of Jews within it as a pressing matter for the nation's rescue. In such conditions it was not merely senseless but verged on the criminal to divide Jews into desirables ("workers") and undesirables ("exploiters"), inflaming a class struggle and class hatred among the Jewish people. At the very beginning of our tragic century, when only the most sensitive and far-sighted individuals could foresee the enormous menace approaching, Jabotinsky called for national unity in order to attain national, and not class, goals. In 1906 he wrote: "I consider all those modish phrases about the Jews not having national but class politics to be ignorant chatter. Jews do not have class politics, but have had and still have (although only in embryonic form) the politics of a national bloc."[10]

Jabotinsky felt that Jewish socialists uncritically borrowed ideas from European socialists and failed to take into account the difference between peoples with ancient and vital traditions of national statehood, whose existence and national rights were in no way mortally threatened, and the situation of the Jewish people. In Jabotinsky's opinion, the new Jewish national ideology, as well as the policy derived from it, should be founded on the idea of national unity, rejecting the idea of class struggle, as well as the general notion of struggle and hatred among the various strata and social groups within a nation. In several of his articles he drew attention to the fact that whenever circumstances obliged Jewish socialists to defend national (rather than "international-class") interests, such socialists would inadvertently betray their ideological principles and find themselves acting as nationalists. Jabotinsky saw this as proof of the incompatibility of Jewish national interests with the principles of socialist politics.[11]

Finally, Jabotinsky considered that conditions in the Jewish political world were symptomatic of an acute lack of national political traditions and of a sound national consciousness not distorted by the grotesque conditions of 2,000 years of dispersion. The true goal of all his activity was that of working out the foundations of a new Jewish consciousness. This would be the consciousness of a nation-state, or, to be more precise, a transition from the consciousness of a "Jew in exile" (*Galut*) to the consciousness of a people with a natural sense of its independent, honorable, and rightful place in the world. Only such an attitude could provide the psychological foundation for the elaboration of an independent national policy.

"Rightful place in the world" meant a place in the community of nations and states. The idea that Jewish politics, no matter how typically Jewish its features might be, should be one of the building blocks in the construction of worldwide international coexistence was as natural to Jabotinsky as the view that every national culture was a resplendent and indispensable tile in the mosaic of world culture. In *The Jewish State*, written in 1937 and deliberately given the same title as Herzl's book, Jabotinsky wrote:

> One of the most important conclusions...is the fact that the Jewish tragedy is not an exclusively Jewish question. It is a problem that is international in character. If our material situation is bad, then the society in which we live will also be suffering from this. If we are without rights, then this disenfranchisement will promote the destruction and demoralization of the country's whole system of government. If racial intolerance rules in the street or in the office, then it is capable of ruining the whole society. One could list even more terrible dangers, but this is hardly necessary. One thing is undeniable: if one fine morning the phenomenon of exile were to disappear and all Jews were established on their own land by sheer magic, without any doubt the benefits and the gains would be mutual.[12]

An individual with such a profound grasp of the mutual dependence and interconnection of world events and processes cannot reject understanding and cooperation with any people, even if the history of relations between that people and the Jews is replete with tragedies. (This also applies to the Arabs, although that problem has, naturally, some unique features. In relations with the Arabs, Jabotinsky insisted on the recognition of their national rights and vital interests on condition that they also recognize the national rights and vital interests of the Jewish people. This is another expression of Jabotinsky's characteristic principle of reciprocity in relations between nations.)

Proceeding from this idea that the various nations of the world have mutual ties of interest and destiny, Jabotinsky considered that anti-Semitism, disseminated in one nation or another (and it would be difficult to find a nation completely free of anti-Semitism), could not serve as a basis for condemning a nation or refusing to cooperate with it. Jewish oversensitivity to anti-Semitism was, in Jabotinsky's view, harmful to Jews themselves, because it encouraged the development of those features in the Jewish character that he sarcastically called the "pogrom philosophy." That is not, of course, a "philosophy" at all, but simply a feeling of humiliation, helplessness, and despair. Jabotinsky pointed out that "all Jews, even passionate Zionists, are very sensitive to every insinuation against us that our existence in exile is displeasing to someone."[13] However, he went on to say that the fact of anti-Semitism "is a natural thing and even an inevitable one: it is the path of every social defect." Such a "defect" is living in the Diaspora, which inevitably gives rise to anti-Semitism. This perception that the Diaspora is precisely the circumstance that creates anti-Semitism is the basis of Jabotinsky's theory of the "anti-Semitism of circumstances." This leads to the conclusion that the psychological basis of Jewish policy should not be feelings of degradation, insult, and fury against nations in which anti-Semitism is widespread. That basis ought to be national self-awareness, spiritual liberation, and territorial and political independence. At the same time, there should be maximum cooperation and understanding with other nations, circumstances permitting.

In characterizing Jews whose reaction to anti-Semitic atrocities was so morbid as to transform wisdom and enlightenment into a type of "pogrom philosophy," Jabotinsky wrote as follows:

> One Jewish journalist recently took advantage of Białystok [the Białystok pogrom] to thrust his fingers into my soul and test what my "pogrom philosophy" was like. He discovered that I am allegedly indifferent to Jewish grief. I did not reply to him. I understand the mood of people of his type too well to take offense at them over injustice or insults. This was a repetition of the old Jewish story: a man sacrificed the best years of his life to plough foreign fields. At the last minute, the landlords killed his brothers and used their corpses to fertilize their field. Reeling from this offense, the person heatedly grabs at straws, becomes angry with everyone at every word of truth uttered, and believes it vital to prove or correct something in minute detail, although one can hardly understand what that something is. I did not reply to him, and there was nothing to say, for I do not have any pogrom philosophy.[14]

This did not, of course, imply justification for the anti-Jewish atrocities produced by anti-Semitism. It was merely an attempt at sober analysis in order to blaze a trail toward a society in which such atrocities would become totally impossible. Jabotinsky argued that the nation's salvation required neither immersing itself in the injustices from which it suffered nor allowing its wounds to fester, but consciously working out a course of action appropriate to the situation, that is, a political line: "When the details of pogroms are recounted to me, my attention strays involuntarily and slips onto other paths. I feel the urge to resolve the following question for myself: all right, let us suppose that I hear the story out and learn where, when, and who was killed. But that is not the point; the point is what to do next—what can be done against pogroms?"[15]

It was these ideas that shaped Jabotinsky's attitude toward the Ukrainian problem and Jewish-Ukrainian relations, and generally toward relations with any nation. Joseph Schechtman tried to sum up Jabotinsky's attitude toward the non-Jewish world by stressing his desire for cooperation based on a convergence of interests and on mutual practical benefit:

> In his concept, the non-Jewish world was a great and creative force, from which the Jewish national movement had a lot to learn in the field of political thought and action. The Jewish problem must be integrated into the general framework of the problems the world is facing. The Jews must study the methods the Gentile had been applying to their solution; must learn the Gentile's way and look for avenues of mutually advantageous cooperation in the solution of the Jewish question. A fervent apostle of Jewish self-reliance, Jabotinsky was at the same time aware that in this complex world of ours no nation is capable of standing alone and solving its major problems on its own, without allies. Such allies must be sought not on the basis of sympathy or compassion, but solely on the basis of community of interests. His contention was that there exists a way of understanding and cooperation between the Jewish national movement and the Gentile world. The politically conscious Gentile is not necessarily an anti-Semite. For the sake of Jews, he would not swerve in the least from the course which he deems best to serve his interests, or even his foibles. But if the Jews come with a reasonable scheme which happens to coincide with his own aims, he may listen to it and even endorse it; he may become a partner in a common undertaking, not necessarily because of friendship, but because of well-understood self-interest. And this is the only thing that counts in the realm of real politics.[16]

Here it is likely that Schechtman was deliberately abstracting himself from the wealth of evidence that Jabotinsky was not a cold, cynical politician who operated only on the basis of political expediency. On the contrary, he had an ardent love for his people and for humanity as the collective bearer and creator of culture. But that did not prevent him from differentiating between emotion and harsh reality in political practice. This is one more lesson in the legacy that Jabotinsky left to Jewish politics.

Joseph Schechtman was undoubtedly right when he wrote in the introduction to his book on Jabotinsky: "We live in an age that, some people tell us, should be the age of the *Common Man*. This is the story of the life of an *uncommon* man—uncommon by any standards."[17] It was, in truth, necessary to rise high above the ordinary in order for Jabotinsky to scorn traditional hostility and make the Ukrainian problem one of the important themes of his work. It is very easy to call upon Jews to cooperate with the Danish people, for example, and to take Danish interests into account, since attitudes toward the Jews have always been good in Denmark. It is incomparably more difficult to call for cooperation with a people whose historical relations with the Jews have been filled with sorrowful, often even bloody, events, but in Jabotinsky's day almost a third of world Jewry lived on such a people's territory. It was precisely by using relations with such a people as an example that Jabotinsky could outline a schema of Jewish policy to serve as a model for relations with other peoples of the world.

Jabotinsky consistently elaborated such a fundamental schema and, however tragic the events in Ukraine may have been, that country's changing situation gave him the opportunity to present multifaceted examples of thoroughly considered political action unfettered by negative emotions. It also furnished opportunities for displays of brilliance in the realm of political writing. This was true of his discussion of Jewish-Ukrainian relations in Galicia, during the debate surrounding the Shevchenko anniversary, in negotiating the agreement with Slavinsky, in the debate within Jewish circles concerning the project of Jewish colonization in Ukraine and the Crimea, and also, in essence, during the Schwartzbard trial, even if in the latter instance Jabotinsky did not prove completely impervious to the pressure of the "street." Thus for Jabotinsky the problem of Jewish-Ukrainian relations offered a clear example that enabled him to develop a concept of relations between Jewry and other peoples.

Jabotinsky's indisputable merit lies in his refusal to avoid the Ukrainian problem, as some Jewish leaders did, and in his elaboration of an unprejudiced political assessment of the Ukrainian question. His second achievement in this field was to grasp, much earlier than many others, the significance of the Ukrainian problem within the complex of problems in the Russian Empire and Eastern Europe generally and to discern accurately how this problem correlated with Jewish interests. Solomon Goldelman bears witness to the extent to which the Ukrainian question remained a closed book to the community at large: "When at the beginning of the revolution in 1917 Ukrainians in Petrograd and Kyiv came out into the streets in many thousands, the Russians in Petrograd and the Jews in Kyiv could not believe their eyes; they simply could not believe that there existed a large nation whose people were known as 'Ukrainians' and a large country known as 'Ukraine.'"[18]

At the very outset of his political activity, Jabotinsky appreciated the existence of this large nation and country. He understood that the destiny of the Russian Empire—with all its implicit consequences for Jewry and for the world—depended on whether Ukraine remained within the framework of the empire or gained its independence. When Jabotinsky wrote in 1911 that the "resolution of the dispute about Russia's national character depends almost entirely on the position taken by the 30–million-strong Ukrainian nation,"[19] he showed a profound understanding of conditions in the Russian Empire and of the significance of the Ukrainian problem for the destiny of Russian imperialism. In order to attain such an understanding, Jabotinsky had to possess—besides a developed political sense—an aptitude for unprejudiced thought, for viewing matters analytically. He had to be free from the pressure of negative Jewish social tradition, which was oriented toward the dominant nation and the ruling culture, even when that nation had no wish to recognize the rights and interests of the Jewish people on its territory.

It is particularly noteworthy that Jabotinsky, though a nationalist with views that his political opponents even today dub "extreme right-wing," was sufficiently free from any traces of chauvinism or prejudice against any nation that it did not even occur to him to blame the persecution of the Jews on any nation as a whole, i.e., on all the representatives of a given people because of their national or racial identity. Some contemporary Jewish authors do, of course, consider themselves to be progressive and in no way tainted with chauvinism. Yet they do not hesitate to blame every Ukrainian for anti-Semitism and to call someone a pogromist just because he is Ukrainian. This tendency is particularly apparent in Saul Friedman's *Pogromchik,* which has been discussed above.[20] Perhaps such authors feel that by doing this they are taking revenge for the injustice that was meted out to the Jewish people. In Jabotinsky's phrases, they remain in the clutches of the "pogrom philosophy," standing "on the terrible ash heap of their nation with a tear-stained handkerchief in their hands,"[21] finding nothing in their souls except pathos for their unfortunate situation. This psychology is a consequence of 2,000 years of disenfranchisement in the Diaspora. It is understandable, and one can express the deepest sympathy for such people, but their stance is hardly worth adopting. Whatever the subjective urges that move these authors, to compromise a whole nation or an individual strictly on the basis of national identity is nothing other than an expression of racism. It is paradoxical that the Jews, who have suffered from racism more than any other people, can be infected, even if unconsciously, with this malady.

Another thesis that is widespread in Jewish historical and political literature is the identification of Ukrainian nationalism with the pogrom movement.[22] By this means the national consciousness and national-liberation struggle of one of Europe's most numerous peoples is branded as a crime against Jewry. If the national-liberation movement of any nation is represented as tainted with banditry, this casts a shadow over the very idea of a national-liberation movement, over every national movement, including Zionism. Jabotinsky, on the contrary, considered that every non-chauvinist and democratic national-liberation or national-cultural movement was ideologically and spiritually affiliated with the Jewish national movement—Zionism. He clearly differentiated between the Ukrainian national movement, which was inspired by the ideas of democracy and international brotherhood, and the activity of pogromists, who appeared on the territory of the Russian Empire for a host of reasons (foremost among them being the anti-Semitic policies of the tsarist government and the activity of the

Black Hundred organizations, which enjoyed official support). Jabotinsky understood that the activity of pogromists in no way reflected the tenets of Ukrainian nationalism, and expressed this very clearly in many of his works.

It is especially characteristic and symptomatic that the authors who write about pogroms never identify pogromist or anti-Semitic activity in general among the Russians, Germans, Poles, Lithuanians or other peoples with those peoples' national consciousness or national-liberation struggles. That remains the exclusive "privilege" of the Ukrainian national movement. Can there be a clearer example of mass prejudice? This is very distant from the views and ideas of Jabotinsky and, unhappily, it is equally far removed from scholarly objectivity and political realism.

In attempting to identify the distinctive feature of Jabotinsky's world-view that places him above the general Zionist current, one must conclude that he thought in terms of a nation-state, even though a Jewish state had not yet been created. From the perspective of a political outlook that embraces statehood, there was a flagrantly obvious disparity between the exile psychology of the overwhelming majority of Jews—the psychology of the Jewish shtetl in the Diaspora—and the tasks involved in state-building. Jabotinsky's whole life was occupied with developing a new psychology among the Jewish people. This was his reason for creating the Jewish youth organization Betar. In the programmatic pamphlet that he wrote for the organization, *The Ideology of Betar*, as well as in other works, he highlighted this problem in various ways.[23]

Jabotinsky's nationalism was of a kind that could be called "normal state nationalism." Thus, in every independent state, all citizens, whatever their political views, are nationalists in the sense that they wish to live in their country, are prepared to defend their state, love their language and national culture, and rejoice at their country's achievements. If these people are also filled with respect and good will toward other nations and cultures, then their views are fundamentally similar to Jabotinsky's. This is the nationalism that the Russian philosopher Nikolai Berdiaev called the "second, higher type" of nationalism, as distinct from the chauvinism and national arrogance of the first type. In *The Philosophy of Inequality*, Berdiaev accurately pointed out that this second type of nationalism "demands self-criticism; it calls for self-criticism and reeducation in the name of national existence."[24] Those lines could be dedicated to Jabotinsky, even though Berdiaev did not have him in mind.

The second type of national awareness is difficult to arouse in people who have not yet definitively broken with their attitude of exile and statelessness. That is why Jabotinsky has not yet been accepted by the majority of Jews, either in Israel or in the Diaspora. His calls for self-criticism, for rethinking outdated concepts, and for the development of a new national consciousness are perceived by most people as exaggerated, superfluous, and dangerous fantasies of a right-wing extremist. To accept Jabotinsky would not necessarily mean agreeing with all aspects of his world-view, but it would mean dropping fantastic notions that he was a dangerous extremist (such notions are still held in certain circles in Israel and abroad)[25] and recognizing him as one of the most eminent leaders in Jewish history. There is some basis for predicting that in the realms of national psychology and politics, Jabotinsky's time still lies ahead.

# Notes

1. Wasyl Szczurat, "Wówczas była to jeszcze mrzonką...," *Chwila* (Lviv, 5 August 1937): 5. See also Asher Wilcher, "Ivan Franko and Theodor Herzl: To the Genesis of Franko's *Mojsej*," *Harvard Ukrainian Studies* 6, no. 2 (June 1982): 233–43.

2. Alex Bein, *Theodore Herzl: A Biography* (Philadelphia, 1962), 100 and passim; Israel Cohen, *Theodor Herzl: Founder of Political Zionism* (New York and London, 1959); and Adolf Friedemann, *Das Leben Theodor Herzls* (Berlin, 1919).

3. *Chwila* (5 August 1937): 5.

4. I. Franko, "Państwo żydowskie," *Tydzień*, literary supplement to *Kurjer Lwowski* (Lviv, 9 March 1896).

5. Ivan Franko (1856–1916), one of the most prominent Ukrainian poets, writers, and political leaders. In Ukrainian culture he stands second to Taras Shevchenko. Franko devoted considerable attention to the depiction of Jews in his works. In his novel *Perekhresni stezhky* (Intersecting Paths, 1899) he expressed, in the words of the Jew Wagman, ideas very similar to Jabotinsky's later writings on the harmfulness of assimilation and on the status of the Jews in their dispersion among other peoples. The following excerpt corresponds entirely to Jabotinsky's published views:

   > In my opinion no Jew can or should be either a Polish or a Russian patriot. Let him be a Jew—that is sufficient. It is, after all, possible to be Jewish and to love the country where we were born, to be useful, or at least harmless, to the nation that, although it is not our own, is still closely associated with all the memories of our life. It seems to me that if we adopted such an attitude, then all the assimilation would be unnecessary.

   See the solid work of P. Kudriavtsev, "Ievreistvo, ievreï ta ievreis'ka sprava v tvorakh Ivana Franka," in *Zbirnyk prats' Zhydivs'koï istorychno-arkheolohichnoï komisiï*, vol. 2 (Kyiv, 1929).

6. Herzl's nineteenth-century predecessors in propagating the idea of a Jewish state were Leon Pinsker (see Introduction, note 5) and the German-Jewish philosopher Moses Hess (1812–75). Beginning as a Hegelian, Hess ultimately developed the idea of rebuilding the Jewish state, to which he gave expression in *Rome and Jerusalem* (1862). The book inspired subsequent pioneers of the Zionist idea, including Herzl.

7. T. Herzl, *Der Judenstaat: Versuch einer modernen Lösung der Judenfrage* (Leipzig, 1896).

8. Jabotinsky wrote a whole series of articles in which he argued the incorrectness of the socialist path for the world as a whole and for the Jewish people in particular. A few of his most interesting articles on this subject are the following: "Klass i chelovechnost'," *Rassvet* (30 November 1930); "Krizis proletariata," *Poslednie novosti* (19 April 1932); "From the Social Philosophy of the Bible," in *Nation and Society* (Tel Aviv, 1961); "Das arbeitende Folk," *Der Judenstaat* (Vienna, 29 March 1935); *Die Idee des Betar* (Lyck, 1935).

9. One of Jabotinsky's finest pieces of literary publicism is "Sidia na polu" (the title refers to the Jewish tradition of sitting on the floor as a sign of mourning), which was written upon the death of Herzl. *Evreiskaia zhizn'* (St. Petersburg), no. 6 (June 1904): 14–21.

10. V. Zhabotinskii, "Evreiskaia kramola," in *Fel'etony*, p. 41.

11. V. Zhabotinskii, "Levye," *Rassvet* (25 January 1925): 7–9.

12. V. Zhabotinskii, *Evreiskoe gosudarstvo: razreshenie evreiskogo voprosa* (Tel Aviv, 1974), p. 24.

13. Ibid., p. 25.

14. V. Zhabotinskii, "V traurnye dni," in *Fel'etony*, p. 31.

15. Ibid., p. 26.

16. J. Schechtman, *Rebel and Statesman: The Vladimir Jabotinsky Story*, vol. 2: *Fighter and Prophet* (New York, 1961), pp. 349–50.

17. J. Schechtman, *Rebel and Statesman*, 1: 15.

18. S. Gol'del'man, *Zhydivs'ka natsional'na avtonomiia v Ukraïni, 1917–1920* (Munich, 1967), p. 135; cf. S. Goldelman, *Jewish National Autonomy in Ukraine*, p. 124.

19. V. Zhabotinskii, "O iazykakh i prochem," in *Fel'etony*, p. 219.

20. Friedman, *Pogromchik*, pp. 1–4, 357–75, and passim. This book includes statements that can only be described as insinuations. For example, on pp. 371–72, there is an alleged quotation from Petliura: "The Jews are a pest, and when I am returned to Russia, it will be necessary to slaughter all the Jews. Only then will calm prevail in Russia." Only someone completely unfamiliar with the psychology of Ukrainian nationalists could believe that Petliura said anything of the kind. Petliura could never have spoken in such terms about Russia: for Ukrainian nationalists, Russia was a hostile colonial power, an occupier that was crushing and oppressing their people. Supporters of Giuseppe Garibaldi had a similar attitude to Austria during their struggle for the independence and unification of Italy. Petliura could no more have confused Ukraine with Russia than Garibaldi could have confused Italy with Austria. Thus the source quoted by Friedman contains an obvious insinuation.

21. V. Zhabotinskii, "V traurnye dni," p. 32.

22. In addition to Friedman's *Pogromchik*, see the following articles: S. Spektor, "Haim darush lanu vaad leshituf peula ehudi-ukraini" (Do We Need the Committee for Jewish-Ukrainian Cooperation?), *Davar* (Tel Aviv, 15 January 1981): 13 (the same text, with a few changes, appeared in the Russian-language *Nasha strana* [Tel Aviv, 23 January 1981]); and M. Agursky, "Ukrainian Nationalism Poses Threat to Jews Again," *Jerusalem Post*, 7 March 1977.

23. This brochure was published in English in *From the Pen of Jabotinsky* (Cape Town, 1941).

24. N. Berdiaev, *Filosofiia neravenstva* (Paris, 1970), p. 87.

25. In *Ktavim al Ze'ev Zhabotinski* (Works about Ze'ev Jabotinsky), (Tel Aviv, 1980), there are many dozens of titles of works sharply critical of Jabotinsky or including bitter polemics between his supporters and opponents. A few typical titles: M. Kleinman, "Zhabotinski meaem..." (Jabotinsky Threatens...), *Haolam* (Tel Aviv, 18 August 1938); E. Shostak, "Madua shetmu manhigei 'miflahot hapoalim' et Zhabotinski" (Why the Leaders of 'Workers' Parties' Hate Jabotinsky), *Khazit haoved*, nos. 11–12 (July 1960); D. Ben-Gurion, "Hatsir shealav savav revizionizm" (The Axis around Which Revisionism Turns), *Davar* (Tel Aviv, 1 July 1964). Cf. also chapter 3, n. 52.

APPENDIX

# Vladimir (Ze'ev) Jabotinsky: A Short Biographical Account

Vladimir Jabotinsky was born on 18 October 1880 in Odesa into a Russified Jewish family. He was given the Russian name of Vladimir, whose Hebrew equivalent is Ze'ev. In secondary school he displayed great literary talent, and his Russian translations of poetry by various Western authors were published when he was only seventeen. While still an adolescent, he perfected his knowledge of the major European languages, as well as Hebrew.

Jabotinsky did not complete his last year of secondary school; instead, in 1898, he accepted an offer to become a foreign correspondent for the liberal newspaper *Odesskii listok* (Odesa Leaflet). As a correspondent for that paper, and later for *Odesskie novosti* (Odesa News), he lived for a time in Switzerland and then in Italy, where he remained until 1901. His articles in the Odesa papers made his name popular not only in Odesa but far beyond it, since they were widely read throughout the whole southern part of the Russian Empire. While Jabotinsky was in Europe he also attended university lectures in jurisprudence, wrote poetry and plays, and translated poetry. Some of his plays were staged successfully in Odesa theatres. Italy made such a great impression on him that he later called it his "spiritual fatherland." The liberator of Italy, Giuseppe Garibaldi, always remained a favorite historical hero for Jabotinsky.

Upon his return to Odesa, Jabotinsky joined the editorial board of *Odesskie novosti*. Soon he was generally recognized as the most popular Russian-language political writer in the south of the empire. The most prominent Russian writers and critics took note of his literary talent.

At the beginning of the twentieth century the anti-Semitic movement within the empire, secretly instigated and supported by the tsarist administration, grew significantly. The bloody pogrom in Chişinău in April 1903, which was the forerunner of the terrible wave of pogroms in 1905–6, provoked angry protests throughout the world, while in the Russian Empire it led to the rise of the Jewish national movement. This pogrom was a turning point in Jabotinsky's development. He became a Zionist and remained one for the rest of his life. His first action as a Zionist was to take part in the formation of Jewish self-defense detachments in Odesa. He also began to translate into Russian the poems of the great Jewish national poet Chaim Nachman Bialik. In his political work he turned to the national theme and called for the recognition of national-cultural and political rights for the Jewish people and all the other peoples of the empire. He made a thorough study of the theoretical foundations of the nationality question and within a few years became one of the leading experts in this field.

In 1903 he participated in the Sixth Zionist Congress in Basel, where he met Theodor Herzl for the first and only time, as Herzl died in the following year. Herzl's personality made a great impression on Jabotinsky. Also in 1903, Jabotinsky moved to St. Petersburg, where he joined the editorial board of the monthly *Evreiskaia zhizn'* (Jewish Life), and later of the weekly *Rassvet* (Dawn). He became well known throughout the empire as a political writer and orator. In 1905 he took a leading part in creating the Union for the Attainment of Full Civil Rights for the Jewish People in Russia, and later was very active in the election campaign for the first State Duma.

In 1905–6 Jabotinsky organized three conferences of Jewish journalists. They approved a program calling for Jewish national self-government within the empire. In 1906 the Conference of Russian Zionists, held in Helsinki, adopted the principles of national autonomy formulated by Jabotinsky as the basis of its program. In 1906–7 he campaigned for election to the second and third State Dumas on a Zionist platform, but was defeated owing to various maneuvers by forces hostile to Zionism. He then began his "offensive against assimilation" in print. Besides the Jewish theme, a series of articles from that period encompasses a wide range of nationality problems, including the Ukrainian question. (Later, in 1913, the best of those articles were published in St. Petersburg in a collection titled *Feuilletons*).

In 1907–8 Jabotinsky lived in Vienna, where he continued his political and literary activities. In 1908, in connection with the "Young Turk" revolution, he went to Istanbul to create a network of Zionist newspapers in various languages in the Ottoman Empire. In Istanbul he met with leading Turkish state figures in order to gain permission for mass Jewish colonization of Palestine, which at that time was under Turkish rule. Jabotinsky quickly became convinced that the only way to achieve the Zionist goal in Palestine was through the breakup of the Ottoman Empire, which he predicted.

Returning to Russia, Jabotinsky continued a press campaign against the assimilation of Jewry, for a return to Jewish culture and the Hebrew language, and for the Hebraization of Jewish education. That campaign led to his first conflict with the mainstream of the Zionist movement, which rejected Hebraization.

At the outbreak of World War I, Jabotinsky went to Western Europe as a correspondent for *Russkie vedomosti* (Russian News). When Turkey entered the war at the end of 1914, he traveled throughout North Africa to meet local Jews and refugees from Palestine. At this time he conceived the idea of creating Jewish armed forces in the British Army. He considered that the participation of Jewish units in the war would give the Jews greater influence during the post-war territorial partitions, helping to resolve the fate of Palestine in favor of Zionism.

Through lengthy negotiations with British government officials, Jabotinsky succeeded in convincing the British to permit the formation of the Jewish Legion within the British Army. Jabotinsky became an officer in the Legion and fought against the Turks in Palestine. His activity and the participation of Jewish armed forces in the war contributed greatly, along with other factors, to the British government's decision in 1917 to issue the Balfour Declaration, which promised to create a legally protected refuge for Jews in Palestine.

After the war, despite his low military rank, Jabotinsky protested to the British military command and government that they had not kept their solemn promises to Jewry. This led to a conflict in which Jabotinsky ultimately prevailed. In order to bury the affair—an unhappy one for Britain—the British government decided to award Jabotinsky the Order of the British Empire, but he refused it.

Having left the army, Jabotinsky settled in Jerusalem and engaged in journalistic work. He warned the British administration that Arab extremists were preparing a pogrom against the Jews, but the British did nothing to prevent it. Jabotinsky then created armed units for Jewish self-defense, the Haganah (Defense). (When the state of Israel was established, these detachments became the embryo of a regular Israeli army.) In 1920 Arab extremists carried out a pogrom at Easter, but the Haganah fought back. The British administration deemed the resistance illegal, arrested Jabotinsky, and sentenced him to fifteen years at hard labour. This sentence provoked great indignation throughout the world, and Jabotinsky demanded its annulment. Soon a second court changed the sentence to a year's imprisonment. Jabotinsky obtained an annulment in that instance as well.

In 1921 Jabotinsky was elected to the Executive of the World Zionist Organization. He sought the creation of Jewish armed units recognized by the British Mandate authorities in Palestine in order to defend the Jewish population against pogroms. The proposal met with opposition both from the British and from a section of the Zionist community. In September 1921 the Twelfth Zionist Congress took place in Karlovy Vary (Karlsbad). Jabotinsky was harshly criticized by some delegates at the congress, and this marked the beginning of his open conflict with the World Zionist Organization.

During the Twelfth Congress, Jabotinsky met with a representative of the Ukrainian People's Republic government-in-exile, Maksym Slavinsky, a friend of his youth in Odesa. Jabotinsky made an agreement with Slavinsky to create a Jewish armed force, a gendarmerie, attached to the Ukrainian army. The gendarmerie was to defend the Jewish population from possible pogroms in the event of a new incursion by the Ukrainian army into the Ukrainian territories under Bolshevik rule. The agreement provoked a storm of attacks on Jabotinsky from his political opponents. Soon his relations with the World Zionist Organization became so strained that he left its ranks.

Once Jabotinsky had decided to abandon political activity, he founded the publishing house Hasefer (Book) to publish literature in Hebrew and textbooks for Jewish schools. He also became a correspondent for the Zionist Russian-language journal *Rassvet*. (He had been a member of its editorial board in St. Petersburg. After the establishment of Bolshevik rule in Russia, *Rassvet* had moved to Berlin.) His articles in *Rassvet* made a great impression on the Jewish public, and he was invited to give lectures in various countries.

During some of his talks to young audiences, it was suggested that Jabotinsky create and lead a Jewish youth organization. On the basis of a small organization in Riga, he established the world Jewish youth organization Betar (its name was derived from the initials of Berit Joseph Trumpeldor, a Jewish national hero who had organized self-defense units in Palestine and died in a skirmish with Arab extremists). The goal of Betar was to raise a new type of Jew free of the psychology developed in the Diaspora. In every respect, this new Jew would be a morally healthy citizen of the sovereign state that was still to be created.

In October 1924 Jabotinsky announced the creation of a new Zionist organization to gather together all the opposition groups in the Zionist movement. The first conference of that organization took place in April 1925 in Paris. Zionists from nine countries, including Palestine, helped form the Zionist Revisionist organization. This was the birth of the Revisionist movement within Zionism. The movement stood for a united national bloc, against the enflaming of class struggle within Jewry, and for a decisive increase of Jewish emigration to Palestine. The Revisionist organization affiliated itself with the World Zionist Organization, but maintained autonomy within it.

The Revisionist program included a demand for the creation of a democratic Jewish state in Palestine as soon as Jews constituted the majority of the population there. In this state all civil and national rights of the Arab minorities were to be recognized, and Arabs were to enjoy the broadest national-cultural and administrative autonomy. Autonomous Arab national agencies were to be created to administer their cultural, social, and religious life, including such areas as national education, health care, social security, and national tax collection. *Rassvet* became the organ of the Zionist Revisionists. Jabotinsky was elected its editor-in-chief, and the journal moved to Paris.

Jabotinsky traveled to dozens of countries to propagate his views. The Revisionist movement grew and branches emerged in almost all countries with Jewish settlements. Revisionist periodicals appeared in various languages. The successes of the Revisionist movement provoked consistent attacks on Jabotinsky from the left-wing Jewish press, which called him an "enemy of the working class," a "reactionary," and a "militarist."

In 1928 Jabotinsky moved to Palestine and intended to settle there permanently. He became editor of a newspaper in Jerusalem. However, after the pogroms of 1929 carried out by the Arabs, he gave lectures to argue for a more decisive and active Jewish policy. He never came out as an enemy of the Arab people. On the contrary, he insisted on giving Arabs broad rights in all areas of community life, arguing that Arab-Jewish antagonism was being exacerbated by the inappropriate policies of leaders of the Jewish community in Palestine, and that this antagonism should be overcome. However, Jabotinsky's talks did not please the British administration, which canceled his entry visa to Palestine, thus banning him indefinitely.

The coming to power of the Nazis in Germany galvanized the Revisionist movement. Jabotinsky promoted mass Jewish evacuation from Europe to Palestine in order to escape the Nazi menace. In 1935 the Zionist Revisionist Organization became the New Zionist Organization, independent of the World Zionist Organization. The Revisionists also left the military organization Haganah in Palestine and created their own underground military organization, Etzel.

Because he foresaw the catastrophe of European Jewry, Jabotinsky took energetic steps to organize a mass exodus of Jews from European countries to Palestine, but he encountered opposition from some Zionists as well as from a number of Jewish non-Zionist left-wing parties and movements, which adopted a policy of caution and waiting. When the British authorities in Palestine resorted to an anti-Jewish policy, including indulgence toward the pogromists and harsh restrictive quotas on Jewish immigration, Jabotinsky ordered Etzel to undertake an armed struggle against British rule.

In the autumn of 1938 Jabotinsky began intensive negotiations with East European governments on the evacuation of Jewry from Eastern Europe. These negotiations met with some success, especially in Poland, but the outbreak of World War II prevented further steps in that direction. Jabotinsky then traveled to the United States, where he opened negotiations on the formation of a Jewish army for a joint military struggle with the Western Allies against Nazism.

In the midst of this activity, Jabotinsky suddenly died in the United States on 4 August 1940. He requested that his remains be taken to the Jewish state, once it was formed. Opponents of Revisionism in Israel kept delaying the fulfillment of his wish, hence it was not until 1964 that Jabotinsky's coffin was transported to Jerusalem. It was buried on Herzl Mountain, not far from the grave of the founder of the Zionist movement.

The Revisionist movement in time was transformed into the Herut (Freedom) Party, which officially calls itself "the Jabotinsky movement." The party was led by Menachem Begin until 1983.

# Bibliography

## I. Writings of Vladimir (Ze'ev) Jabotinsky

### A. Books


*Avtobiografia*. Jerusalem, 1947.

*Evreiskoe gosudarstvo: razreshenie evreiskogo voprosa*. Tel Aviv, 1974.

*Evreiskoe vospitanie*. Odesa, 1905.

*Fel'etony*. St. Petersburg, 1913. 2d ed. Berlin, 1922. Reprint, Tel Aviv, 1971.

*From the Pen of Jabotinsky*. Cape Town, 1941.

*Die Idee des Betar*. Lyck, 1935.

*Izbrannoe*. Jerusalem, 1978.

*The Jewish War Front*. London, 1940.

*Nedrugam Siona*. Odesa, 1905.

*Slovo o polku: istoriia evreiskogo legiona po vospominaniiam ego initsiatora*. Paris, 1928.

*The Story of the Jewish Legion*. New York, 1945.


### B. Articles


"The Antisemitism of 'Men' and 'Things.'" In *Nation and Society: Selected Articles*, pp. 50–55. Tel Aviv, 1961.

"Das arbeitende Folk." *Der Judenstaat* (Vienna), 29 March 1935.

"Asemitizm." In *Fel'etony*, 2d ed. (St. Petersburg, 1913), pp. 77–83.

"Chetyre stat'i o 'chirikovskom intsidente.'" In *Fel'etony*, 2d ed. (St. Petersburg, 1913), pp. 71–100.

"D. S. Pasmanik." *Rassvet* (Paris), no. 28 (13 July 1930).

"Delo bez Beilisa." *Odesskie novosti*, 27 September 1913.

"Demokratizm i natsionalizm." *Odesskie novosti*, 19 August 1912.

"Dezertiry i khoziaeva." In *Fel'etony*, 2d ed. (St. Petersburg, 1913), pp. 71–76.

"Di 'Krim' kolonizatsie." *Der Morgen Zhornal* (New York), 4 June 1926.

Zimri (pseud. of V. Jabotinsky). "Evrei i rusiny." *Evreiskaia mysl'* (Odesa), no. 1 (5 October 1906).

"Evreiskaia kramola." In *Fel'etony*, 2d ed. (St. Petersburg, 1913), pp. 33–43.

"From the Social Philosophy of the Bible." In *Nation and Society*. Tel Aviv, 1961.

"Gel'singforskaia programma." *Odesskie novosti*, 12 August 1912.

"H. Torrès." *Rassvet* (Paris), 7 August 1927.

"Homo homini lupus." In *Fel'etony*, 2d ed. (St. Petersburg, 1913), pp. 101–14.

Interview with *Pariser Haynt*, reprinted in *Rassvet* (Paris), nos. 33–34 (28 August 1927).

Introduction to Chaim Nachman Bialik, *Poems from the Hebrew*. London, 1924.

Introduction to Rudolf Springer (pseud. of Karl Renner), *Gosudarstvo i natsiia*. Odesa, 1906.

Iust (pseud. of V. Jabotinsky). "K istorii proskurovskovo pogroma." *Rassvet* (Paris, 29 May 1927).

"K voprosu o natsionalizme (Otvet g. Izgoevu)." *Obrazovanie* (St. Petersburg), no. 10 (October 1904): 87–98.

"Klass i chelovechnost'." *Rassvet* (Paris), 30 November 1930.

"Krizis proletariata." *Poslednie novosti* (Paris), 19 April 1932.

"Levye." *Rassvet* (Paris, 25 January 1925).

"Medved' iz berlogi." In *Fel'etony*, 2d ed. (St. Petersburg, 1913), pp. 84–90.

"Moia stolitsa." In *Causeries*. Paris, 1930.

"Mrakobes." In *Fel'etony*, 2d ed. (St. Petersburg, 1913), pp. 264–74.

"My burzhui." *Rassvet* (Paris), nos. 15–16 (17 April 1927).

"Na lozhnom puti." In *Fel'etony*, 2d ed. (St. Petersburg, 1913), pp. 248–63.

"Nabroski bez zaglaviia." *Rassvet* (St. Petersburg), 7 June 1909.

"Nashi zadachi." *Khronika evreiskoii zhizni* (St. Petersburg), no. 23 (15 June 1906); no. 25 (29 June 1906); no. 26 (6 July 1906); no. 27 (13 July 1906); no. 28 (20 July 1906).

"Non multum, sed multa." *Ukrainskii vestnik* (St. Petersburg), no. 9 (16 July 1906): 645–50.

"O iazykakh i prochem." In *Fel'etony*, 2d ed. (St. Petersburg, 1913), pp. 218–30.

"O ritual'nom ubiistve." *Odesskie novosti*, 14, 15, 17, and 19–22 September 1913.

"O russkom liberalizme (pis'mo v 'Ukrainskuiu zhizn'')." *Ukrainskaia zhizn'* (Moscow), no. 7–8 (1912): 47–55.

"Otpor." In *Poliaki i evrei*. St. Petersburg, 1913.

"Otvet M. M. Vinaveru." *Evreiskaia mysl'* (Odesa), no. 3 (25 January 1907).

"O zheleznoi stene." *Rassvet* (Berlin), nos. 42–43 (4 October 1923).

"Petliura i pogromy (Pis'mo v redaktsiiu)." *Poslednie novosti* (Paris), 11 October 1927.

"Pis'ma o natsional'nostiakh i oblastiakh. Evreistvo i ego nastroeniia." *Russkaia mysl'* (Moscow), no. 1 (1911): 95–114.

"Poliaki i evrei." In *Fel'etony*, 2d ed. (St. Petersburg, 1913), pp. 139–51.

"Russkaia laska." In *Fel'etony*, 2d ed. (St. Petersburg, 1913), pp. 91–100.

"Samoupravlenie natsional'nogo men'shinstva." *Vestnik Evropy* (St. Petersburg), (September 1913): 117–38; (October 1913): 131–58.

"Shiva." In *From the Pen of Jabotinsky*. Cape Town, 1941.

"Sidia na polu." *Evreiskaia zhizn'* (St. Petersburg), no. 6 (June 1904): 14–21.

"So storony." *Odesskie novosti*, 29 October 1910.

"Struve i ukrainskii vopros." *Odesskie novosti*, 2 March 1912.

"Tochka nad i." *Ukrainskii vestnik* (St. Petersburg), no. 7 (2 July 1906): 399–404.

"Urok iubileia Shevchenko." In *Fel'etony*, 2d ed. (St. Petersburg, 1913), pp. 231–41.

"V. E. Zhabotinskii ob interv'iu g. Torresa." *Rassvet* (Paris), nos. 33–34 (28 August 1927).

"Vmesto apologii." In *Fel'etony*, 2d ed. (St. Petersburg, 1913), pp. 195–205.

"Vopros o Petliure." *Rassvet* (Paris), 8 March 1925.

"V traurnye dni." In *Fel'etony*, 2d ed. (St. Petersburg, 1913), pp. 25–32.

## II. Other Primary Sources

*Igerot Ze'ev Zhabotinski: reshima u-mafteakh* (Ze'ev Jabotinsky's Letters: Summaries and Index), vol. 1. Tel Aviv, 1972.

Iust (pseud. of V. Jabotinsky). "Frantsuzskie antisemity i delo Shvartsbarda," *Rassvet* (Paris, 5 June 1927): 9–10.

*Ktavim al Ze'ev Zhabotinski* (Works about Ze'ev Jabotinsky). Tel Aviv, 1980.

Slavins'kyi, Maksym. "Znosyny z sionistamy," 16 September 1921. Archives of the Jabotinsky Institute in Tel Aviv.

*Stenographisches Protokoll der Verhandlungen des XII Zionisten-Kongresses in Karlsbad vom 1 bis 14 September 1921*. Berlin, 1922.

## III. Secondary Sources

### A. Books

Altshuler, Mordechai, ed. *Russian Publications on Jews and Judaism in the Soviet Union, 1917–1967: A Bibliography*. Jerusalem, 1970.

Baron, Salo W. *The Russian Jew under Tsars and Soviets*. New York and London, 1964.

Baturinskii, D. A. *Zemel'noe ustroenie evreiskoi bednoty*. Moscow, 1929.

Beilis, Mendel. *The Story of My Sufferings*. New York, 1926.

Bein, Alex. *Theodore Herzl: A Biography*. Trans. Maurice Samuel. Philadelphia, 1962.

Benari, Yehuda. *Zeev Vladimir Jabotinsky: A Biographical Sketch*. Tel Aviv, 1977.

——. *Zeev Zhabotinskii: Kratkii biograficheskii ocherk*. 2d ed. Tel Aviv, 1974.

Ben-Gurion, David. *Chaluzischer Zionismus oder Revisionismus*. Berlin, 1934.

Berdiaev, Nikolai. *Filosofiia neravenstva*. Paris, 1970.

——. *Istoki i smysl russkogo kommunizma*. Paris, 1955.

——. *The Meaning of History*. Trans. George Reavey. Cleveland and New York, 1962.

——. *Smysl istorii*. Paris, 1969.

*Bogdan Khmel'nitskii: Letopis' evreia-sovremennika Natana Gannovera*. Leipzig, 1883.

Butmi, G. *Oblichitel'nye rechi: Vragi roda chelovecheskogo. Posviashchaetsia Soiuzu Russkogo Naroda*. St. Petersburg, 1906.

Bykovs'kyi, Lev. *Solomon Izraïlevych Gol'del'man, 1885–1974: bio-bibliohrafichni materiialy*. Denver, 1976.

Chamberlin, William H. *The Russian Revolution*. 2 vols. New York, 1965.

Cherikover, I. M. *Antisemitizm i pogromy na Ukraine 1917–1918 gg.: k istorii ukrainsko-evreiskikh otnoshenii*. Berlin, 1923.

Chernovskii, A. *Soiuz russkogo naroda: po materialam Chrezvychainoi sledstvennoi komissii Vremennogo pravitel'stva 1917 g*. Ed. and introduction by V. P. Viktorov. Moscow, 1929.

Chykalenko, Ievhen. *Shchodennyk (1907–1917)*. Lviv, 1931.

Cohen, Israel. *Theodor Herzl: Founder of Political Zionism*. New York and London, 1959.

Cohn, Norman. *Warrant for Genocide: The Myth of the Jewish World-Conspiracy and the Protocols of the Elders of Zion*. Chico, CA, 1981.

Committee of the Jewish Delegations. *The Pogroms in the Ukraine under the Ukrainian Governments, 1917–1920*. London, 1927.

Conquest, Robert. *The Great Terror: A Reassessment*. New York, 1990.

*Dnevnik imperatora Nikolaia II*. Berlin, 1923.

*Dokument sudovoï pomylky: protses Shvartsbarda*. Paris, 1958.

Doroshenko, Dmytro. *Narys istoriï Ukraïny*. Munich, 1966.

Dubnow, Simon. *Noveishaia istoriia evreiskogo naroda*. 3 vols. Berlin, 1923.

——. *Die Weltgeschichte des jüdischen Volkes*. 10 vols. Berlin, 1925–30.

Ettinger, Shmuel, ed. *Anti-Semitism in the Soviet Union: Its Roots and Consequences*. 3 vols. Jerusalem, 1979–83.

Fischer, George. *Russian Liberalism: From Gentry to Intelligentsia*. Cambridge, MA, 1958.

Frenkin, Mikhail. *Russkaia armiia i revoliutsiia, 1917–1918*. Munich, 1978.

——. *Zakhvat vlasti bol'shevikami v Rossii i rol' tylovykh garnizonov armii: podgotovka i provedenie oktiabr'skogo miatezha, 1917–1918 gg*. Jerusalem, 1982.

Friedemann, Adolf. *Das Leben Theodor Herzls*. Berlin, 1919.

Friedman, Saul S. *Pogromchik: The Assassination of Simon Petlura*. New York, 1976.

Goldelman, Solomon. *Jewish National Autonomy in Ukraine, 1917–1920*. Chicago, 1968.

——. *Juden und Ukrainer: Briefe eines jüdischen Sozialdemokraten*. Vienna, 1921.

——. *Lysty zhydivs'koho sotsiial-demokrata pro Ukraïnu*. Vienna, 1921.

Herzl, Theodor. *Der Judenstaat: Versuch einer modernen Lösung der Judenfrage*. Leipzig, 1896.

Horn, Maurycy. *Żydzi na Rusi Czerwonej w XVI i pierwszej połowie XVII w.: działalność gospodarcza na tle rozwoju demograficznego*. Warsaw, 1975.

*In Memory of Sholem Schwarzbard*. Johannesburg, 1938.

*Istoricheskaia spravka o ritual'nykh ubiistvakh*. St. Petersburg, 1911.

*Itogi vsesoiuznoi perepisi naseleniia 1989 g*. Minneapolis, 1993.

*Iz dumskikh otchetov: Rechi M. M. Vinavera (partii narodnoi svobody)*. St. Petersburg, 1907.

*The Jewish Question in the Duma: Speeches by Deputies*. London, 1915.

Kalinin, M. I., and P. G. Smidovich. *O zemel'nom ustroistve trudiashchikhsia evreev v SSSR*. Moscow, 1927.

Kantor, I. *Evreiskoe zemleustroenie na Ukraine*. Moscow, 1929.

Kleiner, Israel. *Natsional'ni problemy ostann'oï imperiï: natsional'ne pytannia v SRSR ochyma radians'kykh dysydentiv*. Paris, 1978.

*Kniga o russkom evreistve, 1917–1967*. Ed. Ia. G. Frumkin, G. Ia. Aronson and A. A. Gol'denveizer. New York, 1968.

Korshunov, P. S. *Pereselenie evreev v Krym: mogut li evrei rabotat' na zemle?* 2d ed. Moscow, 1930.

Kychko, Trokhym. *Iudaïzm bez prykras*. Kyiv, 1963.

Lecache, Bernard. *Au pays des pogromes: quand Israël meurt*. Paris, 1927.

——. *Kogda Izrail' umiraet*. Leningrad, 1928.

*M. M. Vinaver i russkaia obshchestvennost' nachala XX veka: sbornik statei*. Paris, 1937.

Maor, Yitzhak. *Gatnua gatsionit berusiia* (The Zionist Movement in Russia). Jerusalem, 1973.

Margolin, Arnold. *From a Political Diary: Russia, the Ukraine, and America, 1905–1945*. New York, 1946.

——. *The Jews of Eastern Europe*. New York, 1926.

——. *Natsional'noe dvizhenie v evreistve, 1881–1913*. Petrograd, 1917.

——. *Ukraina i politika Antanty: zapiski evreia i grazhdanina*. Berlin, 1921.

——. *Ukraine and Policy of the Entente*. New York, 1977.

Margolin, I. B. *Kak bylo likvidirovano sionistskoe dvizhenie v Sovetskoi Rossii*. Jerusalem, 1968.

Miliukov, P. N. *Istoriia vtoroi russkoi revoliutsii*. 3 vols. Sofia, 1921–24.

Mytsiuk, Oleksander. *Agraryzatsiia zhydivstva Ukraïny*. Prague, 1933.

Nordau, Max. *Evreistvo v XIX i XX stoletiiakh*. Odesa, 1912.

*Obshchii svod po imperii rezul'tatov razrabotki dannykh pervoi vse-obshchei perepisi naseleniia, proizvedennoi 28 ianvaria 1897 g*. Ed. N. A. Troinitskii. St. Petersburg, 1905.

Pasmanik, D. S. *Russkaia revoliutsiia i evreistvo: bol'shevizm i iudaizm*. Paris, 1923.

*Peterburz'ka Akademiia Nauk v spravi znesennia zaborony ukraïns'koho slova*. Lviv, 1905.

Petliura, Symon. *Statti, lysty, dokumenty*. 2 vols. New York, 1956–79.

Petrazhitskii, L. I. *O ritual'nykh ubiistvakh i dele Beilisa*. St. Petersburg, 1913.

Pipes, Richard. *Struve: Liberal on the Left, 1870–1905*. Cambridge, MA, 1970.

——. *Struve: Liberal on the Right, 1905–1944*. Cambridge, MA, 1980.

*Pogromy v Rossii po ofitsial'nym dokumentam*. Berlin, n.d.

*Protocols of the Meetings of the Learned Elders of Zion*. London, 1925.

Rafes, M. G. *Oifn shvel fun der kontrrevoliutsie* (On the Threshold of Counterrevolution). Kyiv, 1918.

Raisin, Max. *Great Jews I Have Known*. New York, 1952.

*Rakhel' Pavlovna Margolina i ee perepiska s Korneem Ivanovichem Chukovskim*. Jerusalem, 1978.

*Revoliutsionnoe dvizhenie sredi evreev: sbornik pervyi*. Moscow, 1930.

Ruppin, Artur. *Evrei nashego vremeni*. Moscow, 1918.

*Russkomu narodu*. St. Petersburg, 2 September 1906.

Samuel, Maurice. *Blood Accusation: The Strange History of the Beiliss Case*. New York, 1966.

*Sbornik materialov ob ėkonomicheskom polozhenii evreev v Rossii*. 2 vols. St. Petersburg, 1904.

Schechtman, Joseph (Shekhtman, Iosif). *Evrei i ukraintsy*. Odesa, 1917.

——. *Pogromy Dobrovol'cheskoi armii na Ukraine: k istorii antisemitizma na Ukraine v 1919–1920 g.g.* Berlin, 1932.

——. *Rebel and Statesman: The Vladimir Jabotinsky Story*. Vol. 1, *The Early Years*. New York, 1956. Vol. 2, *Fighter and Prophet: The Last Years*. New York, 1961.

——. *Zionism and Zionists in Soviet Russia: Greatness and Drama*. New York, 1966.

Shchegolev, S. *Sovremennoe ukrainstvo: ego proiskhozhdenie, rost i zadachi*. Kyiv, 1914.

——. *Ukrainskoė dvizhenie kak sovremennyi ėtap iuzhnorusskogo separatizma*. Kyiv, 1912.

Shevchenko, Taras. *The Poetical Works of Taras Shevchenko: The Kobzar*. Trans. C. H. Andrusyshen and Watson Kirkconnell. Toronto, 1964.

Sudarskii, I. *Birobidzhan*. Kharkiv, 1933.

Tokarzewski, Jean de Tokary. *Simon Petliura*. Paris, 1926.

Torrès, Henry. *Le procès des pogromes*. Paris, 1928.

Voronel, Aleksander, and Viktor Yakhot, eds. *I Am a Jew: Essays on Jewish Identity in the Soviet Union*. New York, 1973.

## B. Articles

"A Short List of Anti-Semitic and Anti-Israeli Publications in the USSR in the 1960s and 1970s." In *Anti-Semitism in the Soviet Union: Its Roots and Consequences*, ed. Shmuel Ettinger, 1: 345–52. Jerusalem, 1979–83.

Abramovich, G. "Genezis natsional'noi idei i sushchnost' natsionalizma," *Evreiskaia zhizn'* (St. Petersburg), no. 11 (October 1904).

Abramskii, Sh. "Birobidzhanskii proekt, 1927–1959." In *Evrei v Sovetskoi Rossii, 1917–1967* ([Jerusalem, 1975]), pp. 107–25.

Antonovich, V. (Volodymyr Antonovych). "Akty o gaidamakakh (1700–1768)," *Arkhiv Iugo-Zapadnoi Rossii* (Kyiv), part 3, vol. 2 (1876): 128–897.

——. "Poslednie vremena kazachestva na pravoi storone Dnepra," *Arkhiv Iugo-Zapadnoi Rossii* (Kyiv), part 3, vol. 2 (1868): 1–787.

Berenshtein, L. Iu. "Krytyka sionists'kykh fal'syfikatsii istoriï Velykoï Zhovtnevoï sotsialistychnoï revoliutsiï," *Ukraïns'kyi istorychnyi zhurnal*, no. 1 (January 1978): 128–34.

Bikerman, I. M. "Rossiia i russkoe evreistvo." In *Rossiia i evrei: sbornik pervyi* (Berlin, 1923), pp. 9–96.

Buber, Martin. "Die drängende Stunde (über Leo Pinsker und Theodor Herzl)." In M. Buber, *Israel und Palästina*. Zurich, 1950.

——. "The Pressing Demand of the Hour (On Leo Pinsker and Theodore Herzl)." In *On Zion: The History of an Idea*, pp. 123–42. Trans. Stanley Godman. New York, 1973.

Dontsov, Dmytro. "Russkii imperializm i ukrainstvo." *Ukrainskaia zhizn'* (Moscow), no. 2 (1913).

——. "Russkii liberalizm i ukrainskoe dvizhenie," *Ukrainskaia zhizn'* (Moscow), no. 5 (1912).

Franko, Ivan. "Państwo żydowskie," *Tydzień*, literary supplement to *Kurjer Lwowski* (Lviv), 9 March 1896.

Frenkin, Mikhail. "Some Observations on Russian Jewry and Russia's Political Parties (1917–1921)," *Crossroads* (Jerusalem), no. 3 (Spring 1979): 103–38.

Gepshtein, S. K. "Russkie sionisty v bor'be za Palestinu." In *Kniga o russkom evreistve, 1917–1967* (New York, 1968), pp. 386–98.

Gol'del'man, S. "K voprosu ob assimiliatsii i denatsionalizatsii evreev v Sovetskom soiuze." In *XII Konferentsiia Instituta po izucheniiu SSSR* (Munich, 1960), pp. 125–51.

Iakovliv, Andrii. "Paryz'ka trahediia." In *Zbirnyk pamiaty Symona Petliury (1879–1926)*, pp. 228–58. Prague, 1930. Repr. Kyiv, 1992.

Idel'son, A. "Samosokhranenie natsii." In *Natsional'nyi vopros* (Petrograd, 1917), pp. 32–50.

"Interv'iu s Israèlem Èl'dadom," *22* (Tel Aviv), December 1980.

Kleiner, Israel. "On Lenin's Attitude toward the Right of Nations to Self-Determination," *Crossroads* (Jerusalem), no. 5 (Winter 1980): 177–97.

——. "The Soviet Ukrainian Press on Zionism and Israel," *Soviet Jewish Affairs* 4, no. 2 (1974): 46–52.

Koestler, Arthur. "The Magnetism of Jabotinsky," *The Jewish Herald* (Johannesburg, 1954).

Koval's'kyi, M. "Tvortsi antysemityzmu," *Tryzub* (Paris), 24 October 1926: 4–8.

Kudriavtsev, P. "Ievreistvo, ievreï ta ievreis'ka sprava v tvorakh Ivana Franka." In *Zbirnyk prats' Zhydivs'koï istorychno-arkheolohichnoï komisiï*, vol. 2. Kyiv, 1929.

Kul'chyts'kyi, Iurii. "Symon Petliura i pohromy." In *Symon Petliura: Zbirnyk studiino-naukovoï konferentsiï v Paryzhi*, ed. Volodymyr Kosyk, pp. 137–59. Munich and Paris, 1980.

Landau, G. A. "Revoliutsionnye idei v evreiskoi obshchestvennosti." In *Rossiia i evrei: sbornik pervyi* (Berlin, 1923), pp. 97–119.

Levin, I. O. "Evrei v revoliutsii." In *Rossiia i evrei: sbornik pervyi* (Berlin, 1923), pp. 121–38.

Levin, N. "Jabotinsky and the Petliura Agreement," *Jewish Standard* (London), 16 August 1940.

Margolin, A. "Derzhava Kalinina chy respublika Bragina," *Tryzub* (Paris), no. 14 (3 April 1927): 11–15.

"Materialy i issledovaniia," *Evrei v SSSR*, no. 4 (Moscow, 1929).

Nordau, Max. "Speech to the First Zionist Congress (1897)." In *The Zionist Idea: A Historical Analysis and Reader*, ed. and introduction by Arthur Hertzberg, pp. 235–41. New York, 1971.

Orbach, A. "Jewish Intellectuals in Odesa in the Late Nineteenth Century: The Nationalist Theories of Ahad Ha'am and Simon Dubnov," *Nationalities Papers* 6, no. 2 (Fall 1978).

Pasmanik, D. S. "Ėkonomicheskoe polozhenie russkogo evreistva," *Evreiskaia zhizn'*, nos. 11 and 12 (November and December 1904).

——. "Natsional'naia bor'ba evreev v Avstrii," *Evreiskaia zhizn'* (St. Petersburg), no. 4 (1906).

——. "Sionizm ili seimizm," *Evreiskaia zhizn'* (St. Petersburg), no. 6 (1906).

Rabinovich, Yitzhak. "Heskem Zhabotinski-Slavinski bifnei mishpat ha-bolshevikim" (The Jabotinsky-Slavinsky Agreement on Trial by the Bolsheviks), *Ha-olam* (London), 5 August 1943.

Schapiro, Leonard. "The Role of the Jews in the Russian Revolutionary Movement," *Slavic and East European Journal* 11, no. 94 (December 1961).

Schechtman, Joseph (Shekhtman, Iosif). "Evreiskaia obshchestvennost' na Ukraine (1917–1919 g.g.)." In *Kniga o russkom evreistve, 1917–1967* (New York, 1968), pp. 22–43.

——. "The Jabotinsky-Slavinsky Agreement," *Jewish Social Studies* 17, no. 4 (1955).

——. "Nash isk," *Rassvet* (Paris), no. 37 (12 September 1926).

——. "Sovetskaia Rossiia, sionizm i Izrail'." In *Kniga o russkom evreistve, 1917–1967* (New York, 1968), pp. 315–43.

Shub, David. "Evrei v russkoi revoliutsii." In *Politicheskie deiateli Rossii 1850–kh—1920–kh g.g.* (New York, 1969), pp. 353–76.

——. "Parvus, Lenin i Vil'gel'm II (Germano-bol'shevistskii zagovor 1917 g.)" In *Politicheskie deiateli Rossii 1850–kh—1920–kh g.g.* (New York, 1969), pp. 180–243.

Shul'hyn, Oleksander. "Odpovid' Zhabotyns'komu," *Tryzub* (Paris), 16 October 1927: 15–18.

Shvarts, S. M. "Birobidzhan." In *Kniga o russkom evreistve, 1917–1967* (New York, 1968), pp. 160–203.

Slavinskii, M. "Imperiia narodov," *Ukrainskii vestnik* (St. Petersburg), no. 1 (21 May 1906).

Struve, Petr. "Obshcherusskaia kul'tura i ukrainskii partikuliarizm. Otvet Ukraintsu," *Russkaia mysl'* (Moscow, January 1912): 65–86.

Szczurat, Wasyl. "Wówczas była to jeszcze mrzonką...," *Chwila* (Lviv, 5 August 1937).

Trivus, I. "Evreiskaia kolonizatsiia v SSSR," *Rassvet* (Paris), no. 42 (18 October 1925): 3–5.

Trotskii, I. M. "Evreiskie pogromy na Ukraine i v Belorussii (1918–1920 g.g.)." In *Kniga o russkom evreistve, 1917–1967* (New York, 1968), pp. 56–69.

Ukrainets. "K voprosu o samostoiatel'nosti ukrainskoi kul'tury: Pis'mo v redaktsiiu," *Russkaia mysl'* (Moscow, May 1911): 131–46.

Weinryb, Bernard D. "The Hebrew Chronicles on Bohdan Khmel'nyts'kyi and the Cossack-Polish War," *Harvard Ukrainian Studies* 1, no. 2 (June 1977): 153–77.

Wilcher, Asher. "Ivan Franko and Theodor Herzl: To the Genesis of Franko's *Mojsej*," *Harvard Ukrainian Studies* 6, no. 2 (June 1982): 233–43.

## IV. Reference Works

*Encyclopaedia Judaica.* Ed. Cecil Roth and Geoffrey Wigoder. 16 vols. Jerusalem, 1972.

*Encyclopedia of Ukraine.* Ed. Volodymyr Kubijovyč and Danylo Husar Struk. 5 vols. Toronto, 1984–93.

*Entsyklopediia ukraïnoznavstva.* Ed. Volodymyr Kubijovyč and Zenon Kuzelia. 2 parts, 13 vols. Munich, Paris and New York, 1949–84.

*Evreiskaia ėntsiklopediia.* Ed. L. I. Katsenel'son et al. 16 vols. St. Petersburg, [1906–13].

*Evreiskoe naselenie Rossii po dannym perepisi 1917 g. i po noveishim istochnikam.* Petrograd, 1917.

# Index